Researching the Small Enterprise

Researching the Small Enterprise

James Curran and Robert A. Blackburn

SAGE Publications
London • Thousand Oaks • New Delhi

SAGE Publications Ltd
6 Bonhill Street
London EC2A 4PU

SAGE Publications Inc
2455 Teller Road
Thousand Oaks, California 91320

SAGE Publications India Pvt Ltd
32, M-Block Market
Greater Kailash – I
New Delhi 110 048

British Library Cataloguing in Publication data

A catalogue record for this book is available
from the British Library

ISBN 0 7619 5394 2
ISBN 0 7619 5395 0 (pbk)

Library of Congress catalog card record available

Typeset by Mayhew Typesetting, Rhayader, Powys
Printed in Great Britain by The Cromwell Press Ltd,
Trowbridge, Wiltshire

Contents

List of Tables and Figures

Tables

Figures

Preface

The small enterprise has experienced a remarkable revival as a focus of business, political and research interest in recent decades. From being seen as a disappearing relic of nineteenth century industrialization, surviving only where market forces and new technology had not yet restructured the economy, it is now often seen more positively as the generator of the enterprise economy and integral to economic regeneration. Governments of all the main parties, for example, have seized on small-scale enterprises as job creators, innovators and, above all, as vehicles for entrepreneurial aspiration. Although all this enthusiasm may exaggerate the role of the small firm, the statistics of the revival are striking. The number of small and medium-sized enterprises in the UK, for example, increased by 50 per cent in the last quarter of the twentieth century and these are now responsible for over half of all jobs and turnover in the economy.

Growth in research on the small enterprise has reflected the increased interest and recognition of its contribution to the economy. Like any area of academic enquiry the small enterprise is distinctive in the kinds of research problems it poses. Newcomers to small business research, for instance, are often disconcerted by how difficult it seems to be to construct and access a representative sample of small businesses for a research project, something which would be considered routine in many other areas of research. Nor do new researchers find it easy to ferret out what previous research on the small enterprise has established in relation to their selected topic. One reason for this is that small business research is at the intersection of so many disciplines and areas of professional practice that it is easy to overlook previous work.

This book focuses on the problems and challenges of researching the small enterprise. It explores and offers solutions to the problems of selecting topics, designing research projects, conducting fieldwork, analysing data and constructing explanations and interpretations. To illustrate these processes, it draws on a very wide range of examples from small business research. These have been chosen, not just to show how successful research has been undertaken but also to show how easy, as in any other area of research, it is to trip up. Fortunately, avoiding or recovering from failure in a research project is often possible using the right approach. Essentially, the aim is to offer a source book on researching the small enterprise that covers each of the stages of a project from topic selection to the final presentation of results.

One problem facing authors of texts aimed at helping those engaged in researching a specific area is how narrow or wide a focus they should adopt. At one extreme, they can restrict their coverage strictly to the problems likely to arise in the area, leaving the reader to inquire into more general issues, for example, of epistemology or techniques for analysing data, as they feel the need. The opposite would be a (very long) book which tried not only to offer guidance on the specifics of small business research but also to cover all other aspects of the research process. Inevitably, authors have to compromise, pitching their text somewhere between these two extremes. In this book, the specifics of small enterprise research are firmly stage centre but it was also felt strongly that links with some of the fundamental issues of research needed to be made. For example, epistemological issues are as important in small business research as in any other area of research. However, rather than try to explore these exhaustively (something we had neither the space nor the skills to undertake), the book shows why these issues are important and presents some of the alternatives which might be adopted before referring readers to sources which can help them further in relation to their research. A similar position has been adopted in relation to quantitative and qualitative research techniques: the reader is introduced to a variety of techniques, offered pointers on the strengths and weaknesses of these and then directed to specialist sources for further information.

The book also gives more attention than is customary in research texts to certain issues. For example, a chapter is devoted to the presentation of results. Most research texts appear to assume that researchers will have few problems in communicating their results and ideas to audiences of various kinds. Here the view is that presenting research results is much more difficult than it looks and because of this research often fails to reach or convince audiences. In small business research this problem is especially acute because of the range of audiences it strives to reach. Small business researchers, like all researchers, need to convince their peers of the value of their research. Yet, they also often want to reach others such as policy-makers, support agency staff, small business service providers (such as the high street banks) as well as small business owners themselves and the general public. The style of presentation of results, which some of these audiences find stimulating and convincing, does not suit some of the others. Indeed, researchers are often accused of the over use of jargon or of an inability to communicate their work clearly and succinctly by some of their audiences. If findings are not communicated effectively, then the hard work of the researcher can all too easily be wasted.

Much of this book draws on the research in which we have been involved, especially to illustrate problems and their possible solutions. Research is a co-operative activity and most of the projects in which we have been involved have been with others whose creative gifts and research skills have helped bring the projects to successful fulfilment. Although this co-operation is acknowledged implicitly in the references, where publications resulting from this research are cited, we would also like to acknowledge the contributions of colleagues here. We would particularly like to mention: Brian Abbott; Roger Burrows; Steve Downing; Mark Hart; Richard Harrison; Robin Jarvis; John Kitching; Geoffrey Lightfoot; Stephen Lloyd Smith; Lew Perren; John Stanworth; David Storey; and Adrian Woods. All of these are colleagues with whom we have co-authored publications but this does not, by any means, exhaust the list of those from whose ideas, skills and other contributions our research has benefitted. We have been engaged in small business research for a long time and much of how we think about the small business has come from others. This is part of being in any research community: all members come to owe each other intellectual and other research debts which can never be repaid.

We hope that this book will help and stimulate those involved in small business research. The area is one which we find enormously stimulating and worthwhile. The range of topics which can be linked to the small business is huge. Few areas offer such a range, a range that is constantly being renewed as the UK economy, society and small enterprise develops. This richness is a resource and a promise: a resource offering a never ending stream of subjects for research and a promise that intellectually those undertaking the research are unlikely to ever feel they have short changed themselves or their audiences.

Finally, we would finally like to thank our respective partners, Audrey and Helen, who have often endured with us the pleasures and pains of researching the smaller enterprise and writing this book.

About the Authors

James Curran is Emeritus Professor of Small Business Studies at Kingston University. In 1987 he was the founder and first Director of the Small Business Research Centre in the University's Business School becoming Midland (now HSBC) Bank Professor of Small Business Studies as part of the Bank's long-term support for the Centre. From 1989 to 1992 he was also Director of the ESRC Centre for Research on Small Service Sector Enterprises, which was located at the Centre. This was part of the ESRC Small Business Initiative, which lasted over the three years from 1989 to 1992. His career in small business research started in the late 1960s and he had undertaken projects on a very wide range of topics linked to the small enterprise, publishing extensively in article and book form. His last book was *The Quality Business, Quality Issues and Small Firms* (co-authored with R.A. Blackburn and Julian North). He is a Consulting Editor of the *International Small Business Journal* and a Fellow of the Institute of Small Business Affairs, the British Academy of Management and the Royal Society of Arts.

Robert A. Blackburn is the HSBC Professor of Small Business Studies and Director of the Small Business Research Centre, Kingston University. He has extensive experience of researching the smaller enterprise, using a variety of methodological approaches. Most recently he has been involved in an ESRC-funded project on the management of intellectual property in small and medium-sized enterprises and a longitudinal focus group programme with business owners, sponsored by Horwath Clark Whitehill. His recent publications include *Small Firms: Contributions to Economic Regeneration* (Paul Chapman/Sage, 1996) (co-edited with Peter Jennings), *The Quality Business, Quality Issues and Small Firms* (co-authored with Julian North and James Curran) and *Intellectual Property and Innovation Management in the SME* (editor). He has also published numerous conference and refereed journal articles. He is Abstracts and Book Reviews Editor of the *International Small Business Journal*; a member of the Council of the Small Business Research Trust; a Director of the Institute of Small Business Affairs, and has acted as advisor to the corporate sector, government bodies, political parties and interest groups.

1

The Need for Small Business Research

Interest in small-scale enterprise in the UK has increased enormously in recent years. This has been parallelled with an equally large increase in research on this form of economic activity. Regrettably, much of the research has not been high quality, due mainly to failures to recognize the special problems studying the small business poses for researchers. The main aims of this book are to explore these problems and suggest ways in which sound research practice can further understanding of this fascinating area of economic activity.

Why Research the Small Business?

Despite the great increase in interest in the small business in the UK,[1] its importance in the economy is often still underestimated (Storey, 1994). One reason for this is that there remains a tendency to see small businesses as less central to economic activities than large businesses, particularly the multinationals whose activities are the focus of newspapers and television business programmes. But another reason, and one which poses serious problems for researchers, is that there have been considerable difficulties in estimating the number of small businesses in the UK. The problem is compounded by the question – discussed at length later in the chapter – of just what should be seen as a 'small' business.

Leaving aside the niceties of what constitutes a small business for the moment, if we adopt the EU approach, it is possible to offer an indication of the importance of small-scale enterprise in the UK. The EU classifies businesses as: micro firms (businesses with less than 10 people); small firms (10–49 employees); and medium-sized firms (50–249 employees). Frequently, researchers and policy makers combine these into a single category: 'small and medium-sized enterprises' or SMEs. The remainder, those with 250 or more employees, are the large firms.

The Department of Trade and Industry's Small Firms Statistics Unit (DTI, 1999a) suggested there were an estimated 3.7m businesses in the UK at the start of 1998. Of these 94.8 per cent were micro businesses and

Table 1.1   *Size distribution of businesses in the UK at the start of 1998*

Size (Number of employees)	Share of total businesses (%)	Share of employment (%)	Share of turnover (%)
0	64.0	12.7	4.6
1–4	25.2	10.9	11.1
5–9	5.6	6.9	6.4
10–19	3.1	7.3	8.0
20–49	1.3	6.9	7.9
50–99	0.4	4.8	5.8
100–99	0.2	5.2	6.1
200–49	[1]–	1.6	2.0
250–499	0.1	5.2	8.0
500+	0.1	38.5	40.1
	100.0	100.0	100.0
Total	3,657,885	21,595,000	£1,926,987m

[1] The – against 200–49 in the share of total business column means share was less than 0.5 per cent. Turnover excludes VAT and the finance sector.

Source: Department of Trade and Industry (1999a)

a further 4.4 per cent were small firms (see Table 1.1). Only 0.6 per cent were classified as medium-sized and only 0.2 per cent (under 7,000 firms) as large. In other words, less than one per cent of *all* businesses (just over 31,000 firms) in the UK are *not* small or micro businesses. In numerical terms, therefore, small and micro businesses are far from marginal to the UK economy and this becomes even truer if the SME category is used.

It might be surmised, on the other hand, that although SMEs comprise over 99.8 per cent of UK businesses, their contributions to employment and business turnover are much less significant. The DTI estimates, however, do not support this suggestion very strongly. At the beginning of 1998, there were approximately 21.6m people working in the 3.7m private sector businesses (DTI, 1999a). SMEs employed 12.1m, which is almost 57 per cent of jobs in the private sector. If only small and micro businesses are considered, then SMEs were responsible for 9.6m or 44 per cent of these jobs.[2] The contribution to business turnover of SMEs was also substantial. At the start of 1998, SMEs contributed almost 52 per cent of total business turnover (DTI, 1999a).[3] If the contribution is confined to micro and small businesses it falls to 38 per cent, which is still a substantial proportion.

Put another way, if the employment and turnover shares of SMEs are set against the UK's large enterprise sector (using the EU definition of a large firm as one employing more than 249 employees) SMEs are more important in terms of jobs and contribution, to private sector turnover. Taken by themselves, micro and small businesses are less important yet are still responsible for well over 40 per cent of jobs and over a third of private sector turnover. In short, it is difficult to argue that SMEs or small and micro businesses are marginal to the UK economy and any assessment of its functioning cannot ignore them.

What is more, due to a range of influences, such as the alleged rise of the enterprise culture in the 1980s, technological change, outsourcing by larger enterprise and economic restructuring more generally,[4] there has been a remarkable increase in small-scale enterprise since 1980. The DTI estimates, for example, that in 1980 there were just over 2.4m businesses in Britain (DTI, 1999a: 3). The very considerable growth since (1.3m additional businesses) consisted almost entirely of micro and small businesses.

SMEs are likely to be key to the UK's economic future because they are very important in many knowledge-based sectors, the sectors upon which the economy will be very dependent for its place in the future world economy (DTI, 1998). The attention to SMEs in high-technology activities, for instance, has led to them being seen as a special category, known as new technology-based firms (NTBFs), with a considerable literature devoted to it. (See, for example, the collections of papers edited by Oakey, 1996; Oakey and Mukhtar, 1997; During and Oakey, 1998; Oakey and During, 1998.) Other research (Keeble et al., 1992) has highlighted the increasing importance of SMEs in business services such as consultancy and market research. These are areas where economic development comes from brain power and creativity rather than size advantages. SMEs and established large enterprises, in other words, are on a much more equal footing in these areas. Certainly, government sees these areas as crucial to a high-performing economy (DTI, 1998).

If the above arguments are at all persuasive, the case for more well-conducted, rigorous research on SMEs is enhanced further. But even if some of the arguments are overstated, the importance of SMEs in terms of employment and business turnover makes the case for small business research important in understanding the functioning of the UK economy. At the very least, research devoted to the small enterprise ought to approach much more the volume devoted to larger enterprises as measured, for example, by the content of academic journals.

The History and Development of Contemporary Small Business Research

The beginning of serious small business research in the UK is conventionally seen as the Bolton Report (1971). This was the last full official inquiry in to the role of the small business in the UK economy. What was particularly important about the Inquiry was that it had a Director of Research (Graham Bannock) and produced a good deal of data drawn upon in the Report as well as 18 separate research reports (the Bolton Report, 1971: Appendix 3). There had been previous research (see, for example, Acton Society Trust, 1953 and 1956; Revans, 1956) and some with a good level of theoretical sophistication (see, for example, Ingham, 1970) but the Bolton Report undoubtedly raised the profile of the small firm and small firm research.

It might have been thought that the USA, with its earlier and stronger tradition of academic business research and emphasis on entrepreneurship, would have taken an early lead in small business research. There was certainly notable and influential research and theorizing in the USA prior to 1970 (see, for example, McClelland, 1961; Collins et al., 1964; Smith, 1967). However, arguably, this was still much less than might have been expected. Although it is the home of some of the largest businesses in the world, the USA has a huge number of SMEs which play a particularly important role in its strongly developed regional economies. As in the UK, however, academics have tended to devote much more attention to the large enterprise.

As the Bolton Committee was deliberating and perhaps reflecting the increase of interest in the small business, there was an upsurge in research in the UK (see, for example, Boswell 1973; Stanworth and Curran, 1973). By 1980, the London Business School (LBS) had started a Small Business Bibliography. In the Second Edition the compiler wrote:

> If the 1970s saw the emergence of what was in effect a new field of study, the early 1980s have seen its consolidation. The First Edition contained 2592 entries, compared to 4356 in this, of which approximately 25 per cent are dated 1980 or after . . . (LBS, 1983: 5)

The 1989 Edition of the *Bibliography* (1990) added another 1,500 entries to the 12,000 in the previous editions. Unfortunately, this appears to have been the last edition of the bibliography. More recently, the Institute of Small Business Affairs (ISBA) and the Small Business Research Trust produced a *Register of Small Business Researchers* (SBRT, 1998a) which listed over 260 individuals and their research interests in the UK. The Trust and ISBA have also produced an *SME Research Database* sponsored by the DTI (SBRT, 1998b) with over 400 abstracts describing and evaluating small business research projects. Although the register and abstracts have fewer entries than the LBS *Bibliography*, they offer a good indication of the range of contemporary small business research in the UK.

While the volume of publications has grown tremendously since the early 1970s, it has to be admitted that much of it has been of poor quality. One of the largest sections in the 1989 edition of the LBS *Bibliography*, for instance, was headed 'Managing the On-Going Small Business' and consisted almost entirely of 'how to do it' texts with no foundation in well-conducted research. Of the rest, the quality varied with many publications based on atheoretical approaches and/or poor-quality empirical work. At best, it could be argued that there was a discernable, if weak, trend towards stronger theorizing and better methodological strategies but a continuing failure to match rising standards of social and business research generally. The situation has improved since but there is still a need to reach the highest standards.

The Distinctiveness and Richness of Small Business Research

One of the reasons why small business research has had problems in achieving higher quality (and academic status) as well as greater influence on policy makers, is that it is a difficult area in which to conduct research. At first sight this might sound like an excuse for poor performance. After all, what could be simpler to research than a small business? It contains, by definition, relatively few people, is unlikely to have a complex organizational structure or elaborate dealings with the outside environment and its activities are likely to be much more transparent than those of larger enterprises. It might even be seen as a very accessible 'laboratory' for the study of business activities. Its core operations occur in a simple, easily observable fashion enabling researchers to isolate key variables and their effects. Researchers, in fact, should find investigating small businesses a doddle.

However, the apparent simplicity of the small business has tripped up a lot of researchers. Small does not mean simple. Neither is a small business merely a scaled-down version of a large business. A small number of human beings engaged in a common endeavour can create very complex, subtle interactions. Unravelling the underlying meanings and patterns of these interactions can be far from straightforward. The motivations of those involved, for example, can be very diverse and complex. Even when they declare their goals, close observation often reveals actions apparently at variance with these avowed goals, or which appear governed by motivational repertoires difficult to decipher. Much small business research, for example, concentrates on the motivations and actions of just one person, the entrepreneur or owner–manager, but invariably others are involved who also shape the enterprise and its destiny.

Indeed, it can be argued that smaller enterprises are actually *more* difficult to study than larger enterprises. Where activities lack clear structures and recording procedures, measurement is much more difficult and propositions more difficult to test. In larger enterprises researchers can access paper- or computer-based quantitative data or records of how decisions were made.[5] Where respondents offer accounts discrepant with these so-called 'objective' data, researchers normally attempt to reconcile the differences. Given the strong cultural emphasis favouring quantitative over other kinds of data, the end-products of quantitative enquiries are often accepted as conclusive even when, intuitively, the results look suspect. Small firm researchers, on the other hand, often find they are not let off the hook in this way. They have to work with the available data, struggling to generate explanations which may be superior as accounts of what is happening in the firm but which others see as inferior simply because they are not quantitative enough.

Small enterprises have an extreme range of forms. They operate in every sector of the economy, from computer software to candle-making and from insurance broking to instrument manufacturing. Entrepreneurs and owner–managers come from different genders and/or a wide range of ethnic, cultural and educational backgrounds and from every age group. While some start their own businesses from scratch, others inherit or buy an on-going business. Some are sole owners while others run their businesses with partners or other directors. Some are family businesses with owners, partners or fellow directors and even employees linked by blood or marriage. Others are run by people who have come together solely because they share common goals, complementary skills or access to capital.

Recently, some researchers (see, for example, Scott and Rosa, 1996 and 1997; Harding, 1998) have questioned the academic and media emphasis on the 'lone entrepreneur' model of the small business. Commonly, 'the firm' and 'the entrepreneur' have been treated as coterminous but, in fact, a high proportion of small firms, perhaps approaching 40 per cent, have two or more owner–managers/partners/directors (DTI, 1999a: Table 23).[6] This means that even at the owner–manager level, investigating managerial strategies and practices in SMEs will be complex (Harding, 1998). Each owner–manager/partner/director will have his or her personal goals, as well as goals for the business and differing managerial skills and practices. Enterprises linked through cross-ownership may operate significantly differently to enterprises that have no such linkages.

Just over 1.3m SMEs had employees at the start of 1998 (DTI, 1999a: 7).[7] While employees are less important in determining the course of the business, they still influence it as an economic and social entity. Again, they are highly variable. Age, gender, skill and educational levels vary as well as the employees' commitment to the enterprise. Skill levels are especially important in knowledge-based small businesses. In small service businesses where high levels of formal qualifications may not be needed, the personal and social skills of employees and their commitment can be crucial to business success. Employees, in other words, add to the heterogeneity of the enterprise and, hence, the complexities of research.

Nor can small business researchers forget that small businesses have economic, social, cultural, geographical and political environments. No small business can survive without exchanges with the environment. At the simplest, a small business, like any business, obtains resources (capital, supplies and human resources) from the wider environment, uses these to create products and services and returns them to the environment through the market. Given the extreme variety of economic activities in which small businesses engage, the complexities of relations with the wider environment are potentially enormous. Moreover, these relations will often be very unstable or change greatly over time. Unlike larger enterprises, small businesses usually have less ability to influence their wider environment. They are, in fact, much closer to the ideal type of the classical economist's model of the individual business whose activities are dictated completely by the market.

With such diverse phenomena as subject matter, small business research is never going to be easy. Generalization is also going to be difficult. A study of one kind of small enterprise such as 'start-ups' or 'family small businesses', however well-conducted, will always offer conclusions whose wider applicability will be easy to challenge. Were, for example, the start-ups all from the same region? Was the region representative of other regions? Were the owners educationally representative of the population of small business owners as a whole? Did they have any, or the same, training or experience for running a small business? Did they all have access to the same amounts and kinds of finance? Were the start-ups in a range of sectors representative of the economy as a whole or in a selection of sectors or in one sector only? Was the economy in recession or expanding at the time of start-up? Researchers may also argue about the criteria to be used in testing their conclusions. For example, qualitative researchers will frequently argue that statistical tests are inappropriate for assessing their research.

Whatever the criteria applied, questions like those above and similar ones are likely to be asked in assessing the quality and value of any research. Given the complexities and range of influences listed above, all studies are bound to fail on one or more criteria, limiting the generalizability of their results. In other words, there are no perfect, unchallengeable outcomes from research on SMEs (or any other business phenomena). The test of quality of any research is the *extent* to which its conclusions can be generalized convincingly to any wider audience and especially to fellow researchers. Some find this inherent inconclusiveness of research profoundly irritating: they want reliable, durable, straight answers to their questions. But the findings from any research are never more than provisional if only because the real world is constantly changing.

On the other hand, because small businesses are complex, they offer an immense range of topics to investigate. With such a huge variety of subject matter, no researcher could live long enough to exhaust the possibilities and challenges of the small business as research subject. For all the major topics of contemporary social and business research there is a small business dimension. For example, small business researchers have contributed to research on: the impact of economic restructuring on the UK economy (Curran, 1990; Harrison, 1994); small firm–large firm relations (Curran and Blackburn, 1994); employment and unemployment (Storey, 1994; Chapter 4, *passim*); ethnicity and ethnic economic involvement in economic activities (Ward and Jenkins, 1984); gender involvement in economic activities (Carter and Cannon, 1988); the analysis of businesses as organizations (Curran and Stanworth, 1986; Goffee and Scase, 1995); regional economic development (Barkham et al., 1996); economic globalization (Harrison, 1994); entrepreneurship in modern economies (Chell et al., 1991; Burrows, 1991a); intellectual property issues (Kitching and Blackburn, 1999a); business ethics (Spence, 2000), and the rural–urban debate (Curran and Storey, 1994). Further topics are discussed later in the book but the above give an indication of the opportunities for research.

Small business research is not a discipline in a conventional academic sense. Rather it is an area which can be described more accurately as multi- or cross-disciplinary to a degree rare elsewhere in social and business research. Many research areas are described as multi- or cross-disciplinary but it is often difficult to find much evidence of either being typical practice. Small business research, on the other hand, is genuinely multi-disciplinary. This is shown in the way all the major social science disciplines – anthropology, economics, psychology, sociology, geography, politics, as well as history – have been drawn upon to explore how small enterprises function (see Table 1.2). Nor should the professions be left out. Accountancy is the most obvious one contributing to knowledge on the smaller enterprise (see, for example, Keasey and Watson, 1993) but others such as law have also made their contributions (see, for example, Freedman and Godwin, 1994).

Drawing on a single discipline is an easier option than cross-disciplinary research. Where research is based on a single discipline or area of professional practice, the topic can be explored as if no other way of looking at the small firm has any relevance. This is inherently undesirable because it oversimplifies. By imposing what are arbitrary disciplinary or practice boundaries, it discourages researchers from taking account of the real-life links across such boundaries. Cross-disciplinary research, on the other hand, seeks to tackle topics by bringing together the conceptual and theoretical power of two or more social science disciplines and/or professional practices in a single research design. For example, a study of small businesses and their links with local economies (Curran and Blackburn, 1994) employed concepts and theories from sociology, economics, geography and psychology in its research design. These cross-disciplinary inputs continued in the final overall interpretation of the results from the research.

Revisiting the Problem of Defining the Small Business: Devising Solutions

The problem of what a 'small' business is was raised earlier when the importance of SMEs in the UK economy was highlighted. EU definitions

Table 1.2 *Small business research and contributions from social science disciplines*

Discipline	Researchers	Details of study
Anthropology	Harding and Jenkins (1989)	A mainly theoretical study of the operation of the informal economy which is largely composed of small enterprises.
Economics	Reid et al. (1993)	Study of a sample of 73 small firms in manufacturing and services with both strong theoretical and applied emphases.
Psychology	Chell et al. (1991)	Uses a psychological framework and case studies to attempt to a neural network approach to the entrepreneur.
Sociology	Scase and Goffee (1982)	Well-known and much cited study of small business owners which was theoretically innovative and empirically based.
Geography	Barkham et al. (1996)	Inter-regional study of small-firm growth in four UK regions showing the relations between firm and the area in which it is located.
Politics	McGregor and Fletcher (1993)	Empirical examination of enterprise policies in disadvantaged areas in six UK cities.
History	Foreman-Peck (1985)	Theoretical and secondary analysis which compares small business revival in the 1980s with the recession period of the 1930s.

Even though each study is attributed to a single discipline, this is often the primary disciplinary emphasis with theories and contributions from other disciplines incorporated into the overall analysis. This multi-disciplinary aspect demonstrates the admirable refusal of experienced researchers to be bound by conventional disciplinary boundaries. Full citations for all of the above are given in the References.

of 'micro', 'small' and 'medium' businesses were used but numerical definitions of these kinds are often semi-arbitrary. In fact, there is no established, widely accepted definition, official or otherwise, of the small firm. This has created problems for small business research. The result has been considerable debate which, if it has not produced any neat solutions, has clarified the issues involved and encouraged researchers to offer reasoned justifications for the definitions they adopt.

Definitions Based on Numbers Employed

Definitions based on numbers employed in the enterprise are extremely popular with researchers and policy-makers alike. The obvious reasons for this are their apparent simplicity and that they are quantitative. Quantitative definitions are seen as 'objective' and are amenable to statistical manipulation. Quantitative definitions are also liked by policy-makers because they appear to be objective and transparent. Employment data is also convenient because it is collected anyway for national statistical purposes and so already exists for researchers to use. It has, therefore, considerable appeal as a surrogate for size of business. It is also relatively easy to collect directly from firms where necessary.

But the advantages of basing definitions of size of firm on numbers employed have to be set against some serious disadvantages. The most obvious is that employment measures are likely to be very sector dependent. A 'small' oil refinery, for example, might employ several hundred people (and be capitalized at several million pounds). Can this be compared with a small independent backstreet garage that employs three people besides the owner (and has a capitalization of perhaps £150,000)? If we include both in a sample of 'small firms' for research purposes, are we really categorizing and comparing like with like to produce an analysis with sensible generalizable conclusions?

The apparent simplicity of numbers employed as a measure of business size is becoming more and more problematic in practice. Full-time employment is becoming less common in the UK, for example, with part-timers, casual and temporary workers and the self-employed becoming more widely used by employers. For example, between 1981 and 1996 the proportion of part-time employees (those working 30 hours a week or less) in the active labour force rose from 21 to 29 per cent (DfEE, 1997). Between 1980 and 1990, the number of self-employed people in the UK increased by 1.5m and is projected to rise to over 4m by 2007 (DfEE, 1998: 8). As discussed earlier, a substantial proportion of these are, in effect, employees and many of these work for SMEs.

A measure of size, such as 'numbers employed' is also difficult to use where part-time, casual and temporary labour is not evenly spread across the size distribution of businesses. For example, Labour Force Survey (Spring, 1996) data reported that over 40 per cent of employees in workplaces with between one and 10 employees were part-timers compared with an all workplace average of just under 34 per cent. The mix of different kinds of labour also varies by sector. Data on the use of full-time, temporary and self-employed labour in small firms in different sectors is less easily come by but some which have large numbers of small firms such as tourism and hospitality, are known to use temporary and casual workers extensively (DfEE, 1998: 10).

Overall, therefore, 'employee' as a unit of size measure for defining the small firm has limitations. It does not, of course, rule it out as an approach – it is too popular and easy to use – but clearly it needs to be used with some care. In a single-sector study, for example, particularly one with good quality data on workforce composition, these problems are much less serious. But even here acceptable conventions on the use of employment measures will be required. One common convention, for instance, is to treat a part-time employee as the equivalent of half a full-time employee.[8] But this will only be a rough equivalence where, for instance, Firm A employs mostly part-timers who work, on average, 25 hours a week and Firm B employs the same number of full-time employees working a 35 hour week. Such differences could, for example, render productivity comparisons between the firms questionable.

Definitions Based on Financial Turnover

An alternative and, again, apparently attractive measure of size, is turnover. But turnover has much the same problems as employment except that they are worse. Turnover, like employment, has sector characteristics so a 'small' independently owned retail outlet selling newspapers, confectionary and, cigarettes, for example, might have an annual turnover of well under £100,000 but a 'small' precision instrument manufacturer, selling throughout the UK and abroad, might easily have a turnover of £2,000,000 or more a year, which is twenty times greater. An even bigger problem is finding out firms' turnovers. Unless a business is registered as a company – and it is estimated that over half are not (DTI, 1999a: 111)[9] – there is no requirement to make accounts public.[10] Many small business owners themselves use differing financial management conventions and practices (Jarvis et al., 1996) which may not produce comparable data. Similarly, accountants may employ differing conventions in preparing accounts for firms, resulting again in non-comparable turnover totals.

Owner–managers themselves may not even have precise data on their annual turnover and not be able to provide accurate information to researchers. Many, for example, do not regard turnover as very important: cash flow is seen as much more important for monitoring the progress of the business. Finally, owner–managers are sometimes reluctant to supply turnover data to outsiders, including researchers, because they consider it too personal to divulge or fear that such information may reach competitors and other outsiders, including the Inland Revenue.

One solution frequently used by researchers collecting turnover data from small firms is to ask respondents to indicate a particular category within which the firm's turnover falls. For instance, a mail questionnaire might have the categories 'under £25,000', '£25,000–£49,999', etc., and this has been found to produce better response rates than asking for more exact information. For studies within a single sector or a group of separate sectors, this approach offers one way of approaching the definitional problem[11] although, of course, it does not indicate which category or categories should be labelled 'micro', 'small' etc.: this remains a separate issue. Nor does it permit much in the way of quantitative analysis because the data is only for the *range* within which turnovers fall with no data on the average (mean or median) or distribution within the categories selected.

As the earlier discussion made clear, official estimates now include data on turnover in UK businesses (see Table 1.1) but while this may be reasonably accurate as an indicator of relativities between the smallest and largest enterprises, it cannot be disagregated down to the level of the firm. For any of the employment size categories employed in the official data (1–4, 5–9, 10–19 etc.) the distribution of turnover within the category is likely to be wide and skewed so making assumptions about, for example, turnover in the 'typical' firm with 1–4 employees is dubious.

A further serious problem with turnover-based definitions is dealing with the problem of inflation – especially where the analysis compares firms over time. If the intention is a 'snapshot' study of small firms at a particular point in time then turnover may be useful (by itself or combined with other criteria) in generating a definition, providing data of sufficient quality is available. Data on the population from which the sample is to be recruited, as well as the firms actually investigated, however, is required to ensure the firms studied are representative. Even then some care is needed in selecting the *relevant* population in order to avoid over generalization.

Where a turnover definition is used over time or intended to be relevant for later researchers, turnover-based definitions are less useful. The Bolton Committee, for example, used turnover-based definitions for four of the sectors it covered. The effects of inflation on definitions of these kind can be illustrated by seeing what happened in the case of retailing. Only a few years after the Report was published, the Wilson Committee (which was concerned with the financing of small firms) found it necessary to adjust the definition for small retailing firms to allow for inflation. It raised the upper limit for seeing a firm as 'small' in this sector from £50,000 to £150,000 (Wilson Committee, 1979: 48). Obviously, the longer the period the greater the adjustment required but the problem is that this very easily produces a figure which is unrealistic because inflation affects different sectors at different rates. In retailing, for example, continuing to adjust for inflation to update the Bolton Committee definition produces an upper turnover level way above what most single outlet retailers typically experience because their turnovers have not risen in line with inflation.[12]

Early Qualitative Definitions and the Bolton Committee's Solutions

The above bases for defining the small business are quantitative but there are alternative qualitative approaches. One of the best known was offered by the Bolton Committee. This was in the form of an ideal type combining three key elements:

First, in economic terms, a small firm is one that has a relatively small share of its market. Secondly, an essential characteristic of a small firm is that it is managed by its owners or part-owners in a personalized way, and not through the medium of a formalized management structure. Thirdly, it is also independent in the sense that it does not form part of a larger enterprise and that the owner–managers should be free from outside control in taking their principal decisions. (1971: 1)

The clear intention here was to capture the distinctive characteristics of the small firm compared with larger enterprises. Few would disagree with the second and third elements but the first is trickier and more subjective. Some small firms do have large shares of particular 'markets' (depending on how 'market', another very slippery term, is defined). In some high-technology areas, a single small firm might pioneer a new product or service and, at least initially, dominate the market. But even quite common kinds of small firms may operate with few *effective* competitors in the sense that an economist would use the latter term. A small garage in a small town or community with little public transport, for instance, might have few competitors within easy distance.[13]

The Bolton Committee was quick to acknowledge that the weakness of its qualitative definition was that it was not easy to operationalize. There was not in 1971, nor is there today, any remotely comprehensive data on the '. . . business population in terms of ownership, management, organizational structure and market shares. . .' (Bolton Report, 1971: 3). Instead, the Committee adopted non-comparable, quantitative definitions selected on what appears to have been a common-sense basis for each of the nine sectors of economic activity it elected to cover in its inquiry (see Table 1.3).[14] In short, the qualitative approach was quickly converted into a quantitative one.

The Bolton Committee's definitions and the ways in which they were constructed are highly instructive in relation to the issue of defining the small firm. The problems which arise from turnover-based definitions when used to compare firms at different points in time have already been discussed. Another result of the Bolton approach, which some more recent conceptualizations suffer from also, is that, by selecting sector-specific definitions, comparisons between sectors becomes difficult. A small transport firm (one with five or fewer vehicles) may not be easy to compare with a small construction firm (defined as one with 25 or less employees). As Storey (1994: 12) points out, definitions of this kind also make international comparisons difficult if researchers in other countries do not adopt the same definitions or size distributions in other countries differ. This problem is now more serious given the development of the EU single market where comparisons between members become important for assessing the way the market operates and for policy-making.

Table 1.3   *The Bolton Report definitions of the small firm*

Sector	Definition
Manufacturing	200 employees or less
Retailing	Turnover of £50,000 p.a. or less
Wholesale trades	Turnover of £200,000 p.a. or less
Construction	25 employees or less
Mining/quarrying	25 employees or less
Motor trades	Turnover of £100,000 p.a. or less
Miscellaneous services	Turnover of £50,000 p.a. or less
Road transport	5 vehicles or less
Catering	All excluding multiples and brewery-managed pubs

Source: The Bolton Report (1971)

The Bolton Report definitions display indications that the quantitative limits were selected fairly arbitrarily. This approach is questionable if it is not based on a sound knowledge of the kind of enterprise to which they refer. Take, for instance, the Bolton definition of a small manufacturing firm (up to 200 employees). Subsequent research (see, for example, Curran and Stanworth, 1979; Storey, 1994: 10) has suggested that this upper limit is high and contradicts the qualitative ideal type the Committee initially preferred. A small manufacturing firm, for instance, with close to 200 employees would be difficult to manage '. . . by its owners or part-owners in a personalized way, and not through the medium of a formalized management structure' (Bolton Report, 1971: 1).

More Recent Qualitative Approaches

Subsequent researchers have not given up so easily in attempting to formulate qualitative definitions of the small firm. What underpins these attempts is a key assumption that small firms are fundamentally different to large firms and any definition needs to capture this difference. In one of the classics of small business theorizing (Penrose, 1959) this assumption was summed up neatly in the analogy that small and large firms were as fundamentally different from each other as caterpillars are from butterflies. Even if one metamorphoses into the other, it would not simply be a larger version of the other and, it might be added, in the case of small firms there is no certainty that metamorphosis will take place at all. As the extreme skewness of the size distribution of businesses in the UK demonstrates, most small firms never grow beyond a small size: most of the 'caterpillars' never become 'butterflies'.

An example of an attempt to isolate the basic differences between small and large firms on qualitative criteria is provided by Wynarczyk et al. (1993). They argue that the three central ways in which small firms differ from large firms are related to uncertainty, innovation and evolution.

Uncertainty is linked to small firms being price-takers, a vulnerability associated with having a limited customer base, lack of resources and general inability to withstand external influences on the way businesses are run.

Innovation and small firms are often linked but rather than expensive research-based breakthrough innovations, small firms are much more likely to be distinguished by offering marginally differentiated or non-standardized varieties of products or services. Only a small proportion will be responsible for more important innovatory activities. This can occur where the small firm trailblazes radically new products or services and/or market solutions ahead of slower larger firms. But the key point here, it is argued, is the constant, active engagement in innovation processes by small firms.

Evolution refers to the greater likelihood of small firms experiencing a greater range of changes than occurs in larger firms when – and if – they grow. These changes are manifested in the multifarious, complex processes which occur when, in Penrose's terms, they evolve from caterpillar to butterfly, from small firm to large firm.

Wynarczyk et al. (1993) were attempting a conceptualization of the small firm which, firstly, marks it as fundamentally different to the large business and, secondly, implies that it therefore requires its own theorization rather than merely being seen as a miniature version of the large firm. This latter point is centrally important to conceptualizing and theorizing the role and activities of small firms but is only slowly gaining acceptance. More often researchers, neglecting this issue, rush straight to a simple 'number-of-employees' or turnover definition and base their theorizations on some borrowed, off-the-shelf model originally developed with large firms in mind.[15]

The weakness of the Wynarczyk et al. construct is that it is evocative rather than conceptually robust. We might agree that it is touching on genuinely key differences between small and large firms related to the impact of uncertainty, innovation and evolution but the focus is not sharp enough. Levels of uncertainty vary enormously between small firms and some, particularly in newer knowledge-based sectors, may feel they can take on all comers in their market, whether large or small. Innovation, as researchers have discovered, is extremely difficult to conceptualize clearly enough to use reliably in research (Harrison, 1994: 56–8). Evolution from small to medium to large does mean enormous changes in a wide range of key aspects of the enterprise but, in practice, few small firms evolve to become large firms. So this criterion touches on changes which affect only a minority of small firms and even when they do occur, the variety of ways in which this evolutionary process can happen are enormous.[16] All these points add up to considerable problems in using the approach for research purposes. For these reasons, it is not surprising that Wynarczyk et al's. approach has not inspired much further development or wider adoption.

Combining the Qualitative and Quantitative in Defining the Small Firm

Some researchers have argued that the curse of small business research is that size can, superficially, be so *easily* measured. Size, as measured by employment or turnover, it is argued, all too often leads to 'size reductionism' (Curran and Stanworth, 1986: 140–1). By this is meant that the tendency is to attempt to explain every aspect of small firms by reference to whatever size criterion has been selected. But:

> Size whether measured in terms of number of employees, turnover, market share or whatever, is *not* a sufficiently robust criterion to allow 'small firms' to be isolated and analysed as having an economic and social specificity. (Burrows and Curran, 1989: 530; emphasis in the original)

These authors go on to argue that smallness *per se* is not technically a necessary characteristic of an organization but a *contingent* one. That is, in principle, it has the same status as a wide range of other characteristics such as legal form, type of economic activity in which the firm is engaged, the technology employed, the region or local economy in which the firm is situated, the age, gender, ethnicity and educational level of the persons who own or work in the firm, etc. To privilege size over these other criteria begs important questions about what most influences the operation and structure of economic enterprises and under what conditions. In practice, the emphasis on size often leads to other criteria being neglected or being treated as secondary. This is not to say that size has no influence but merely that it is only one of a range of possible factors which can shape the firm. This suggests, therefore, that despite the popularity of simple employment/turnover definitions in small business research and policy-making, sticking so closely to such definitions may hamper the development of more powerful[17] conceptualizations and, worse, of more powerful theories and explanations of the operation and role of the small firm in economic activities.

Burrows and Curran were members of a research team investigating small service-sector businesses in an Economic and Social Research Council (ESRC)-sponsored research initiative. From the above thinking the team developed a set of definitions for their research programme which combined the qualitative and quantitative.[18] First, they noted that size is usually linked with legal independence, though this is not always adhered to in small business research. For example, researchers sometimes treat small establishments and small independent enterprises as equivalents. This is unsatisfactory on a number of grounds. A small establishment is often a branch of some much larger firm, which usually means its operational procedures are dictated by head office rather than by those running the establishment. This can have all kinds of other ramifications also. For instance, the establishment may be able to draw on the parent for access to capital, supplies, financial and other resources. This will make it very different to an independently owned, single-outlet enterprise. Legal independence was therefore selected as a first criterion in their definitions.

Building on legal independence, the researchers linked this with what they termed a grounded notion of size for the particular varieties of small-scale enterprise included in the research programme. This grounded element was generated by investigating how 'smallness' was perceived by those engaged in the economic activities being investigated. A wide range of people working in each sector and their associated activities – managers and owners of firms of all sizes, representatives of trade associations, suppliers etc. – were interviewed to find out how 'smallness' was defined within the sector's culture.[19] From these interviews it was possible to extract a sector consensus on what was regarded as a 'small' enterprise in each of the sectors to be investigated. These qualitative beliefs were then expressed in quantitative terms to make them operational (see Table 1.4).

This grounded qualitative/quantitative approach has not been widely used by other researchers. The originators noted that it was not without disadvantages. For instance, where a number of sectors are to be studied, constructing sector-based, grounded definitions for each is time-consuming and makes comparisons between sectors difficult, if not impossible. Burrows and Curran (1989: 531) however, argued that returning to simple, across-the-board numerical definitions based on employment or turnover alone also means, almost inevitably, a return to what they regarded as discredited size-reductionist analyses. Researchers and especially policy-makers and support agencies often want to treat 'the small business sector' as a single entity and non-comparable, sector-based definitions prevent this, but the price paid for the simplicity and convenience of across-the-board definitions is high.

Lumping together all businesses with under 50 employees as 'small businesses' implies that besides having below this number of employees, they also share enough other characteristics to be treated as members of the same category for research and policy purposes. But proponents of a grounded approach to defining small enterprises argue that to include furniture restorers, corner shops, computer software firms and restaurants in the same category merely because they employ less than some stipulated number of employees or their turnover falls below some level, is to ignore a wide range of sector characteristics that make them very different from each other.

Some would go further, arguing that this multitude of differences between firms defined as 'small' for official or statistical purposes, means that, in effect, chalk, cheese and wrapping paper are being mixed together, resulting in a spurious analytical category. The results of research based on such a category are bound to be flawed. For instance, Storey (1994: 16) notes that research has shown consistently that there is

Table 1.4 *Some grounded definitions of small firms in the service sector*

Type of enterprise	No. of outlets	Employment criteria (FTEs)	Special conditions
Free houses,	1	None	Not brewery-owned
wine bars and	1	10 or less	Premises owned or rented
restaurants	1	10 or less	
Video-hire outlets	Up to 3	None	None
Leisure businesses	1	10 or less	None
Vehicle repairs and servicing	Not specified	10 or less	New car selling franchisees excluded but other franchised activities permitted
Market research	1	25 or less	None
advertising	1	25 or less	Must not be in *Campaign*'s top 50 agencies list or annual list of top 300 agencies
Employment, secretarial and training agencies	1 or 2	10 or less	None
Computer services	Not specified	20 or less	None
Plant and equipment hire	Not specified	10 or less	Excludes businesses solely engaged in car hire or the hire of agricultural machinery or industrial plant for manufacturing

All enterprises must have at least one employee or equivalent full-time or part-time labour. Where business types are grouped as, for example, free houses, wine bars and restaurants, they are treated as related types of business for sample construction purposes. Employment upper limit for employment, secretarial and training agencies excludes any people registered solely for obtaining temporary work with client firms of the agencies.

Source: Curran, Blackburn and Woods (1991)

no neat relationship between size and performance. An obvious reason for this is that firms differ greatly between sectors and sector characteristics are more important in influencing performance than size defined by employee numbers or turnover.[20]

Despite the above, however, there are circumstances where simple definitions of the 'small firm' have clear utility. For example, the DTI's Small Firms Statistics Unit estimates of the size distribution of the UK business population using EU size definitions, are undoubtedly useful both to researchers and policy-makers. They offer a broad picture of the employment and turnover shares of differently sized firms in the UK economy. There is also political and administrative utility in using simple criteria to separate smaller enterprises from larger enterprises. It would be difficult politically and administratively expensive, for example, to have separate VAT thresholds for every different kind of economic activity in the UK. But the key point is that researchers need to avoid rushing to adopt simple, quantitative definitions, especially for cross-sectoral samples, and to think much more carefully about how they define 'small businesses'.

A slightly tongue-in-cheek but not entirely illogical approach to solving the problem of defining 'the small firm' is to suggest that it is really a non-problem, not worth all the effort it excites. As underlined earlier, the DTI estimates show that less than 7,000 businesses (0.1 per cent) were 'large' (250 or more employees) (DTI, 1999a: 4). In other words, the economy is composed virtually solely of SMEs. It follows, that any sample of firms selected randomly should contain about 99 per cent SMEs. It should, therefore, be easy to strip out the one per cent or so 'large' firms and get on with the research. In effect, the definition prob-lem disappears.[21] Unfortunately, this appealing solution does not solve the sector issues discussed above. Nor does it eliminate the important other differences correlated with size (such as differences in organiza-tional structure) which remain even if the size distribution is restricted to firms with under 50 or 250 employees.

From Theoretical Considerations to Good Practice

Given all the above problems of constructing a reasoned conceptualiza-tion of 'the small firm', researchers still have to solve the *practical* problems of carrying out research. Researchers have to decide how the 'the small firm' is to be defined for their particular project. Moreover, the definition will have to be *usable* in relation to the aims of the research and the resources available. In practice, a variety of approaches are used. A good indication of how researchers go about this can be seen in the work for the ESRC Small Business Research Initiative cited earlier, which supported 16 projects (Storey, 1994). The projects employed a wide variety of definitions (see Table 1.5). In some cases, there was a clear link between the subject and the definition adopted. For instance, the study of co-operatives simply took any co-operative as the unit of enterprise. There are very few co-operatives which would not be regarded as 'small' businesses so a size criterion was not required. On the other hand, taking the unit as any firm with between one and 500 employees, as Hughes et al. (Small Business Research Centre, 1992) did for their mail survey of SMEs, seems unduly wide given the size distribution of businesses in the UK. In 1998, for instance, only just under 3,500 firms (under 0.3 per cent) out of the 1.3m UK firms with at least one employee would be excluded (DTI, 1999a: 7). Some of the other definitions also look poorly related to the size distribution of the UK business population.

What the table also shows is that several of the definitions showed little sensitivity to issues such as sector differences or the utility of

Table 1.5 *Definitions of the small firm used in various studies*

Subject of research	Main research strategy	Sector/sectors	Definition	Sample size
Services small businesses	Face-to-face interviews	Services	Grounded	350
National survey of SMEs	Mail survey	Manufacturing and services	1–500 employees	2,028
Small firms and labour markets	Mail survey	All sectors	Establishments with under 200 employees	3,309
Small start-ups in rural areas	Mail survey	All sectors	Small start-ups	559
Longitudinal study of manufacturing firms	Face-to-face interviews	8 manufacturing sectors	Independent firms with less than 100 employees	306
International study	Mail survey	Manufacturing and services	Less than 300 employees	467
Self-employed people	General household survey data	All sectors	Individuals	N/A
Cross national study of co-operatives	Local face-to-face studies	All sectors	Co-operatives and matched private firms	200
Ethnic-owned businesses	Face-to-face	Retailing, wholesaling and manufacturing	Ethnic-owned businesses	403
Legal forms of businesses	Mail survey	All sectors	Incorporated and unincorporated businesses with under £1m turnover	429
Community enterprises and businesses in managed workspaces	Face-to-face	All sectors	Community enterprises and managed workspaces	346
Subcontractors	Postal survey	All sectors	Under 100 employees	
Family-owned businesses 1861–1891	Historical records	All sectors	Family businesses	781
Financial management	Face-to-face	All sectors	Under 10 employees	200
Policy and small firms	Telephone	All sectors	Under 100 employees	294
Informal venture capital	Postal	All sectors	Users of informal capital	297

Source: Storey (1994)

adopting definitions which might be comparable across studies. Where a definition has 'All Sectors' next to it, for example, it often means the researcher(s) did not take the sector into account at all. Where a type of activity was selected such as 'subcontractor' this may lump together firms involved in a wide range of differing economic activities. One study used 'establishments' rather than 'enterprises' as the unit of analysis. As pointed out earlier, establishments and enterprises are not comparable even when they employ similar numbers.[22]

It would be unrealistic to demand uniformity of approach to defining the small enterprise for research purposes. The only semi-official definitions at all widely used – the EU definitions of 'micro', 'small', 'medium' and 'large' – are simple numerical definitions which, as the earlier discussion showed, are barely adequate. Nevertheless, if that is all that it is possible to employ, then they might be used rather than alternatives if only to promote comparability between studies. Often particular studies require samples selected to serve the specific aims of the research. For example, Oakey et al. (1990) studied new firms in the biotechnology industry and opted for a definition suited to this type of enterprise following a careful investigation of the whole population of such firms. This was possible because this population was small at that time.

Studies of particular localities and local economies may aim to provide a full account of all firms in all sectors. Size definitions here can be simple numerical definitions of the EU variety or be sector-sensitive. They will also probably reflect the actual size distribution of enterprises within the locality. Thus, a 'large' manufacturing firm in a locality might be one with 75 employees if all comparable firms employ ten or fewer. Approaches of this kind may therefore suit the actual sample and the needs of the research even if they lose comparability with other studies.

Despite the importance of sector, it is not always easy to classify a business as being in one sector rather than another. For instance, firms producing a range of products or services may operate in more than one 'sector' (depending on how the latter is defined). NTBSs, for instance, may be pioneers whose products or services cannot easily be placed in existing sector categories. Small firms may throw up this kind of problem less often than larger enterprises because they have a limited range of products or services due to their small size. One solution is to classify the firm according to its main product or service measure by contribution to turnover and/or profits. Another might be to take the sector definition of the owner–manager or managing director: if the firm 'behaves' as part of a particular sector, this may be critical when comparing its strategies, structures and performance with other firms.

In practice, therefore, there are no hard and fast rules to defining 'the small firm' for the aims of any specific project. However, there are some good-practice principles which can be derived from the forgoing discussion. These are summarized in Figure 1.1. The aim is to promote thoughtful, clearly reasoned approaches to the problem and greater

1 Where the simplest definition only can be used, adopt DTI/EU size categories:
   – Micro enterprises firms 0–9 employees
   – Small enterprises 10–49 employees
   – Medium-sized enterprises 50–249 employees
   – Large enterprises 250+ employees
2 While other numerical indicators such as turnover, number of units produced or number of units of capacity (e.g. number of vehicles used by distribution firms or number of hotel rooms in the tourist sector) may be used with advantage, care should be taken that sampling frames will contain all information required to a reasonable level of accuracy.
3 Where possible, attempt to ground the definition in the culture of the sector(s) being investigated. This will require some preliminary study of the kinds of economic activities in which firms in the study will be engaged. The official Standard Industrial Classification codes are useful for defining 'sector' but may not always be suitable for the needs of the research because they often group together quite disparate kinds of activities. (This is very likely where single digit SIC categories are used.) Any attempt is better than leaving 'sector' to define itself. Where a firm's products or services are in more than one SIC, adopt a clear convention such as classifying the firm in the product/service group from which it derives the largest proportion of its turnover. Sector-sensitive definitions may be combined with numerical definitions such as the EU definitions but there may be others such as official or legal definitions applicable to the specific sector.
4 Definitions adopted may depend on available sampling frames so preliminary investigation on the type and quality of such frames (see discussion in Chapter 3) may be required before a final definition is adopted. Inadequate sampling frames may restrict the kinds of definitional strategies which can be used. Ignoring these issues can lead to adopting definitions which lead to poor or inaccurate analyses.
5 Do a literature search to ascertain how other researchers have defined small firms, particularly in studies of the same kind of small enterprise. This a) avoids obvious mistakes in approach and b) increases the comparability of results with previous relevant studies.
6 After formulating a preliminary definition, check the resulting sample against known populations such as DTI SME statistics to assess whether the definition is producing a sample which is representative. Where the sample departs from known sample characteristics, is this expected? It may, for instance, reflect the character of businesses in the specific sector or locality.
7 Where secondary data, such as the General Household Survey, is to be used check whether coding categories employed in the original analyses can be converted to produce a suitable definition of a small enterprise.

Figure 1.1   *Good-practice principles for defining the small enterprise*

consistency between researchers. More issues which can affect definition construction, such as sampling frames and sample selection, are examined in later chapters.

The Audiences for Small Business Research

Researchers need an audience or audiences for their efforts: research is hard work and few would bother if the results were likely to be of no interest to others. Put another way, research has to have relevance. But the question has to be put: relevance for whom? It can be argued that there are five main audiences for small business research.

1 *Academics and other researchers*. The results of research through theorization, proposition testing and the generalization of findings, help us to understand how small businesses function and relate to the wider economy and community. In turn this knowledge may be translated into teaching materials, consultancy and policy advice. The papers presented at the annual Institute of Small Business Affairs (ISBA) National Small Firms Policy and Research Conference always contain plenty of examples of this kind.

2 *Policy-makers*. A primary audience are policy-makers who need well-founded knowledge on the small business to formulate effective policies which use public resources as economically as possible. For example, the Department for Education and Employment commissioned a national survey of training in small firms from the Small Business Research Centre at Kingston University in 1996 (Curran et al., 1996). Equally, policies need to be evaluated and policy-makers often sponsor research-based evaluations (see, for example, DfEE, 1999).

3 *Support bodies*. Enterprise agencies, Business Links and the Small Business Service as well as trade associations also sponsor and use research on small enterprises. The Forum of Private Business, for example, sponsored research on small business owners and BS 5750/ISO 9000 in 1994 carried out by the Manchester Business School (Chittenden et al., 1996).

4 *Private business sponsors*. Larger businesses such as banks may sponsor research on small firms for marketing purposes. For larger businesses such as the high-street banks, small firms are a major market for their services. Other large enterprises sponsor regular small business surveys whose results provide findings on small firms' views on issues such as the National Minimum Wage and how well the economy is performing. Some of these sponsorships can be long lasting. The HSBC financial group, for example, has sponsored the Kingston University Small Business Research Centre for almost 15 years.

5 *Small business owners*. It might seem surprising to put small business owners last here but most people who run their own businesses do not have much time (or perhaps inclination) to read the results of small business research. Nevertheless, they still benefit from research where it influences support agencies and policy. For example, an evaluation of soft loan schemes (Curran et al., 1994) produced good practice recommendations based on its findings to improve the help such schemes give to those starting and developing a small business.

In the UK there has long been a divide between those who 'theorize' and those who 'do' such as practitioners. In small business matters this emerges particularly clearly between academic researchers and the staff of support agencies. Doubts about the value of theorizing or research are often seen as characteristic of British culture. Frequently, such doubts surface in questions of the 'what use is research?' kind. Anti-theorizers (including some small business owners), for instance, argue that if researchers really knew about small businesses and how they can be run successfully, they would be doing just this and making themselves a fortune. But even those who deride 'airy fairy' theory and see themselves as thoroughly practical people, often use a great deal of 'theory' and 'research' (labelled 'common-sense', 'practical experience' etc.) to guide their decision-making.

The problem with common-sense and relying on individual experience is that it is easy to show that they are often poor or limited guides. Common-sense, for example, might suggest that cutting rates of income tax might motivate small business owners to work harder and expand their businesses. Research on the impact of lower marginal rates of taxation on small businesses owners in the 1980s (Rees and Shah, 1993) suggested, however, that they worked fewer hours in the 1980s than in the 1970s. This might have been the result of hardworking business owners taking more time off for leisure and family interests rather than accepting more income. Alternatively, it might have been due to other influences such as shortages of skilled labour making expansion difficult or the additional risks and difficulties such as finding larger premises which often accompany expansion. In other words, personal taxation levels may have been one factor in deciding whether to expand but not the most important one. Researchers would contend that neither common-sense nor personal experience are substitutes for testing accepted views under a wide range of conditions with well-designed rigorous research.

A result of the reluctance of practitioners (and policy-makers) to keep up with research on the small business, the 'I don't need to read all the turgid tosh produced by academics' attitude, is a tendency to continually reinvent the wheel. Projects are undertaken or policies adopted without finding out whether similar projects have been undertaken before or similar policies tried and what research has suggested are the likely results. Often the result is research or policies that not only reinvent the wheel but are inferior to what has been done previously. One key aim of good research, including small business research, is that its results should be cumulative, that is, successive work should build on what has gone before to add to our understanding.

One issue which undertaking research for different audiences raises can be summed up in the question: 'Whose side are we on?' What this refers to is the aims and benefits of research. One view, for example, is that all small business research ought to be dedicated solely to helping small business owners run their businesses more successfully. This is clearly highly worthwhile but should it be the *sole* aim of small business research? Certainly it does not encompass all the topics small business research might cover. For example, there are other stakeholders in small businesses than owner–managers. These include, at the least, customers, employees and the general public. The interests of other stakeholders are not always the same as those of owner–managers.

An easy example of the possible conflict between employer and employee interests in the small firms is linked to employee training. Employees may wish to raise their skill levels to increase their chances of finding better paid and/or more interesting jobs. Small employers often find they cannot afford high levels of employee training. In particular, they often find it very difficult to give employees time off for training away from the business without the business suffering (Curran et al., 1996). Employers have interests in the form of keeping the business in profit; employees have interests in furthering their careers; government has an interest in raising the overall skill level of the labour force to ensure the economy as a whole performs better. Whose 'side' should researchers favour? Or again, in some sectors, small business owners are sometimes accused of routinely evading taxes or health and safety regulations designed to protect employees and consumers. It can be argued that research into such topics is not only legitimate but if the accusations are supported by the findings, then researchers have a duty to report their findings publicly even though some small businesses and their owners will suffer as a result.

The above touches centrally on the issue of research ethics. In any research, the commitment to being as objective[23] as possible in the way questions are asked, in devising the research designs employed and in the analysis of the results, has to be as strong as possible. Equally, the same commitment should guide the presentation of results and their implications. Moreover, this is not simply a matter of ethics *per se*: research which fails to live up to these commitments will, at best, be misleading or simply propaganda. At worst, it leads to wasted resources, ineffective and inappropriate policies, unfounded advice leading to poor practice (by small business owners and support providers) and poor performance. Good theorizing supported by high quality research and analysis has immense practical pay-offs even where not all those affected like the results. Researchers are on the side of understanding and knowledge, not of this or that group of people.

All research is incomplete. No project ever provides a definitive answer to the problems it seeks to understand. Indeed, research sometimes results in having to accept that we know less than we thought we did. What sound research achieves is *more* understanding not complete understanding. Those who expect research to always provide conclusive answers are asking for the impossible. Research chips away at ignorance about whatever topic it focuses upon and seeks to provide more knowledge. But there can be no guarantee that this knowledge will not be superseded by future and better research. This is no less true in physics, medicine and engineering than it is in social and business research, including small business research.

Notes

1 The terms 'business', 'firm' and 'enterprise' are used interchangeably through-out except where otherwise indicated. There is an important distinction between any of the above and the term 'establishment'. This is discussed later in the chapter.

2 There has been a debate on whether the self-employed without employees should be included here. While most, if not all, would accept there are 'businesses' with no employees, such as consultants, designers and furniture restorers, there are others included in the DTI's 'size class zero' where doubts might be raised. For instance, the construction industry has many 'labour only subcontractors' – bricklayers, carpenters, plasterers, etc. – who, although self-employed for tax and social security purposes, are to all intents and purposes employees (Drucker and Macallan, 1996). It might be argued that, at best, these people 'own their jobs' but to describe them as 'businesses' is wrong. Similar arguments are sometimes made in relation to journalists, dancers and artists who are registered as self-employed. By including all the self-employed, it could be said the DTI statistics exaggerate the importance of small businesses in the UK economy. But even if all the size class zero category is excluded, the economic significance of SMEs remains. SMEs with at least one employee would constitute 99.5 per cent of all businesses with employees and be responsible for half the jobs and turnover in the private sector. If only micro and small businesses are considered, they constitute 97.6 per cent of all businesses with employees, provide just under 37 per cent of all jobs and contribute 35 per cent of turnover.

3 These estimates exclude VAT and the base excludes data from enterprises in SIC category J 'financial intermediation'.

4 The precise effect of these (and other) influences on the size distribution of UK businesses is complex and a matter of some controversy. For discussions see Storey (1994: 34–43) and Curran (1999: 9–23).

5 Often in-house data is augmented by other macro-economic data which does not exist for the small firm. Official data, for example, sometimes has a minimum size of firm cut-off or is less detailed than for larger enterprises. The DTI (1999a: Chapter 5), for example, stated that the official Inter Departmental Business Register included around 2m businesses but '. . . its coverage is known to be incomplete among the very smallest businesses' (125). Even where data is offered, the accuracy is often admitted to be suspect for smaller enterprises.

6 This estimate based on DTI data can only be approximate. It was calculated by subtracting all SMEs registered as sole proprietorships from the total number of SMEs in the DTI estimates (1999a: Table 24). It may well overstate because some enterprises recorded as partnerships or as incorporated may still only be run by a single person. Other partners/directors may have 'sleeping' roles with no responsibilities for the running or development of the business. But both Scott and Rosa (1997) and Harding (1998) offer evidence of significant levels of multiple ownership in SMEs in the UK in the form of two or more people owning and running the same firm or a single person owning and running more than one enterprise.

7 Again, this estimate should be treated with care. 'Employee' here refers to anybody recorded as an 'employee' and covers people who were part-time,

temporary or casual workers as well as full-time permanent employees when the data was collected. In addition it also includes self-employed people who run a business which falls within the SME category. It also contains people who are employees in any business (whatever the size) who are self-employed. People running two businesses are counted twice (DTI, 1999a: 128). If only micro and small businesses are considered, the 1.3m total falls only marginally because of the skewed distribution of employment in small firms.

8 However, this convention is at odds with the definition of a part-time employee used by government which stipulates that an employee is part-time if he or she works up to 30 hours a week. If we take a standard working week as 40 hours then on the official definition some part-time employees are really three quarters of a full-time employee.

9 This DTI estimate is for businesses with at least one employee. As Storey (1994: 20) points out, incorporation also varies by sector.

10 Moreover, accounts on public record are often out of date or difficult to use for comparison or aggregation. Directors of SMEs have a number of options in preparing accounts for submission to the Registrar of Companies and some provide less information than in a full set of accounts. See the further discussion in Jarvis (1996).

11 In practice, this approach benefits from prior investigation of the likely range of turnovers in the sector/sectors being investigated. Those new to small business research are sometimes surprised at just how low turnover is in some small businesses. A preliminary investigation can also help in selecting suitable categories to maximize the value of the information collected. For example, rather than offering '£50,000 but under £100,000', prior investigation might suggest most of the businesses fall within this category and therefore two or three categories within this range will produce more revealing data.

12 For example, in 1989 the Department of Employment offered updated versions of the Bolton Committee turnover definitions to allow for inflation. For retailing the original £50,000 was raised to £410,000 (Department of Employment, 1989: 9). A lot of small retailers would have been very pleased indeed to have a turnover of £410,000 in 1989. For example, data from the Midland Bank for 1988 (supplied to the Small Business Research Centre, Kingston University) showed that 70 per cent of *all* the Bank's business accounts had turnovers of less than £70,000. More recently, economists have begun to argue that in both the USA and the UK, price indices of which the UK's version is called the Retail Price Index, have seriously overestimated inflation (see *The Observer*, 20.7.97). This might be another reason why adjustments for inflation used for turnover size definitions appear to grow faster than actual turnover levels of businesses in at least some sectors.

13 Some researchers (see, for example, Curran and Blackburn, 1994) have argued that it is easy to overstate the levels of competition faced by small firms. In interviews small business owners often find it difficult to name any significant competitors. One reason for this is that owners frequently strive to differentiate their businesses from potential competitors by combining a highly personalized, non-standard service with whatever product they offer. In service-based businesses this differentiating strategy is often even more apparent.

14 The Committee decided to exclude agriculture and professional and financial services from their deliberations on the grounds that they considered their

problems too highly specialized to be grouped with the other kinds of small firms covered. A case can be made for excluding agriculture because it is relatively unimportant in the UK economy and treated very differently to other forms of enterprise by government and the EU. But excluding professional and especially financial services appears strange looking back from the year 2000. Professional services are now increasingly regarded as being a businesses like any other even though they may have 'clients' or 'patients' rather than customers. Doctors in general practice, for example, have been pushed to become more business-minded especially where they have become fund holders. Like other advanced market economies, the UK has moved strongly towards a greater emphasis on services and especially financial and business services. Indeed, these sectors had the biggest increase in the numbers of small firms since 1980 of any sector (Keeble et al., 1992).

15 A common example of this approach is using Michael Porter's business strategy model (Porter, 1985) (or some similar business strategy model developed mainly with larger firms in mind) and applying this to small firms for which it is manifestly unsuitable.

16 Besides the obvious 'linear' growth model, that is, the firm growing by adding capital, capacity, employees or entering new markets, offering new products and services, etc. (which still implies a variety of ways of growing even when the firm remains a recognizable single entity), firms may also grow by propagating independent but related enterprises or the owner–manager may dissolve one firm to found another larger enterprise or two or more independent firms may merge or amalgamate or a single firm may expand rapidly by the reverse takeover of a larger but poorly performing firm. All these forms of 'evolution' deserve careful and rigorous study and a suitable theoretical underpinning.

17 The term 'powerful' is used here in a technical sense to mean having greater conceptual clarity and/or the potential to lead to explanations which are able to encompass a greater range of observations, influences and conditions.

18 The results of the research were reported in an extensive set of publications. Examples are Curran and Blackburn (1994), Curran and Blackburn with associates (1992) and Curran et al. (1995). A fuller list is available from the Small Business Research Centre, Kingston University.

19 By 'sector's culture' here is meant the shared meanings as to how the sector's activities are constituted, implemented and sustained and the values and norms which guide those engaged in the sector's businesses and support organizations. Some of the sector's culture as defined here will be in written form but most will probably be only possible to elicit through the oral accounts of those involved. They normally contain, *inter alia*, notions of relative size ('small', 'medium', etc.) for enterprises in the sector.

20 The fundamental weakness of the categorization, 'the small business sector' is one reason, some have argued, why so many policy initiatives designed to support small businesses have so little impact. It is difficult to construct a policy strategy which will benefit *all* 'small firms' because their circumstances vary so greatly with the result that some initiatives actually have negative effects for some small firms even when they help others.

21 If the research is only on 'small firms' defined as those employing under 50 people the same point holds. Any random sample of UK businesses would expect to include only just under one per cent of firms with 50 or

more employees. If the research is confined to firms employing at least one employee, the position changes very little. A random sample of firms with 1–249 employees would expect to contain about 0.5 per cent of firms with 250 or more employees and about 2.5 per cent of firms with 50 or more employees.

22 Figure 1.1 does not include details of the sampling frame employed (a topic discussed at length later in the book) but a wide range of sampling frames were employed which also greatly reduced comparability between studies even where they appeared similar in other respects.

23 Being 'objective' in research does not mean that the researcher has no opinions or values in relation to the topic being researched: all human beings have values, opinions and prejudices in relation to other people and situations. What 'objective' refers to in research is the use of agreed conventions in the conduct of research and presentation of results. These include honesty in describing the research and its methods and, as far as the researcher is able, the truthful reporting of findings. Interpretation and generalization from the findings should be clearly apparent as such to readers. All research should also be open to peer review wherever possible so that weaknesses in research methods and analysis can be identified by others.

2

First Stages in the Small Business Research Project

Research on the small enterprise has a lot in common with most other kinds of social research. Business and management research relies heavily on the principles and procedures which disciplines such as economics and sociology have developed painstakingly over the last one hundred years. Whatever the topic, there are key steps in setting up a research project if it is to produce fruitful results. These steps are the focus of this chapter. There are different audiences for small business research but whatever the audience, research needs to meet the same quality standards.[1]

Some of the groundwork for research is time-consuming, unexciting, even boring, and all too easily skipped over to get to the more interesting stages. A great deal of research requires what might be best termed a *craft orientation*, a willingness to carefully and meticulously complete tasks to a high standard. This is especially important in the early stages of any project. This emphasis on the craft component of research is intended as something of a counter balance to the attention given to the more glamorous, creative aspects. Research on the small enterprise *is* about creative, new ways of thinking about the small enterprise that will enhance our understanding of how it functions. But this is not the whole story, the craft element is also critical. This is not an attempt to substitute a cookery book, recipe-bound approach in place of the creative, knowledge-generating mission of research. It is a response to what many, especially new, researchers feel a need for – that is, practical advice on how to start their projects. The intellectual elements such as the philosophical choices related to research will not, however, be neglected (as the later sections of the chapter demonstrate) since these are also integral to the groundwork for any research.

Facts and Theories

A lot of so-called common-sense thinking takes what is sometimes called a 'naive empiricist' stance which says, in effect, 'let the facts speak for themselves'. Research, in this view, is fact accumulation: if there is to be any theory attached, it can be generated subsequently to order 'the facts' and produce projections or even predictions. For example, 'facts' on profit retention and investment levels by small business owners can be collected which might then later be translated into growth predictions for small businesses, perhaps even into a 'growth theory of the small firm'.

Despite the long-standing appeal of a 'fact accumulation' approach to research, particularly to those who value a hard-headed 'stick to the facts' style which refuses to be 'just theory', it has been dismissed by philosophers of knowledge.[2] All research has a theoretical context: it can never be theory free. There are no such things as 'facts', in the sense of references to the world 'out there', independent of the ways in which observers think about what is external to themselves. In other words, 'facts' and 'theory' are inextricably linked to each other so that separating 'facts' from any theoretical context is nonsense. The popularity of theory-free research rests on a fundamental confusion about how the external environment is experienced and interpreted. The assertion, for example, that 'small business owners are more entrepreneurial than non-small business owners', is not a simple statement that speaks for itself. It is, to use the appropriate technical phrases, both *theory laden* and *theory dependent*. It is theory laden because, to make such an assertion, it is necessary to draw on previous knowledge and ideas about, for example, what a 'small business owner' is,[3] and what kinds of activities constitute 'entrepreneurial' behaviour.

The assertion is theory dependent because it implies a causal relationship between being a 'small business owner' and being 'entrepreneurial'. This linkage may or may not exist in the way implied by the statement. It might be, for example, that the association between small business ownership and behaving entrepreneurially is not direct. Small business owners are young, old, male, female, ethnically diverse, educated to different levels, religious or non-religious, drawn from deprived or privileged backgrounds, have experienced or not experienced parental loss before puberty, have parents or relatives who are, or are not, in business for themselves, etc. Any one or combination of the above influences might have a prior and stronger impact on whether a person behaves 'entrepreneurially' than simply owning a business. In other words, behaving entrepreneurially and small business ownership might well be the outcomes of some other influence or combination of influences.[4]

The above philosophical points have important practical implications for beginning any research project. If all research is theory laden and theory dependent, then this needs to be kept firmly in mind from the very start. In short, research is not simply a matter of going out and collecting 'the facts': theoretical issues have to be part of the initial development of the project. Thereafter, as the rest of this and subsequent chapters demonstrate, this *theory-data coupling* remains in place right through to the dissemination and publication of results.

The Topic

Choosing a topic is often seen as a problem, especially by first-time researchers such as undergraduates meeting a dissertation requirement. Even graduates sometimes have problems despite having completed a first or Master's degree. Some undergraduate and Master's courses offer little research training. Doctoral students, in particular, often worry a great deal about their research topic. If you are going to invest three or more years of your life (much longer for a part-time registration) in researching a topic, it needs to be one you are confident will offer a better than reasonable chance of a successful thesis.

Selecting a topic can be a matter of serendipity: a topic can 'select itself' as if by accident. But relying on serendipity is not the most efficient way of finding a topic. Two well-tried and effective approaches are discussed below. It needs to be stressed, however, that there is no automatic topic-generating process that will guarantee fruitful, relevant research: whatever the approach, it always needs creativity to produce real advances in thinking on the small firm.

Literature and Database Trawling

A well-tried technique is the traditional literature search approach. This might begin by compiling a list of relevant journals and working through them – initially inspecting the indices of article titles, which takes relatively little time – to see what subjects others have selected as suitable for research. Using this technique, it is sometimes also possible to detect trends in research on particular topics. It may also be possible, by inspecting the most recent copies of journals, to pick out what other researchers currently see as 'hot' topics.

The obvious journals are those which concentrate on the small business such as the *International Small Business Journal*, the *Journal of Business Venturing*, the *Journal of Small Business Management*, the *International Journal of Entrepreneurial Behaviour and Research*, *Entrepreneurship and Regional Development* and the *American Journal of Business*.[5] But any such list would need augmenting by adding mainstream business and management journals such as the *Journal of Management Studies*, *Academy of Management Journal* and the *Strategic Management Journal*.[6] These have the occasional article directly concerned with the small business but, even more importantly, other articles may offer indirect suggestions. Thinking and research on topics such as employment relations in larger enterprises can have applications to the small business though care is needed in moving from one to the other. What may be important for larger enterprises may not be for small firms. Practices in large firms may have no or little application or relevance for small firms: small firms are not large firms writ small. Overall, therefore, there are a large number of journals which could help suggest research topics. Fortunately, the advent of computerized bibliographical databases and journals on-line makes literature searching very much easier.

'Very much easier' – but this does not entirely solve the problem. With literature searches using computer-based bibliographies, a main decision is selecting the key search terms likely to produce the most useful suggestions for topics. Just using 'small business', for instance, is likely to produce several thousand references. Many will be of poor quality and attempting to inspect all of them would be very time-consuming. The search can be narrowed by adding a key search term such as 'finance' or 'employment' but the important point to keep in mind is that, whatever the terms selected, the list is never likely to be comprehensive. For example, a key term such as 'employment' used in conjunction with 'small business' may produce a different list of references than if alternative terms such as 'career' or 'worker' were used.[7] Some bibliographical databases only go back a few years and all are incomplete in the sense that they only cover a finite list of journals, etc. They may well miss out key work, in other words.

Earlier references are often not included in computer-based bibliographical databases but should not be dismissed simply because they are old. Some of the classic studies in small business research date from the 1960s and 1970s.[8] In addition, the Small Business Research Trust and the Institute of Small Business Affairs jointly published a register of small business researchers which provided brief descriptions of projects undertaken, or recently completed, in the UK (SBRT, 1998a). The Department of Trade and Industry also periodically sponsors abstracts of key research with evaluations which are also useful (SBRT, 1998b). Sources such as these date fairly quickly but new ones appear from time to time so it is worth finding out whether anything similar has come out recently. New PhD students should consult the British Library's list of theses submitted for research degrees in the UK to find out what others before them have researched on the small business.

Whatever the references found, the reader still has to assess their content. Topics do not jump off the page readymade. Attention has to be devoted to 'seeing' possibilities, making links between ideas or kinds of research. For example, anybody trawling small business research databases will come across increasing references to quality issues and small firms.[9] An inspection of this literature makes it easy to generate further topics linked to quality issues and small firms. For instance, how do ethnic minority business owners manage quality, particularly if their goods and services are targeted at white or other ethnic groups? Are quality issues, particularly when they are culture-related, a barrier to ethnic minority business owners breaking out of their own minority markets to reach the larger national market? How do such barriers, if they exist, compare with other alleged barriers such as finance?[10]

Even simpler is asking the question: how do owner–managers with businesses in particular sectors manage quality issues? There are literally hundreds of different kinds of economic activities in which small businesses are found and often quality issues are very specific.[11] Are there opportunities for comparative studies between small businesses in different sectors or in different countries such as different members of the EU?

For anybody needing a topic to start a research career, the above approach has much to recommend it. First, a lot of basic thinking will already have been documented (although it should never be accepted at face value: being critical of previous work is a requirement of good-quality research). Second, research designs will have been tested and, where they have been proved effective, can often be adapted to new projects on similar topics. It is also possible to compare the results from the old and the new research if the research designs are similar, adding to the interest and relevance of both projects. Third, it helps new researchers' entry in to the small business research community by offering ready made links with others who have faced similar problems researching the topic. Fourth, older research offers benchmarks against which new researchers can compare their work and ensure standards are at least as high (preferably even higher) than previous work.

Brainstorming Strategies

These are another way to generate research topics and can be employed alongside literature-based approaches. The simplest technique is to take a sheet of paper and list words and phrases as they come to mind. Often, even after the first few items, it is already possible to start associating or linking words and phrases to become more complex ideas for a project. While individuals can easily brainstorm in this way, it is more powerful if a group is involved, particularly if they are drawn from different disciplinary backgrounds or areas of business experience. Tape recording sessions ensures nothing significant is lost.

Brainstorming approaches can be rather more formal than just sitting around freely associating words and phrases. Two examples are 'relevance trees' and 'morphological analysis'. Relevance trees (see, for instance, Howard and Sharp, 1983; Mason, 1988) are a graphical approach which starts with a broad title and is then developed to branch into three aspects of the broad title. After considering each of the three, a further three branches are added at a level more specific than the first. This iteration is continued until a topic emerges which looks interesting and viable. Again, individuals can do this or it can be a group exercise but, again also, the approach comes with no guarantee of a sound, fruitful project topic.

Morphological analysis (also discussed by Mason, 1988, as well as by Gill and Johnson, 1997: 17–18) sounds very scientific but is based on a simple matrix approach. Given a broad heading such as 'Owner–Managers and Stress', a list of terms, words, adjectives and nouns is generated to form two or more columns in a matrix formation. Ideas for projects are generated by taking combinations of terms or words from each column and viewing them as titles or key phrases suggesting a possible project. Again, it can be an individual or a group process and comes with no guarantees.

Approaches of the above kind should not be seen as short cuts to intellectual profundity. Most would-be researchers will come up with a topic that is interesting and fruitful through reading and informal discussions with others. Moreover, whatever brainstorming approach is employed, the literature trawl still has to be performed. Finding out what previous researchers have achieved is imperative: no research project starts in a vacuum and apart from simply finding out what has already been established previously, it is obvious good sense to avoid repeating previous work, especially failed work.

Student researchers sometimes claim that they have found a completely new subject for their project. They have spent hours in the library going through computer databases and 'found nothing' on the topic. This is never the case in a strict sense but may appear so at first sight if the topic is very narrowly defined ('the management training problems of small businesses engaged in the production of plastic coated wire products in Yorkshire'). If nothing emerges in a first literature trawl, the search may need widening. It may well be that small firms producing plastic coated wire products in Yorkshire do not have a literature devoted to them. But management training in small businesses does (for reviews see Storey and Westhead, 1994; Curran et al., 1996) and, of course, there is a huge literature on management and business training in general.

It is not possible to draw strict limits for a literature search on any specific topic. Even seemingly unlikely journals may have suggestions for small firm research projects. For example, a journal such as *Housing Studies* would probably be passed over by anybody seeking ideas for a small business research project but a look through issues published in the early 1990s would find articles on home ownership in recession. This might stimulate a project linking home ownership and finance for small businesses. A substantial proportion of small businesses are financed by loans secured on the owner–manager's home. In turn, this might stimulate an investigation of how the housing recession of the early 1990s affected the small business and any lasting impact it may have had.[12]

Analogies and Project Generation

It is possible to develop ideas for projects by seeing analogies with ideas or themes from all kinds of (sometimes unlikely) sources. For example, anybody familiar with the history of Jewish immigration into Britain from 1850 to the early twentieth century will know that many immigrants entered into small-scale enterprise. However, their children were much more likely to enter the professions rather than small business ownership (Kosmin, 1981). It might be suggested therefore that this path will be followed by other immigrant minorities who have come to the UK since the 1950s. A comparative study of different minorities could establish whether this is indeed the case and, even more interesting, under what conditions it is more or less likely to occur. For a first stab at such a study see Curran and Blackburn (1993).

Project generation by analogy is very common in business and management research. In early organizational analysis, for instance, a common model of the organization was the analogy with a machine: each role and part of the organization were seen as similar to the parts of a machine which work together smoothly to achieve a common end. Small business research has also employed analogy approaches. For instance, 'the life cycle' analogy derived from biological thinking (albeit often rather loosely) is sometimes used to blueprint how small firms develop. Small firms, using this analogy, are 'born', 'develop', 'mature', 'decline' and 'die'. (For examples see: Mueller, 1972; Dewhurst and Burns, 1993: 84–6; Leach, 1994: 17–23.)

Of course, analogies *are* analogies, that is, at best, they stimulate ideas about possible parallels between what are otherwise totally different phenomena. Again, therefore, an analogies approach offers no guarantee of successful outcome. Analogies can mislead as well as illuminate. For example, do small firms inevitably 'die'? Often what is termed 'death', that is, a small firm ceasing to trade, is rather misleading. For instance, a highly successful small firm which has grown rapidly, made large profits and has the potential to grow even further ceases to trade (or 'dies' in the life cycle analogy) because it is the subject of a 'reverse takeover' into another, listed, firm. The small firm has ceased to exist but survives healthily in another form.[13]

Topic generation in small business research, though often seen as difficult, is not really. With a systematic approach, some thought and making use of available resources, particularly previous research, it is not that hard to come up with suitable projects. In fact, even a less than strenuous use of the above strategies would be likely to result in a list of possible projects any of which would produce interesting and worthwhile results. But selecting a topic is only one first step in setting up a research project. Other first-stage steps, discussed below, have to be successfully implemented also if the final outcome is to be productive research. There is also an interactive relationship between choosing the topic and these further steps. For instance, it may be difficult to elaborate a topic into a project which can be tested adequately with the resources available. A research student, for instance, is a one person research unit often with very limited resources. In this case, it might be necessary to rethink the topic entirely or, less drastically, adjust the way it is defined to make it more practical to implement.

Concepts, Hypotheses, Propositions and Theories

The topic, once selected, needs elaborating into a proposal. The main concepts related to the topic and hypotheses or initial propositions about how the concepts are linked, has to be spelt out. This needs to be in some detail before firm decisions about the research design, the methods to be used for collecting new or utilizing existing data, can be made. This will help ensure the research design will investigate the topic adequately. It is no use discovering halfway through the project that basic questions that ought to have been asked in the planning stages were overlooked because there was not enough forethought.

For many people, notions such as 'concepts', 'hypotheses', 'propositions' and 'theories' are rather mysterious, though they may be loath to admit this. All are used frequently in everyday discourse but their precise meanings and how exactly they are formed and used in research may be unclear. There are abstruse philosophical issues associated with these terms but, again, as in the earlier discussion under the heading Facts and Theories, the aim here is not philosophical disquisition but making research an accomplishable activity. It is possible to develop suitable approaches to concept formation, hypothesis or proposition making and theory construction, without being too philosophically crude, while still ensuring good quality research.

Concepts

The most helpful way of thinking about 'concepts' is to see them as basic elements in theory and interpretation construction. Concepts are abstract notions which bundle related ideas together in a shorthand form. 'Small business owner', for instance, is a key concept in small business research. Wrapped up in that phrase are an assortment of ideas which need to be made explicit if the concept is to be used clearly and precisely. One way to do this is to offer a definition of 'the small business owner'. This avoids the problems which frequently arise when researchers simply use a phrase such as 'the small business owner' as if everybody knows what it means. One result of vague concept formation, for instance, is that comparisons between studies are questionable because different concepts of 'the small business owner' were used. The problem can be even more serious if the differences are not noticed because concepts were not stated clearly.

Despite the apparent simplicity of the phrase, 'the small business owner', it is not that easy to define in a way which all would agree upon. As Chapter 1 showed, there can be problems defining those who run so-called 'one-person businesses', the self-employed who employ nobody else directly. Some people registered as self-employed operate what many would accept as a 'business' but others are what are termed 'labour-only subcontractors', that is, they work for other employers in much the same way as employees. At the opposite extreme, it needs to be decided at what size (and how 'size' itself is to be measured) does a business cease to be 'small' and, hence, the owner can no longer be called a *small* business owner'? Some formula, in other words, is needed to produce a precise concept of 'the small business owner'.

Note that not all researchers need agree on the same definition or concept content. There is no single 'true' concept of 'the small business owner': different versions may be adopted for different purposes. For example, a research project concerned with employer–employee relations in the small firm might exclude one-person enterprises on the grounds that to study employer–employee relations, the firm must employ people.[14] Similarly, a study of a specific sector might adopt an upper size limit to reflect the size distribution of firms in the sector: a 'small firm' in one sector might therefore reasonably be taken to employ more people than a 'small firm' in another sector. A study of fast-growth businesses might focus on owners of enterprises which have existed under ten years but have a turnover of over £3m and/or over 250 employees. This produces a narrower definition of 'small business owner' than what others would regard as a 'small business owner'.

Of course, it would be perverse to be too eccentric – especially for very common notions in small business research such as 'the small business owner' – or be different for the sake of being different. If there is a wide consensus among researchers, it is helpful to be a part of that consensus if at all possible because it will make results comparable with those of previous research. But researchers may have good reasons for adopting a new approach to concept formation because they want to look at the issues examined in a new way. For example, Jarvis et al. (1996) investigated the financial-management practices of small business owners with an emphasis on cash flow management. Their initial concept of 'cash flow management' was taken from accounting texts where it is a widely used technical term. But they established that their owner–manager respondents, although using the phrase 'cash flow management', were using it in ways which departed from the textbook definitions. They therefore found it necessary to construct a new concept of 'cash flow management' to reflect the behaviour of the small firm owners. In turn, this led the authors to suggest an alternative theory of cash flow management in small firms to that used in analysing the phenomenon in larger enterprises.

The same concept formation process needs to be undertaken for each of the key concepts relevant to the project. A study of stress among small business owners, for instance, would need to develop a clear concept of 'stress'.[15] This concept-formation process goes with the literature search. Firming up concepts is helped greatly by seeing how others have dealt with the same or similar notions. This is particularly necessary where the concept is a difficult one (such as 'stress'). Any newcomers could otherwise waste a lot of time reinventing the wheel and might well end up with an inferior 'wheel' because they were unaware of how others coped with the problems. Moreover, a literature search in relation to a key concept will often uncover a good deal of theorizing using the concept. This could also be very useful in investigating the phenomenon in relation to the small business.

Operationalizing Concepts

One important consideration which needs to be borne in mind when formulating concepts is operationalization. This refers to the practicality of a concept: can it be *used* in research? The key elements in the bundle of ideas which constitute a concept have to be observable and/or measurable in ways which make them clearly identifiable in the data-collection process. For example, concepts of 'the small business' conventionally include (often with other elements) references to measurable parameters such as number of employees and/or turnover.[16] A widely acceptable conceptualization might be:

> A small firm is a legally independent economic unit with up to 50 employees and £500,000 turnover per year whose owner(s) is/are responsible for all key decisions in the day-to-day operation and forward-planning of the enterprise.

In turn, this would allow a concept of the 'small business owner' to be derived. This concept of 'the small business' would not be too difficult to operationalize. Legal independence is relatively easy to establish, data on the number of employees employed and turnover per annum can usually be obtained and the direct involvement of the owners in the running of the business is again relatively easy to establish.[17] A rather less usable conceptualization, on the other hand, might be:

> An enterprise with up to 250 employees and £5m turnover run by its owner(s) in a visionary way which ensures it is always responsive to changes in technology and the market.

This would be difficult to operationalize for a number of reasons. First, as Table 1.1 in Chapter 1 showed, a 250-employee upper limit excludes only 0.2 per cent of *all* UK businesses and the £5m upper limit on turnover similarly excludes only a minority of UK businesses. But, more seriously, how would the notion of 'visionary way' be operationalized? How could it be measured or even interpreted qualitatively since one person's 'visionary way' might be another's 'reckless decision-making' likely to lead to business failure? To demand that the firm 'is *always* responsive to changes in technology and the market' is not only asking a lot in terms of managerial performance but again there is likely to be problems in measuring 'responsiveness' in either context. Equally, the concept of 'small business owner' stemming from this definition of the small business would also be difficult to operationalize.

Sometimes operationalizing concepts takes ingenuity and what at first sight seems difficult or impossible, can be managed even if only imperfectly. For example, one of the key themes of the 1980s and 1990s was the notion of 'the enterprise culture'. Those then on the right of the political spectrum were keen to argue that a revival of 'the enterprise culture' was central to overcoming the severe economic problems which emerged in the 1970s in the UK.[18] Several of these arguments suggested that 'the enterprise culture' was most clearly epitomized by small business owners and especially those who started new enterprises (see, Goss, 1991; Burrows, 1991a).

However, conceptualizing 'the enterprise culture' in a way which would allow it to be clearly measured or shown to be present or absent, is difficult. As Burrows and Curran (1991: 9) remarked 'Whenever there are attempts to give the "enterprise culture" analytic solidity, it melts. Even its advocates appear confused over its meaning.'[19] One solution to this problem was devised by Blackburn et al. (1990) who wanted to find out how small business owners themselves saw and reacted to the enterprise culture. Because of the vagueness of the concept, the researchers first asked respondents (in face-to-face interviews) what they understood by the phrase 'the enterprise culture' and then to say how the 'enterprise culture', as they understood it, was linked to their businesses. Where respondents were unable or unwilling to offer a definition even after further interviewer encouragement, they were shown a card with a definition derived from statements made by ministers and supporters of the then Conservative government. The result was replies suggesting that most owner–managers were either lukewarm about, or explicitly distanced themselves from, notions of 'the enterprise culture' emphasized in the dominant political discourse of the time.

Problems of operationalization should not be allowed to completely dictate concept formation. Concepts need to be generated creatively by researchers to give flesh to their intuitions and ideas about the phenomenon under study. If measurement is given too much prominence for example (particularly if only quantitative measures are acceptable) it can lead to sterile, mechanical research resulting in boring findings which do not advance understanding very far. Where concept-formation needs to be adventurous, worries about operationalization problems come after not before and often need to be solved ingeniously.

Hypotheses and Propositions

Hypotheses or propositions are statements which assert a relationship between two or more concepts.[20] 'Employees in small firms experience higher levels of job satisfaction than workers doing similar work in large firms', is an example. The key concepts in the statement are easily recognized. They are 'employees', 'small firms', 'experience', 'job satisfaction', 'similar work' and 'large firms'.[21] Sometimes hypotheses or propositions may be constructed in slightly different forms to explore variations in the notions being explored. For instance, the above assertion might be paired with one contending that 'employees who have worked in both large and small firms have higher levels of job satisfaction than those who have only ever worked in small firms'.

The terms 'hypothesis' and 'proposition' have been paired above though essentially there is no real difference between them. Some object to the term 'hypothesis' on the grounds that it implies a particular model of research enquiry, that is, one based on research approaches in the natural sciences. The debate underlying this issue (positivist versus non-positivist models of inquiry) is discussed in detail later in the chapter. The term 'proposition' or variants such as 'sensitizing proposition' are more acceptable to those committed to non-positivist models or research. However, the position adopted here is that whatever label is preferred, assertions about relations between concepts are still being made. Thus the terms 'hypothesis' or 'proposition' (or variants) serve the same function and may be treated as equivalents.

Ethnographic approaches (important kinds of non-positivist approaches discussed later) to social and business phenomena, for example, explore the ways in which patterns of regular events and relations between them might be interpreted. Holliday (1995), for instance, undertook an ethnographic study of the layout of the production area of a small garment manufacturing firm. She found this did not conform to any easily recognizable O&M textbook model. Her observations showed that, in fact, the main influences on the production path followed in the making of garments were related to the firm's informal labour recruitment methods and relations between employees. This formed the basis of her qualitative interpretation of the production process in the firm.

Hypotheses and propositions may also change during the life of a research project. One of the best known theory-generating strategies is 'grounded theory' (Glaser and Strauss, 1967). In this approach, a project commences with loose definitions of the key concepts and some speculative initial hypotheses/propositions. Observations are then made and where these do not fit with the initial hypotheses/propositions, these are either restated to encompass the contrary observations and/or the initial concepts are redefined so as to exclude the wayward observations. These lead to increasingly refined interpretations which are then explored through further observation. This process is repeated until what is held to be a robust interpretation is generated. In practice, this iterative refining of hypotheses/propositions and explanations/interpretations is common in small business research, whatever the epistemological preferences of the researchers.[22]

A very useful working principle – whether a positivist or non-positivist approach is adopted – is always to put any proposition in a form where it can be observed to be false. For example, the statement 'all small businesses started by people born in Cornwall either grow, stay the same or decline' cannot be falsified. All businesses would exhibit one of more of these states at some time so there is no chance of learning anything new, which is the aim of any research. One of the main tasks of the operational criteria associated with concepts, whether quantitative or qualitatively based, should be to supply the means of falsifying a hypothesis or proposition.

The above emphasis on falsification rather than on proving any assertion is correct, might look odd at first sight. It is linked to a widely recognized principle in the philosophy of knowledge commonly associated with Karl Popper (1972). This states that no statement about relations between entities (or, as discussed below, any theory since such statements are integral to any theory or interpretation) can ever be proved. There are two reasons why this always holds. First, to be absolutely sure that a statement was true, it would be necessary to observe every instance of the occurrence asserted. But it is always possible that an instance will occur somewhere, sometime, where the relationship does not occur.[23] Second, where human beings are the subject of the assertion, unlike natural phenomena, they are sentient. They can consider and reflect on their situation, which can result in radical changes in their behaviour even under apparently similar conditions. All it is possible to say with some confidence is that in all cases observed the relationship stated held.[24] If the association has been investigated repeatedly using a variety of research approaches, then clearly confidence increases. But it is never certain. Human beings can be remarkably perverse.

The above means that researchers can never say 'it has been proved that . . .' but only that, 'on the basis of the present research and findings, it seems that . . .'. Where claims of certainty about this or that aspect of small enterprises and the people linked to them are made, this is almost certainly an indication of poor research.[25] The refusal of responsible researchers to say something has been 'proved' and that commonly in research (in the natural sciences as well as in social and business research) theories are revised, sometimes radically, often exasperates users of research. One task of researchers is educating users that certainties are no more possible in research than they are in any other area of human activity.

Theory, Explanation and Interpretation

The third of our key terms, theory (sometimes labelled alternatively as 'explanation' or 'interpretation'), is simply the hypothesis(es) or proposition(s) together with additional statements which collectively suggest *why* something occurs. For example, it might be proposed that there is a link between the productivity of employees in small enterprises and the gender of the owner–manager. Assuming that the key concepts have been defined clearly and operationalized, if the results are positive, then the interpretation would suggest why such a relationship exists. In practice, it is likely that further propositions would be added to widen the scope of the project. For example, these might specify under what conditions gender is likely to be linked with higher or lower productivity. For example, it might be theorized that women are more effective in managing businesses where the outputs include a substantial emotional content. This would enable the theory to be more powerful, that is, offer an explanation of a wider range of situations.

Models of Explanation and Interpretation

In discussing concepts, hypotheses, propositions, etc. above, mention was made of positivist and non-positivist approaches to research. These refer to different ways of thinking about what is meant by 'research' and an 'explanation' or 'interpretation' and how research should be conducted. The following three models are especially important.

Hypothetical-deductive. In this positivist approach, commonly associated with the natural sciences, the conceptual and theoretical framework which offers an explanation are formulated in advance of any testing or observation. A research design is developed which operationalizes the key concepts and links between them in the theory. The research process follows, testing the hypotheses and relationships asserted in the theory. If the tests agree with the theory it is accepted even if, strictly, it is seen as provisional since, as noted above, it is unwise to assume a theory is proved in any final sense.

Inductive. This is a mirror image of the hypothetical-deductive approach but may be positivist or non-positivist. Here the bones of the process are intuitions and observations which lead to concept formation, thence to hypotheses and theories. In other words, theory is the outcome of processes of thinking and observation. Earlier an outline of the grounded-theory approach associated with Glaser and Strauss (1967) was given. This is a clear example of an inductive approach to theory.[26] In practice, small business research much more commonly follows some variant of the inductive rather than the hypothetico-deductive approach but examples of the latter can be found, particularly in economics (see, for example, Reid et al., 1993).

Ethnographic or qualitative. This model rests on a fundamentally different notion of research. The hypothetico-deductive, and some versions of the inductive models outlined above, were labelled 'positivist' because of the way they are apparently modelled on approaches in the natural sciences and especially physics. Advocates of ethnographic or qualitative models (as well as some of the inductive approaches used in social and business research) argue that the subject matter of social research is fundamentally different from that of the natural sciences. The subject matter of the natural sciences are non-sentient, that is, they may be said to behave but they do not have a conscious awareness of the environment in which they exist.[27] The subject matter of the social sciences, including much of the subject matter of interest to business research, has awareness, that is, the subjects are conscious of their environment and can even restructure it significantly. Their behaviour reflects this and their internal states and purposefulness must be taken into account in explaining or interpreting why they act in the ways that they do. In this model, human action can only be understood in terms of the perceptions and internal logics which arise from this special consciousness and awareness of the environment which human beings possess. Thus, while the subject matter of the natural sciences can be studied and understood by imposing an external logic or theory on it, the subject matter of the social sciences cannot be understood in this way: the meanings, interpretations, intentions and world views of the subject matter (human beings) must also be incorporated. This model has gained enormous ground since the 1960s in the social sciences and business research, though less so in the latter.

The importance of the distinction between the non-positivist ethnographic or qualitative models, on the one hand, and positivist models on the other, cannot be over-stated and the implications for small business research need to be considered carefully. A great deal of theorizing and research employing both positivist and non-positivist models has been devoted to the small business. But even though the two approaches co-exist, the distinction between them remains profound.

An example of a positivist approach is the study by Storey et al. (1987) of small business performance that attempted to generate a model to predict small business success and failure. The approach was essentially quantitative using publicly available financial, employment and other data on businesses and their owner–managers from 636 single-plant manufacturing companies in the north of England. The data was subjected to extensive statistical analyses to produce predictive statements, particularly in relation to business failure. The authors make very clear the limitations of both the data and sample as well as of the final model. Overall, it is fair to say that models of this kind, though common in small business research, have not been found to have any great predictive power.

A non-positivist approach would argue that a major reason for the weak predictive power of positivist analyses of the small business is that they largely fail to give due weight to the key person in the enterprise:

the owner–manager. *Because* the business is small, owner–managers' motivations, aims and the 'logics' they construct upon which they run their businesses are very important in determining the performance of the business. Moreover, in incorporating owner–manager motivations and aims into any interpretation of the way the business operates, it is necessary to investigate those of real life business owners rather than *assume* what they are. For example, it is common in economic studies of small business performance to assume owner–managers are profit maximizers reflecting the assumptions fundamental to classical economic theory.[28] However, studies of real-life small business owners show that profit maximization is rarely a prime motivation in the way they operate their businesses (see, for example, Scase and Goffee, 1980; Jarvis et al., 1996).

An example of a non-positivist, ethnographic study of small business owners which highlights the importance of their motivational patterns and respondents' internal logics, is Curran et al. (1993a). They studied small business owner motivations in relation to what they termed 'critical incidents'. The latter refers to any kind of event which could severely disrupt the business. Events of this kind could include a serious dispute between two or more partners/directors of a business, the loss of major customer, family problems such as severe illness or death of a spouse or making a crucial investment decision for the business. The main proposition tested was that although previous research suggested small business owners were normally reluctant to seek outside help and support, when a critical incident arose such help would be sought to assist the business through its difficulties.

In fact, the findings suggested the opposite: owner–managers were no more and often *less* likely to seek help in solving critical incident problems. The authors argued that the reasons for the unexpected finding were related closely to the meanings and values attached to small business ownership. Owner–managers frequently display an exceptional commitment to independence and autonomy. Seeking external help, even in a crisis, is resisted because of a reluctance to compromise or even appear to compromise, this independence. Many owner–managers worked long hours and found it difficult to find the time to go outside the business for advice on, for example, investment in new equipment. Some owner–managers were also reluctant to let outsiders know that the business had a serious problem for fear their reputation and that of the business, might be hurt. The authors concluded that only an ethnographic approach would produce an interpretation of this kind and that positivist approaches would find it very difficult to explain many of the decisions made by small business owners in such situations.

There is no need to adopt a view *a priori* that only a positivist or a non-positivist approach is valid in small business research. Rather it is horses for courses: each is appropriate for particular kinds of topics. For example, since 1980 there has been a great deal of interest in the job creating propensities of small firms both in the USA and the UK (see reviews in Harrison, 1994: Chapter 2; Storey, 1994: Chapter 6). One important theme in this research has been that while large firms have been net losers of jobs for most of this period, small firms have been net creators. Testing this proposition has been most easily achieved using positivist, quantitative approaches.

On the other hand, finding out about the *quality* of jobs in small firms in terms of levels of involvement and satisfaction among employees and how they gauge their relations with employers would be an excellent topic for qualitative research. A participant observation approach, for instance, might be very effective (see, for example, Holliday, 1995) or semi-structured, face-to-face interviews with carefully selected samples of employees and their employers might be used (see, for example, Kitching, 1997). Often research on small firms benefits strongly from a mix of quantitative and qualitative approaches, a form of 'methodological triangulation' (Denzin, 1970: 308). The use of a mix of methods helps by ensuring that the weaknesses and blind spots of one approach are compensated by the strengths of one or more other approaches. Confidence in the conclusions will be higher if different approaches have produced similar results.

Constructing Theories and Interpretations

As the above makes clear, theories or interpretations are made up of one or more hypotheses or propositions linked by additional statements so that, together, they offer an answer to 'why' questions.[29] The hypotheses/propositions need to be investigated by whatever form of observation are seen as appropriate. This will depend, in part, on whether a positivist or non-positivist approach has been adopted. But regardless of the approach, the testing processes need to be rigorous: only theories or interpretations which have withstood close examination are given real respect by others. Almost always, developing a theory or interpretation supported by sufficient relevant findings is hard work and expensive if only in researcher's time. One aim, therefore, should be to avoid the trivial.

One of the most common criticisms of research – especially research for a PhD – is that it often involves a detailed investigation of some trivial or minor topic of little or no importance or interest to anybody except the researcher, if even to him or her. Critics of small business research seize on any examples which they believe show that publicly funded support is often a waste of taxpayers' money or that commercial sponsors are paying to be told the obvious. As argued earlier, selecting interesting and worthwhile topics is not actually that difficult. Attention, consequently, should be given to avoiding the trivial when selecting and designing research projects.

Essentially, non-trivial proposals mean that the project should be defined in such a way that, whatever the results, they should still be interesting. Gill and Johnson refer to this as ensuring 'a symmetry of potential outcomes' (1997: 14–15). For example, a small business research project might test the idea that the businesses of owner–managers who have undertaken financial management training will have higher rates of growth than those of owner–managers who have no such training. If the results show that, in fact, the reverse is the case or that there is no difference then that would be interesting. But if the findings show that the proposition is correct, the results will not be nearly so interesting or even be seen by critics of research as a good example of resources wasted 'proving the obvious'.

In contrast, in a study whose central proposition stated that 'where a business has two or more owner–managers, faster growth is achieved where there is a strict division and centralization of key managerial functions between the owner–managers', it would not make much difference what the results showed. Either way, the study would produce interesting findings. If the findings supported the proposition, it would have implications not only for small business growth but for management and organizational theory more generally since recent thinking has tended to favour decentralized, team approaches to management decision-making and a reduction in functional demarcation (Goffee and Scase, 1995). If, on the other hand, the findings did not support the proposition, they might suggest what alternative patterns of managerial division of labour in multi-owned small firms were most associated with rapid growth.

In describing the project it is always useful to make links with other research and thinking as well as policy. Often influential theorizing in business research is based on the large enterprise with little or no reference to the small business. For instance, total quality management (TQM) has been advocated as a solution to a wide range of organizational problems (Barad, 1996). But the discussion has been large firm-centred with little research on the usefulness of TQM in smaller businesses.[30] In other words, the neglect of the small business in much contemporary business and management thinking offers opportunities for small business researchers.

Most small business research has policy implications. There is a great deal of policy aimed at helping the small enterprise (see Storey, 1994: Chapter 8; DTI, 1999b). The link between research and policy may not always be obvious at first sight but a little thought usually shows a connection. For instance, a study which improved the ability to predict small business failure has obvious implications for support policies but the 'critical incidents' study described briefly above might seem less relevant. Yet the authors argued that the findings help explain why it is apparently so difficult to persuade small business owners to take advantage of the help (often free or subsidized) offered by support agencies such as the Small Business Service. If small business owners are so reluctant to seek outside help even when the business is experiencing some kind of crisis, it might be even more difficult to reach them when the business is running reasonably smoothly.

Putting it Down on Paper

Having selected a topic, identified and defined the main concepts, set up some initial hypotheses or propositions and perhaps formed a preliminary theory or interpretation, one of the most helpful next steps is to write the whole thing up as a proposal or working paper. If the project is to form the basis of a PhD, then a proposal will almost certainly be needed. Equally, if outside funding is sought from, for instance, ESRC, a written proposal – with costings – will be needed. But even for a project which has no sponsor, the value of putting the proposal on paper cannot be urged too strongly. ESRC and other funding bodies usually insist that proposals should be brief, perhaps six or so A4 pages. This means the proposal requires a succinct, effective presentation. A working paper would usually be longer and incorporate a more detailed literature review than a proposal to a funding source.[31]

A working paper or proposal needs to maximize its value in developing a research project (and win funding where it seeks this also). Four main areas should be covered.

Title and introduction   Emphasizing attention to the title might seem trite but having to come up with a brief form of words for a title does help in crystallizing the main concerns of the project. In winning outside funding, a title can hint at the intellectually important and exciting focus of the proposed project. Other sponsors, such as those in industry, might be impressed with any obvious practical dividends the title suggests. For a research student, the title will probably end up as the title of the thesis also so a little care at this stage is in order. It should give a clear idea of the concerns of the thesis but should be elastic enough to accommodate any of the unforseen developments which commonly occur as the fieldwork and analysis progress. The introduction itself should give a brief general statement on why the research is potentially interesting, that is, place the project in a wider context, making links with other intellectual concerns, users' problems or policy.

The project stated more precisely   The next section should focus more narrowly on the topic. For example, a project might be concerned with small business training but no research project can cover *all* small business training. So here the specific aspects of small business training that will be investigated and the reasons for choosing them, need to be explained. Relevant previous thinking and research will be referred to and commented upon critically to show how the proposed project will develop understanding on the topic. The key hypotheses/propositions to be investigated together with any supporting reasoning, should be stated. This section, though longer than the opening section, need not be very long: being succinct is important.

Research design   The research design, that is, how the research will be conducted concentrating on the mechanics of the process – how the data will be collected, what kinds of secondary sources will be used, etc. – needs to be specified clearly.[32] The design has to appear practicable and manageable. A research student who proposes to personally conduct 500 two-hour, face-to-face interviews with owner–managers throughout the UK over nine months would be attempting the near impossible. As argued earlier, the practical aspects of research are as important as the intellectual in achieving a successful outcome. A clearly thought out, systematic research design showing an awareness of the difficulties likely to be encountered and how they might be solved, is very helpful in persuading a research committee or potential sponsor. A timetable should be included showing the time to be devoted to each stage of the project, the outcomes or 'milestones' to be achieved at each stage and the overall time to completion. Again assessors, who will frequently be experienced researchers, will use this to gauge the practicality of the project and the capabilities of the researcher.

Outcomes   The proposal or working paper should end by stating the expected outcomes of the project. These will not, of course, state the precise results: if this were possible there would be no point in carrying out the research. But outlining the expected outcomes is a good way of testing whether the project meets the symmetry of outcomes criterion discussed above. Research students need to state how their work will contribute significantly to advancing knowledge. Research for support agencies or commercial sponsors should state how the results will meet the sponsor's aims. Sometimes it is possible to offer a sponsor extra results without incurring any extra work or costs. This could give a winning edge to a bid when competing against other bids.

Costings where needed are usually presented separately. It is difficult to give advice on costings. Many research proposals are distinctive, which makes them difficult to price. Advice from experienced researchers or quotes from commercial research agencies can be helpful. The market is imperfect here in the sense that market prices, even for routine projects, are hard to come by. Sponsors are often reluctant to reveal their budget to keep the price down. Research teams often regard their pricing policies as secret to keep potential rivals in the dark. But keep in mind that offering to undertake a project at too low a price may win funding but is likely to produce serious problems later. Researchers need to be sure that not only can they deliver at the price they tender, but the price allows the research to reach the quality standards by which they would wish to be judged by their peers. It is foolish and self-defeating to do research for a price which will not allow these criteria to be met.

Conclusions

This chapter has covered the early stages of developing a small business research project. It has stressed that all research is both a craft and an intellectual activity. Research needs to be creative to produce new ways of thinking and new findings about the small business but it also has to be well-executed. Often the craft element is neglected in favour of the more glamorous, creative aspects but here, and in the rest of this book, the two elements are treated as equally important and as mutually supporting of each other.

A popular and naive view of research is that it is essentially concerned with collecting facts. A more sophisticated view shows that all research – no matter what the audience is for its results – is theory-laden and theory-dependent: there is no such thing as fact separated from theory. This means that the researcher has to be conscious of the need to integrate observation and theory at every stage of the project.

Choosing a research topic sometimes appears difficult, particularly to first-time researchers. The chapter offered advice on topic selection based on established methods. The discussion showed that, in fact, given some initial reading and thought, it might well be that the first-time small business researcher will end up with the problem of which one from a list of attractive topics to choose. Certainly, the small business is an area exceptionally rich in research topics.

Small business research is now a well-established area of social and business enquiry. Any new project needs to grow out of what has gone before even if it takes a radically different view, rejecting previous approaches. Even where there are no obvious links with previous small business research, there are links with other business and social research which will be relevant. Indeed, taking ideas from what is often at first sight totally unrelated thinking and research, can be a very fruitful source of new approaches to small business issues. But this should never be an unthinking borrowing of ideas. For instance, theories and approaches developed to analyse large enterprise behaviour may not translate easily to the small firm context.

Several core elements of the first stage of the research process – 'concepts', 'hypotheses', 'propositions', 'theories' and 'interpretations' – were discussed in detail. Although all are familiar terms in everyday discourse, their precise meaning in research is not always clear. Yet a sound understanding of what they refer to and the role they play, is indispensable. 'Concepts' were defined as basic elements in theory construction. They refer to bundles of ideas summed up in short-hand terms or phrases ('the small business', 'the small business owner', etc.). They have to be clearly defined if the research is to be a successful addition to understanding the small business and the way it functions. Even something as apparently obvious as 'the small business owner' was shown to be a concept which could be defined in several ways depending on the research project's needs. In short, there is no single 'true' concept of 'the small business', 'the small business owner', etc. This variation is an additional reason why definitions need to be clear.

Concepts need to be operationalized, that is, some measures or indicators are needed to be able to use them in research. 'Small business performance' can mean a lot of different things and each definition needs criteria for using it in any study of small businesses. In other words, a concept is made operational by generating rules for how it is to be used in real-world situations. 'Business performance', for example, might be measured by year-on-year changes in the return on capital employed by the business or the value of the output produced by each employee. Different measures might be used in different studies for different reasons. Again, therefore, there is no 'true' or 'universal' measure or indicator for any concept: it depends on the research issue and theory being generated. But whatever the measures or indicators, they need to be as unambiguous as possible. Operationalizing concepts can demand as much creativity as any other aspect of research.

Hypotheses and propositions link concepts. They assert possible relationships which will be investigated in the research project. The terms 'hypothesis' and 'proposition' were treated as equivalents. However, some researchers dislike the term 'hypothesis' because they see it as too closely linked to positivist models of the research process, which they argue are inappropriate to social and business research. But those who take a non-positivist position still focus on links between concepts as defined above but employ fundamentally different approaches to analysing how the links occur. 'Proposition' or similar labels such as 'sensitizing proposition', etc., serve very much the same purpose in their approaches. Hypotheses or propositions are not fixed. They may well be revised and revised again as a research project develops and data and observations are accumulated.

In investigating hypotheses or propositions, it was stressed that the aim should not be, as is sometimes popularly supposed, to prove they are true or correct. On the contrary, a good rule of research is that the emphasis should be on falsification, on showing them to be wrong. The reason for this is that, strictly, proving a hypothesis is true is impossible when a positivist approach is adopted. The relationship stated in the hypothesis might be observed 10,000 times but it is always possible that a further observation will show it to be false. On the other hand, only one observation that it is false is needed to show it needs revising. A similar principle is helpful in non-positivist approaches. Where human beings are involved, the chances of relationships between concepts holding permanently is always going to be low because human beings can reflect on their situations and change their behaviour. Human beings inherit their environments and situations but they also create and sustain them through their thinking and actions. So any proposition will produce provisional results at best but by looking for exceptions or contrary observations, any interpretation will be challenged. The result is usually a stimulus to a more insightful interpretation. But whatever model is favoured – positivist or non-positivist – all hypotheses or propositions are provisional.

Theory, the last of the key terms examined, is simply hypotheses or propositions, usually combined with additional statements, to form an explanation or interpretation. In positivist models they lead to 'if A then B' type statements with related predictions. In qualitative research the equivalent is the propositions and the linking statements which form an overall interpretation but with a much lower emphasis on prediction. The reason for these differences is that positivist and non-positivist approaches are based on different models of explanation. The differences between these models relate to the debate about how a knowledge of human action and social phenomena is produced. The *hypothetical*, *inductive* and *ethnographic* or *qualitative* models were outlined to show these distinctions. While the differences between them are profound, with some researchers only ever using a positivist or a non-positivist approach, the position adopted here was that each has a role to play in generating knowledge about the functioning of the small business.

Research projects usually start with provisional theories/interpretations and it was stressed that care should be taken to ensure a 'symmetry of possible outcomes'. This means that in setting up the project it is wise to do so in such a way that whatever the findings, the outcome will be of interest. This avoids the risk of trivial research whose results are not very exciting, even to the researcher. This is important for any research but is particularly important for those committing a lot of time and effort to a PhD, or where the research is resource-expensive.

Finally the chapter discussed the construction of research proposals and the value of an initial working paper that helps researchers to be really clear about what they want to achieve. Just as important, it minimizes the chances that a major fault in the thinking underlying the project will emerge later, thus rendering the results worthless. Being able to translate the research project into a research proposal is usually necessary for registering for a research degree and is essential to win funding from bodies such as ESRC or other sponsors.

This chapter has covered the initial stages in the development of the small business research project, trying to ensure that these are based on a clear, well-thought out approach. The following chapters concentrate on the next stages and the analysis and writing up of the results. But the importance of sound preparation is difficult to overstate. It is the bedrock upon which interesting, worthwhile research is built to add significantly to knowledge and to meeting the needs of research users such as support providers and policy-makers.

Notes

1 Some object that some clients do not want 'over-academic' research with its jargon-ridden presentation, footnotes, references and reluctance to offer unambiguous conclusions. What clients in the business world want, it is argued, is down-to-earth, results-centred reports which solve their problems. But we should not confuse presentation with research quality standards: the two are not mutually exclusive. It also needs to be kept in mind that non-academic clients are not necessarily the most informed consumers of research.

2 Given this book focuses primarily on small business research as a practical activity, the discussion does not enter too deeply into philosophical discussions of how knowledge is established. This is not because such issues are not important: on the contrary they are among the most important addressed by philosophers. But they are also highly technical and only a working knowledge is required for the accomplishment of competent research. For those who wish to investigate philosophical issues in more detail, the following offer introductions: Hughes (1992), Sayer (1992), Gill and Johnson (1997).

3 As the discussion in the last chapter showed, deciding what is a 'small business' is itself problematic and logically requires settlement before deciding what a 'small business owner' should be taken to mean.

4 In fact, there is a lot of research exploring links between the influences listed above and small business ownership. For example, Burrows (1991b), Meager (1991) and Gray (1998) summarize findings linking small business ownership with gender, age, ethnic origin, educational achievement, class origin and parental experience of small business ownership. One of the best known of all sociological theories is that of Weber (1952) who linked Protestant religious beliefs with the kind of people who pioneered modern business ownership from the seventeenth century onwards.

5 This is not a complete list of specialist small business journals and new journals appear from time to time. As a rule of thumb, older journals are likely to contain more important work since new journals take time to establish themselves.

6 In addition, some more general journals in the social sciences such as *Human Relations*, and *Work, Employment and Society* often contain articles concerned with small business issues. Some social science disciplines also have specialist journals devoted to the small business such as *Small Business Economics*.

7 Similarly, if 'company' is used in place of 'business' or 'enterprise', the same result might happen. A smart move is to enlist the help of a specialist-information librarian in setting up the search.

8 The London Business School's *Small Business Bibliography* mentioned in Chapter 1, contains most of the earlier research on the small business and provides references to a great deal of the work not on computer-based bibliographic sources.

9 Much of this research has been concerned with ISO 9000 (formerly BS 5750) or 'Total Quality Management' (TQM) and small businesses. More recent research, however, has widened investigation to encompass quality management strategies in small firms more generally. Examples are Chittenden et al. (1996); Roper et al. (1997); North et al. (1998).

10 Some topics are inherently more difficult to investigate than others. Investigating quality management strategies among ethnic small business owners, for example, might be much more easily undertaken by somebody who is able to use their knowledge of the minority's language and culture. Besides easier access, this will make it easier to cope with the subtleties of quality issues where they cross cultural boundaries.

11 The authors supervised a research student studying service delivery in the printing industry which included quality issues. The study compared printing firms and their customers in the UK and Finland and easily generated sufficient data for a doctoral thesis.

12 In fact, just such a link was made by our former colleague, Roger Burrows, now at the Centre for Housing Policy, University of York. This resulted in an article 'Self-Employment and Home Ownership After the Enterprise Culture' (Burrows and Ford, 1998).

13 For another excellent illustration of the limitations of analogy approaches see Ram and Holliday (1993) who demonstrate the care needed in using the analogy between the family and the small firm. The family and family relations have been a very popular way of conceptualizing internal social relations and functioning of the small enterprise.

14 This is not as obvious as it might seem. A project studying how employer–employee relations develop in small firms might wish to define 'the small firm' to include firms which have yet to employ their first employee in order to study how owner–managers cope with the first stage in acquiring a labour force.

15 For an example see Williams (1985). 'Stress' is one of those concepts where a researcher would be very wise to explore the previous literature where this highly problematic concept has been subject to a good deal of refinement.

16 Here 'measurable' clearly refers to quantitative measures (number of employees etc.) but 'measurable' in the social sciences and small business research may be much less precise than this. It may be possible, for example, to say with confidence that one small business owner is 'much more' growth-minded than another but impossible to say by how much in any quantitative form.

17 This is not to say that there will be no operationalization problems in relation to the concept. For example, establishing the number of employees may be difficult where, for example, the firm uses self-employed people to meet most of its labour needs. Should they be seen as 'employees' in operationalizing this concept? Other firms may use mainly casual or temporary labour and, hence, the size of the firm may vary from day to day. Collecting data on turnover may not be easy because owner–managers may be reluctant to give such information. Even when information is offered, it may not be clear how the respondent has estimated turnover. It may refer to gross sales or total sales after allowing for costs of production and in some sectors may be calculated in specific ways. In advertising, for example, it may refer to 'total

billings', that is, the value of the advertising etc. they handle as priced to the client at gross value.

18 It was only in the 1990s that the Labour Party adopted a similar view of the importance of the enterprise culture and its links with the small business. See, for example, Gavron et al. (1998); DTI (1998).

19 Pratt (1990) for example, was unable to elicit a definition of the 'enterprise culture' in the late 1980s from even those among its keenest advocates, such as Conservative Central Office, the Department of Trade and Industry or the then Department of Education and Science (whose ministers were then Conservatives).

20 The meanings of 'hypothesis' or 'proposition' used here are not the only ones but are chosen to make exposition as straightforward as possible. An alternative, for instance, is to make them in forms which imply explanations or interpretations. For example, 'higher levels of training in small firms leads to higher levels of productivity because workers are more satisfied' not only asserts a link between 'training' and 'productivity' but suggests why. Here the assertion also contains a theory or interpretation. In the discussion in this chapter, answers to 'why' questions are dealt with separately below in the section on theories and interpretations. The practical implications of this separation for researchers are not great.

21 'Job satisfaction' is another good example of a concept which is difficult to define but has generated an enormous number of attempts to provide clear, usable notions. Occupational psychologists, in particular, have thought long and hard about the problems of conceptualizing job satisfaction or 'occupational well-being'. For an early example of its use in relation to the small firm see Curran and Stanworth (1981a) which shows a careful approach to concept formation in relation to job satisfaction among small business employees.

22 Refining hypotheses or propositions and generating successive interpretations need not be part of the same project. In much research, it occurs in successive projects conducted by separate researchers. This is one of the ways in which cumulative improvements in understanding occur. For example, a study might focus on the assertion 'when small business owners are offered free management training they will enthusiastically take up the offer' and find that the take up was very low. This might lead to a further project testing the assertion that lack of time or the lack of relevant training courses prevents small business owners from taking up free offers of training and so on.

23 A common example used to illustrate the need to be cautious about claiming certainty about any observation is that until Australia became known to people in Europe, they could assert with total confidence that 'all swans are white'.

24 'With some confidence' is another hint at the need for caution in any assertion no matter how thorough the research. It could be, for instance, that the measuring techniques or indicators used to assess the statement are poor so that instances are not observed reliably. Whether a positivist or non-positivist approach is being employed, this still holds.

25 Sometimes results are reported in a way which implies certainty. Consultants, for example, know clients want decisive recommendations and that anything less is likely to be regarded as the consultant being less than confident or

evasive. Unfortunately, presenting research in this way does not help educate consumers on the limitations of research.

26 Although the most cited text on grounded theory (Glaser and Strauss, 1967) is subtitled 'strategies for qualitative research' and the approach is usually taken as being concerned solely with qualitative approaches (discussed immediately below), Glaser has asserted (in a 1996 workshop at Kingston University) that it can be used in positivist approaches just as effectively.

27 This distinction is not as black and white as indicated here. Some areas of the natural sciences which deal with birds, reptiles and animals (including humans) can be said to deal with sentient beings even if, in the case of non-humans, there may be debate about the degree to which they may be said to be sentient. However, the principle here is that the subject matter is treated *as if* it was not sentient. In some areas, particularly in medical science, some argue that dealing with human beings in this way leads to failures in explanation and inappropriate treatments.

28 For an example, albeit one which is tempered by considerable observation of small business owner behaviour, see Reid et al. (1993: 3). A similar approach is sometimes adopted in theorizing about growth in the small business when it is assumed that small business owners will, except under exceptional conditions, always want to maximize growth. However, research on the motivations and behaviour of real-life small business owners shows that, in fact, most small business owners do not want to grow or, at best, only wish to grow at a slow, manageable rate (see, for example, the discussions in Storey, 1994: Chapter 5; and Goffee and Scase, 1995: 41–50).

29 The term 'interpretation' rather than 'theory' or 'explanation', is often preferred by qualitative researchers for reasons similar to those for their reluctance to use the term 'hypothesis'. They feel that 'theory' or 'explanation' is too closely tied to positivist models and their stress on predictive power. Since human beings can, and frequently do, change their views of what constitutes appropriate behaviour in particular situations, qualitative researchers argue that positivist-type predictions are impossible in social and business research. At best, what can be offered is an interpretation which may allow informed estimates of what is likely to happen when the same or similar actors encounter the same or similar situations in the future. But there can be no guarantee that this will occur and, correspondingly, they put very much less emphasis on the importance of predictive power in any analysis.

30 North et al. (1998) investigated quality management strategies in small businesses and found that TQM in the form taught in business schools, did not have much relevance for small firms. Instead, small firm owner–managers often had strategies which were as, or even more, effective than the benefits claimed to come from TQM but which large enterprises would find hard to use because of their size.

31 There are now numerous generic templates available for preparing research proposals (see, for example, Jankowicz, 1995). Some are included as parts of wordprocessing packages. However useful these may be, a good proposal comes from sound preparation and background research. They certainly cannot be generated merely by filling the appropriate boxes in a pro-forma template.

32 These issues are covered in detail in the following chapters but it is worth noting that small business research often has very specific and sometimes

difficult problems in accessing data. Experienced assessors of small business research proposals often find that proposals they are asked to read have weak research designs which underestimate the difficulty of some of these problems. This can mean that while the project seems interesting, the proposal's worth is doubted because it is deemed impractical.

3

In the Field

The distinctiveness of small business research is nowhere more apparent than in the fieldwork stage. Finding and recruiting samples, collecting and processing data – the essential elements of fieldwork – all have very subject-specific challenges. While most common social research techniques can be used, some are difficult or have to be used in specific ways to work effectively. A great deal of small business research, particularly by first-timers but even by experienced researchers, is rendered superficial by failures to tailor fieldwork procedures to the special characteristics of the small enterprise.

This chapter is concerned with the *research design*. This encompasses the practical procedures for accessing the subjects of the research (small business owners, employees, suppliers, customers, support providers and others) the methods used to collect data (surveys, interviews, secondary data, case studies, etc.) and organizing the data collected for analysis. Like other parts of the research process, there is a craft element involved. This is especially the case for data-collection. Despite the apparent simplicity of interviewing, for example, most people find they are not born interviewers. But there are techniques which can be learnt which, with practice, can make most researchers competent interviewers.

There are an infinite number of possible permutations of the elements which make up a research design. But as the last chapter indicated, the character of a project often narrows the choices. For instance, a project on small business owner economic confidence levels in Scotland aimed at measuring changes over time, would almost certainly be survey-based. It would need to collect responses from a large enough number of owners to be sure of gathering responses across the whole range of economic activities in which small businesses are engaged as well as from owners in different geographical areas. The approach would have to be standardized so that differences in responses over time could be attributed to real changes in views rather than changes in the data-collection process itself. The research design could include other data-collection strategies to support the survey, such as focus groups, to reveal more about why owner–managers held particular views, but if the aim was a periodic snapshot of Scotland's small business owners' views, a survey would probably be the most effective instrument.

On the other hand, a project on how small business owner–managers in the printing industry manage the introduction of new technology could opt for a national survey but this would probably not be the most effective strategy. There are a very large number of general printing firms in the UK.[1] This suggests a relatively large sample would be needed. Large-scale surveys, typically employ standardized 'tick the box' questionnaires, particularly if, as is likely, they are telephone or mail-based because large-scale, in depth face-to-face interview surveys are expensive. But these kinds of large-scale surveys would be unable to investigate in sufficient depth the complex processes involved in introducing new technology in firms.

Instead, the project would be much more likely to use a case study approach based on a small number of firms. Case studies can be very effective when investigating complex change processes (Yin, 1994; Stake, 1995). Not only the business owners but employees, suppliers and customers might also be included so that their experiences could be included in the analysis. Because in-depth case studies are expensive per case and produce large amounts of data with corresponding problems for analysis, sample sizes tend not to be large. In small business research, for instance, case study samples rarely exceed 25 and are often fewer than ten. Although the sample would therefore be much smaller than in a standard survey, a follow-up mail or telephone survey might be used to check the representativeness of the case study firms' experiences.

Since this chapter aims at showing the range of research design issues in small business research, the discussion will not explore technical issues in great depth. So, for example, there is no treatment of data analysis techniques such as SPSS (Statistical Package for the Social Sciences) – a widely used computer package for the analysis of quantitative data or NUDIST (one of the widely used computer packages for qualitative data) or other research instruments, such as attitude scales. It is much easier to refer to specialist publications on these.[2] However, as in the previous chapters, illustrations from small business research will be used to show how research strategies have been used.

Sampling Frames and Samples for Small Business Research

Undoubtedly, one of the most difficult problems in small business research is accessing small businesses. As the first two chapters discussed, there are problems in defining 'small business', 'small business owner' and related concepts but having solved these, accessing suitable samples can be just as difficult. There are three main reasons for these difficulties. First, there are rarely up-to-date lists available of relevant small businesses from which to recruit a convincingly representative sample. Secondly, small business owners are busy people, often under considerable pressure. Understandably, they may not be too sympathetic to requests from researchers for some of their time. Thirdly, some business owners are sceptical about the relevance of research, especially academic research. This puts researchers under pressure to emphasize the usefulness of their projects as well as to sell themselves hard to prospective interviewees. These reasons can all too easily lead to low response undermining claims that those responding are representative of the wider population of small business owners.

To these problems can be added the heterogeneity problem. As the opening chapter showed, not only is the population of SMEs large but there is an exceptionally wide range of different kinds of small businesses from mortgage brokers to medical instrument makers, run by an equally wide range of different kinds of people with a comparably diverse labour force and differing links with the wider economy. Owner–managers engaged in different kinds of activities may be more or less reluctant to participate in research. This causes considerable problems in ensuring samples are representative where the research seeks to offer authoritative conclusions about small businesses generally.

National Sampling Frames

As the opening chapter reported, there is no single publicly accessible register of businesses in the UK. This is a very considerable handicap for researchers, particularly quantitative researchers. Many quantitative analytical procedures require a sample to be drawn systematically from a larger population whose members can be individually identified so that their chances of being selected can be known precisely. Without a complete, publicly available register of businesses, this is not possible in the UK.

Although there is an official Inter Departmental Business Register, which held records of almost 2m businesses at the beginning of 1998, this would be inadequate as a sampling frame because it fails to pick up many micro or small businesses and cannot be up-to-date (DTI, 1999a: 126). New businesses take time to come to official attention and businesses that cease to trade can have done so long before this is known officially. This is more serious than it might seem because the number of businesses entering and leaving the population over, say, any 12-month period, is known to be large. For instance, Barclays Bank publishes estimates of start-ups and closures for England and Wales. These are based on small business accounts opened and closed grossed up to reflect the bank's small business market share. For 1998, for example, it estimates there were 472,000 start-ups and 436,000 closures (Bank of England, 1999: 15). In other words, of the estimated total of 2.6m businesses at the start of 1998 in England and Wales, there were over 900,000 start-ups and closures in the rest of the year, that is, the equivalent of almost 35 per cent of businesses either entered or left the population.

Constructing National Samples

Nevertheless, some small business research projects need a national, representative sample. There are ways in which the problem of constructing a suitable sample can be solved, even if the result may still have weaknesses from a strict quantitative research perspective. One solution is the strategy employed for a national survey of training in small businesses by Curran et al. (1996). The sampling frame used was the records of the business information specialists Dun and Bradstreet. The latter collects information on businesses and has built up a large, continually updated database over a number of years. It collects information in a number of ways. For example, one of the services it provides is credit rating. For this it needs information on any business for which credit information is requested.

Like any small business database, Dun and Bradstreet's will be incomplete and inaccurate. For example, new businesses may not be entered on to the database for some time because there have been no requests for credit information about the businesses. These gaps may be more serious for some kinds of small business than others. Equally, businesses may cease to trade but not be removed from Dun and Bradstreet's database for some time. As with official records, it is the smallest businesses which are most likely to elude the database. Thus, for studies of new or micro businesses, this database is less useful than for studies of larger or mature firms.

Another problem studies of small firms typically experience is that size and response rates are strongly positively related, which leads to response bias.[3] Ensuring that response rates are high is always a problem in small business research. Mail surveys, for example, often achieve very low response rates. For example, a study of rural and urban businesses by Keeble et al. (1992) appeared, at first sight, to be based securely on a large sample, since 1,100 businesses responded. But, in fact, *11,000* questionnaires were sent out, split between 7,500 urban firms and 3,500 rural firms. The response rate was seven per cent for the urban firms and 13 per cent for the rural firms. That means that, overall, almost nine out of ten of those invited to participate declined to do so. Among the urban firms it was well over nine out of ten. This leads to doubts about how representative those who replied were of the populations the samples were supposed to represent.

A closer look at the results from the above survey implies that, in fact, the very common size-related response bias mentioned in the above paragraph, may well have occurred. This takes the form of smaller firms being much less likely to respond than larger small firms. This is suggested by comparing the size distribution of the firms replying with the known size distribution of UK businesses.[4] This means that the results may be misleading. For example, they might well overstate the problems of larger firms and understate those of small firms.

For the national survey of small business training (Curran et al., 1996) mentioned earlier, Dun and Bradstreet were asked to provide a quota sample based on size and sector. Quota samples are a common strategy in social and business research, using the simple idea of ensuring respondents who meet certain criteria will be represented usually in proportion to their known incidence in the population. For example, if it is known that just over 20 per cent of all businesses employing under 50 people are in construction, then a quota sample of businesses with under 50 people would ensure that one in five respondent firms came from that sector. Of course, if too many criteria are used in setting quotas, this can produce problems of filling all the quotas unless the sample (and population) is very large. Quota samples also violate the principle of each member of the population having an equal chance of being selected: respondents are recruited until each quota is filled, so their chances of selection will vary. In other words, quota sampling helps solve some problems of response bias linked to size but may not solve them all.

For the small business training study, Dun and Bradstreet were asked to provide a database with firms in nine different size categories (1–2 workers, 3–5 workers, etc.) covering the size range 1–200 employees and three main types of economic activities: manufacturing, services and construction. The database contained almost 4,000 enterprises and 850 firms were recruited to achieve the quotas for each size and economic activity category. Inevitably, some firms were unsuitable because they had increased or decreased in size to fall outside the specified size range or had gone out of business altogether. Having a much larger number of firms in the database than required meant that other firms could be substituted until all quotas were filled. The final response rate was 78 per cent of all suitable firms contacted.[5]

An alternative strategy in large-scale investigations aimed at covering the whole of the UK, is to use one of the major, national market research and opinion polling firms such as MORI or NOP to conduct the fieldwork. The data can be analysed by the firm or received in a suitable form for analysis. For instance, the data can be coded onto disk and then SSPS, or some other suitable statistical package, can be used to analyse the data. If an outside organization is used, it is very important to discuss the sampling strategies that will be used to ensure that the results will be representative and/or the likely biases can be estimated.

Secondary Data Sources

One way around the above problems is to mine existing data sets. These are of two kinds. First is data collected by previous research solely concerned with the small business. Second are data sets which, while not exclusively concerned with the small business, nevertheless contain subsets of data on small businesses which can be isolated from the larger data set. There are quite a lot of such data sets available but they are under-utilized by small business researchers. One possible reason for this is that many researchers simply do not consider this strategy because they have seen so few examples. However, some social sciences, notably economics, use this approach extensively. Researchers may also feel that their work will not be regarded as original if it uses data collected by others. However, originality stems not from the data but how intellectually ingenious the interpretations generated from it are.

Care needs to be exercised in using secondary data and, inevitably, there are limitations. If the original data set has been poorly constructed, then any secondary analysis will suffer quality problems. If construct definitions were unclear or quixotic or the sampling frames, sample construction strategies and response rates were poor, then it will not be worth reworking the data. In short, any secondary data set, even one offered for free, should be carefully assessed before mounting a secondary project. Sometimes, for instance, a data set turns out on closer inspection to be very 'dirty', that is, has been poorly coded, resulting in a database with lots of errors, missing data, etc.[6] Usually, corrections later are not possible because the original data sources are no longer available or cannot be checked. This means any subsequent analysis will be highly suspect.

A main limitation of any secondary data set is obviously the kind of data collected. Since the original reason for collecting the data will be related to a specific research project or administrative undertaking, it may not provide much useful data for later projects. The questions asked and coding categories used need to be carefully checked to determine whether they can be reinterpreted for a further project. For example, a study of small business growth needs to know size (measured in an appropriate way) of firm at some point in the past compared with a later point in time. Further, this data needs to be able to be related to other data collected on the business, its owner–managers and other variables seen as significant to growth. Missing data will restrict any re-analysis and interpretation or may greatly reduce the value of the latter.

On the other hand, some data sets may be gold mines for secondary analysis. One source of high-quality data sets is the ESRC Data Archive. This consists of data collected for research funded by the Council. Usually the data sets are constructed to high standards and often the original researchers can be contacted to discuss the data. Some of the data sets are directly concerned with small business issues while others may contain data relevant to small firms which can be harvested for further analysis. However, very few small business researchers have used the ESRC Archive in this way. One reason is probably that until about a decade ago only a small proportion of the Council's support went directly to fund small business research. Now, however, data sets from the ESRC Small Business Research Initiative completed in 1992 and other projects, are available.

Some national data sets have been mined very successfully for small business research purposes. Curran and Burrows (1988 and 1989), for example, used data from the General Household Survey (GHS) which is usually conducted annually by the Office of Population Censuses and Surveys (now the Office of National Statistics). In the early 1980s the GHS carried out interviews with around 28,000 people in Great Britain. The surveys were conducted to exceptionally high standards and achieved overall response rates of over 80 per cent and even over 70 per cent among the self-employed and small business owners. Given the known problems of response rates among those engaged in small business, this was outstanding. The preparation of the data set was equally exemplary.

Curran and Burrows were helped by the GHS coding conventions which allowed those working for themselves with no employees and those running a business with under 25 employees, to be isolated and the data on these subsamples to be related to a wide range of other questions asked. Given the high standards of the original survey, it could be assumed that any reasonably sized subsample was representative of the self-employed and small business owners in Britain. The re-analysis by Curran and Burrows produced data on the self-employed and small business owners' age and gender profiles, marital status, education and qualifications, types of economic activities in which they were engaged, ethnic background, hours worked and health.

Some of the data was used to test hypotheses based on accepted views on the self-employed and small business owners. For example, it had been argued that small business ownership was a main upward mobility path for those from disadvantaged backgrounds. While the data supported this view, it also showed that those from higher social strata were even more strongly represented, relative to their numbers in the population as a whole. In other words, self-employment and small business ownership were even more important for those from more privileged backgrounds.[7] Later, Burrows (1991b) carried out a more sophisticated statistical analysis on these issues using the same secondary data set.

A second example of using a secondary data set in a similar way is Meager (1991) who drew on the Labour Force Surveys (LFSs) of 1984–87. The LFS collects information from a much larger number of individuals than the GHS did. Like the GHS, it is conducted officially (this time in conjunction with the EU) and Meager's analysis was very similar to that of Curran and Burrows' although the larger sample led to refinements of the latter's analysis and conclusions. Because the LFS is conducted in association with the EU, it has the additional advantage of allowing comparison with other states in the Union (see, for example, Meager et al., 1992 for a comparison with Germany).[8]

So far secondary analyses of the above kind have been infrequent in small business research. What the above suggests, however, is that there is considerable potential in data sets of this kind. To the extent that more and more economic and social policy-making in the UK recognizes the significance of the small enterprise in the UK, it might be expected that official data will give more attention to the small firm. For instance, the Low Pay Commission needs accurate data on wages and salaries in SMEs in order to make informed recommendations and this might prompt greater attention to collecting data of this kind.[9] In turn, this may provide data sets which independent researchers can mine.

Smaller Scale Samples

Most small business research projects, however, will not attempt national coverage. Large-scale studies are expensive to conduct without support from bodies such as ESRC, government departments or private sector sponsors. Where the research is being conducted by a lone researcher such as a PhD student, a large-scale national sample would be difficult to handle. Beginners will sensibly want to cut their teeth on something more manageable. A lot of commercially or otherwise sponsored research such as that commissioned by local business support agencies, will be aimed at small businesses in particular localities or kinds of businesses.

It might be thought easier to recruit a sample for a small-scale or local study of small businesses but the problems can still be difficult. Just as there are no ready-made national sampling frames for small businesses, there are rarely up-to-date, suitable sampling frames for particular kinds of small firms or localities. Often a researcher will be assured by a trade association, chamber of commerce or local authority economic develop-ment unit that they have up-to-date, comprehensive lists from which firms can be recruited. In practice, such lists are almost always very incomplete and out-of-date. Assembling complete, up-to-date lists of small firms is expensive. Most organizations that keep lists are often unaware of just how deficient they are. To retain their usefulness lists need regularly updating, which is expensive. Many bodies have neither the resources nor a strong belief in the need to keep lists up-to-date.

Some lists are better than others as sampling frames. For instance, a local small business support body may commission a survey of all the firms on its database to canvass opinions on its services. Although its database will probably be incomplete (not every contact with a firm will have been recorded and some firms on the list will be no longer trading or will have moved outside the area) the gaps will probably not be too serious for the survey. If, however, the agency wants to use the findings to generalize about the entire small business population in its catchment area, this would be more questionable. Existing research[10] suggests that Business Links, TECs and similar agencies had contacts with only a minority of firms in their areas and the firms with which they had contacts were often not representative of the larger population of small firms in the locality.

One approach to compiling sampling frames for local small business surveys or particular kinds of small enterprises or even for a national survey, is to use the *Yellow Pages*. This can be either the paper or disc version. Compiling a suitable sampling frame from either is bound to be laborious. First of all, enterprise size needs to be defined together with any other characteristics, such as sector, relevant to the research. Firms then need to be selected from the *Yellow Pages* source to achieve the sample size required. Unfortunately, some of the key information needed such as who owns the business, whether or not it is a branch or subsidiary of a larger enterprise and the number of employees, will be missing. Similarly, if the project needs to recruit women, small business owners or businesses with two or more active owner/directors, the information will not be readily available.

The only solution to problems of the above kind is contacting selected firms to determine whether they fit the desired sample definitions. The easiest (though still time-consuming) way is a preliminary telephone survey. Often basic information on, for instance, whether the firm employs fewer than the upper size limit adopted or whether it is engaged in the specific activities the study wants to cover, etc., can be obtained from whomever answers the phone. If the firm looks suitable, it is essential to obtain the name of the owner–manager or managing director but at this stage it is usually unwise to try to speak to the owner–manager or director directly. One reason is that, as discussed below, attempting respondent recruitment at this stage tends to produce high non-response rates. Owner–managers are much less sympathetic to research when approached on a 'cold call' basis. Another reason is that if the bulk of the sample has not yet been recruited, it may be necessary to adjust the composition of the final sample for one reason or another. For instance, it may be wished to recruit a particular kind of small enterprise in a locality only to find that there are very few such enterprises, thus making it necessary to redefine the coverage of the study. Interviewing too early, therefore, can produce results which cannot be used.

An example of the above sampling frame construction strategy was a study of small firms in seven localities across Britain (Curran and Blackburn, 1994: 67–71).[11] Sampling frames were constructed for nine kinds of economic activities using *Yellow Pages* and, where available, any other local business lists such as those compiled by local authorities. Preliminary telephone interviews were used to screen out unsuitable firms and obtain the names of potential respondents. For each type of activity, in each locality, a quota was set and firms were recruited from the sampling frames for face-to-face interviews until the quotas were met.[12] Although this was very labour-intensive and time-consuming, the researchers believed that the resulting samples were both representative of the kinds of small businesses selected and their involvement in the economies of the seven localities. The final response rate was just under 60 per cent.[13]

Sometimes, especially in very small firms, the owner–manager may answer the telephone or take over the call. For this reason, if the firm appears suitable, it is imperative that the researcher is able to answer questions about the project knowledgeably and confidently and, in effect, 'sell' the project to the potential respondent. If it is a telephone survey and the questionnaire is already prepared, the interview might even be conducted there and then. Again, the person conducting the telephone survey needs to be trained and equipped for this. Normally, however, initial calls to prospective respondents are aimed at constructing the sampling frame.

Case Studies, Focus Groups and Snowballing

Other kinds of studies, not based on large samples, such as case studies or focus groups can also recruit businesses from the *Yellow Pages*. Conversely, studies of these kinds may select participants in other ways which do not rely on statistical representativeness to be convincing. For example, case studies often employ *theoretical sampling* strategies. Here respondents are selected to fit the rationale underlying the research project. For example, a study of possible differences in owner–manager managerial strategies related to gender might recruit firms which were matched closely for sector and market, length of time in business, number of employees, operating in the same or a similar locality, owner–managers' educational level and previous business experiences but owned and run by people of different gender.[14] In constructing a case study sample for such an investigation it might not matter all that much how the sample was recruited provided the main criteria were met and no easily avoidable biases were introduced. The matching of the firms on the range of criteria assumed or known to be relevant with only gender differing, could reasonably theorize that any differences found were related to gender. Local sources, such as chambers of commerce, enterprise agencies and the researcher's personal contacts, might produce suitable firms.

Selecting respondents for *focus groups* is rather more tricky (Blackburn and Stokes, in press). Despite their current popularity among political-opinion researchers, they have limitations as a research tool. In small business research, they are most likely to be used as support in a research design rather than as the main research strategy. For example, in preparing for a study of small business owners' opinions on late payment, one or more focus groups might be used to find out the kinds of issues respondents see as salient. Focus groups can also be used to test researchers' analyses and conclusions from a research project. However, in recruiting participants, theoretical sampling issues arise again. In order to have any confidence in the results, participants need to be representative of the wider population of small businesses relevant to the research. Since the number involved in each group has to be limited (normally a focus group has at least four members but rarely more than ten) given the heterogeneity of the small business population, some studies could well require a number of groups.

Furthermore, good practice in focus group construction demands that respondents should not know each other in advance. The obvious reason for this is that people who know each other before participating in the group may well have shared tacit understandings on the issues being explored whereas the aim of the focus group is that they articulate their views as openly as possible. Recruiting people who have never met before may not be easy if all participants come from the same locality or if they are able to discuss what happens in advance with previous participants. If they are competitors, this may also inhibit their participation, making the results less valuable.[15]

A serious problem in recruiting small business owners for focus groups is time. Typically, participation involves giving up half a day and many small business owners will feel this is simply too much time to give to a research project. Bringing busy small business owners together on the same day at the same time will also always be more difficult than interviewing them individually at a time convenient to them.[16] Size of business may also have an affect: owner–managers of smaller businesses will find it more difficult to find the time than those with larger enterprises who have staff to whom they can delegate responsibility. Similar considerations may arise in relation to sector. Some small business owners feel they need to be present in the business virtually all the time while others feel easier about leaving the business to run itself for half a day. Some owners will not show up even though they have agreed to do so. From experience, the 'no-show' rate can be up to a quarter and should be allowed for when setting up the focus group.

Two other sampling strategies are also worth mentioning, *purposive sampling* and *snowball sampling*. Purposive sampling can take several forms but the most common in small business research is the *key informant* or *Delphi sample*. This involves identifying and recruiting respondents who, because of their experiences and special knowledge, are especially well-informed on the issues central to the research. For example, a study of small business policies in the UK used a Delphi sample of experts to assess the effectiveness of the policies since 1980 (Blackburn et al., 1999). One advantage of this kind of approach is that the sample need not be large. Indeed, there may be very few expert respondents relevant to the topic. On the other hand, they will only be able to give their own views. The owner–managers of small firms may have different views than any expert respondents.

Snowball sampling refers to recruiting samples by word of mouth, particularly by using one respondent to suggest other suitable respondents. Other sources such as chambers of commerce, enterprise agencies and

TECs might also suggest respondents. This is probably best used only when other means of recruiting a representative sample are not available. For instance, studies of ethnic business owners are often difficult to recruit because of the lack of suitable sampling frames and/or doubts about the researchers' aims among members of ethnic minorities. Curran and Blackburn (1993), for instance, set up a project to study the futures of small businesses run by members of three ethnic minority communities – Afro-Caribbeans, Bangladeshis and Greek-Cypriots – in London and Yorkshire. To overcome the problems noted above, they defined the kinds of firms about which they wished to collect data and then recruited experienced researchers from each community. The latter were trained and instructed to recruit firms by appropriate snowballing strategies to fill quotas in the research design.

The main problem with snowball strategies is ensuring the representativeness of the sample. For instance, if a single source is relied upon, this may produce bias. If all respondents are recruited from, say, among chamber of commerce members, they may differ from those who are not members.[17] The solution, wherever possible, is to use several starting points for the snowballing. This will not eliminate bias but will reduce any likely to occur where a single source is used. It follows also, of course, that snowball samples cannot claim representativeness in a statistical sense. What they can do, however, is make possible a project which could not otherwise go ahead.

Accessing Small Business Owner Respondents

Whatever the sampling frame construction strategies employed, the result is a list of potential respondents but they still have to be persuaded to participate in the project. Recruiting the respondents is the next stage. The key problem in virtually all small business research is achieving an acceptable response rate. Mention has been made of mail questionnaire surveys achieving 10 per cent or even lower response rates with suspicions of high levels of response bias. This is simply not satisfactory for research wishing to make confident claims for its findings. The study by Curran and Blackburn (1994) who put considerable effort into recruiting their samples, managed, as noted above, an overall response rate of just under 60 per cent. This is just about the minimum that might be considered respectable for any kind of in-depth quantitative analysis.[18]

Approaching small business owners as potential respondents is best done in two stages. First, given the sampling frame construction included collecting the names of owner–managers/managing directors, those selected should be sent a personal letter explaining the research, suggesting that their participation would be invaluable. Busy people do not like long letters. For a complicated research project, the invitation can be kept short and the project described on a separate sheet. The letter should reassure the recipients that involvement will not take a lot of their time. For instance, they can be told interviews will take, say, 50 minutes or less[19] and can take place at any time during the day or evening convenient to the respondent. They are doing the researcher a favour so it is only right that it should be at a time that suits them even if it is much less convenient for the interviewers.

Academic researchers can stress that the research is for academic purposes to establish that it is not just another market research survey or selling ploy. Yet, at the same time, they need to avoid any suspicion that the research is of no relevance to anybody except the researcher. Stressing the practical and policy values of the research or how it will add to understanding small business problems, can help also. Where the research is sponsored, ethically the prospective respondent should be informed. But whatever the sponsor or source of funding, the confidentiality of the respondent's replies should be stated as absolute, a pledge that should be strictly kept. The letter should end by informing the respondents that the researcher will telephone them in a few days to answer any questions they might have and invite them to take part.

The follow-up telephone call should be made two to four days after the prospective respondent will have received the letter. Since the respondent can be approached by name, every effort should be made to do so. Sometimes this may take two or more telephone calls or it may be difficult to get past a 'gatekeeper', such as a secretary. The respondents should be asked whether they have received the letter and had a chance to read it: some will not have and a further call will be needed. Some will claim they have not received the letter and should be promised another as soon as possible. If the respondent has a fax machine and is amenable, a copy can be sent immediately. But if another letter has to be sent this means the whole process of securing co-operation has to start again in a few days.

Be prepared to explain the project again, even if the respondents state that they have read the letter. Psychologically, this establishes that the researcher knows that he or she is asking a favour and that the respondent's co-operation is important for the research. Again, the researcher is 'selling' the project and needs to be positive about its value and importance. With luck, the conversation ends with the face-to-face interview arranged at a mutually convenient time. For a telephone interview, there is a chance the interview can take place there and then, but another time may need to be arranged. For a mail questionnaire already sent out, follow-up calls at this stage can help raise the response rate. Respondents can be assured the research is important and reminded tactfully that they have the questionnaire or be sent another if they have not received, or have mislaid, the original.

All the above sounds very laborious but gaining the co-operation of small business owners is never easy and low response rates are a serious problem in small business research. High quality research depends on recruiting good quality samples. Even following the above to the letter may only produce a just-acceptable sample. For example, as noted earlier, the study by Curran et al. (1991) for their ESRC-sponsored project on service sector small enterprises carried out in 1990, which used the above methods, achieved a response rate of just under 60 per cent.[20] By the standards of much social science research this might be deemed low but this was the second-highest recorded response rate in any of the 16 projects in the ESRC programme.[21] For very large samples (say, 500 plus) follow-up telephone calls or even letters explaining the project before a mail questionnaire is posted out might be too expensive but the result is likely to be lower response rates. This should be allowed for by starting with a much larger initial sample.[22]

Other Kinds of Respondents in Small Business Research

The above concentrated on small business owners but not all small business research focuses on small business owners. Some research will need to recruit other respondents such as employees, suppliers, customers, consultants or others from trade or support bodies such as enterprise agencies. It may also want to interview the general public about small business issues. Some of these are a good deal easier to recruit than small business owners and can be approached in much the same way as respondents for other kinds of social research. Often accurate sampling frames are easier to come by for these other kinds of respondents than for small business owners.

One exception to the above, that deserves special mention is small firm employees. These are a somewhat neglected group in small business research. Often the impression given in both research and in the media is of the lone entrepreneur responsible for all the achievements of the business. This is clearly nonsense where the firm employs others. A small firm with employees is better conceptualized as a team. There has been research on employment in the small business (Curran, 1991; Goss, 1991: Chap. 4, *passim*; Kitching, 1997) but accessing small business employees is not easy.

The most common strategy for recruiting small business employees is to go through the employer.[23] This is not entirely satisfactory because if employees are aware that they have been approached with the consent of their boss, this may inhibit them from expressing themselves freely. Even worse, the employer may only be willing to nominate employees rather than allow the researcher to approach them directly. This may lead to sample bias because those nominated are not representative of all employees in the firm. Approaching employees directly is superior, particularly if the design requires employees to be selected according to specific criteria.

Research Design Choices

From the above it is clear that research designs in small business research can utilize a wide range of means of constructing samples of owners and other respondents. As has been argued, in part the research design will depend on the kind of problem being studied. Quantitatively based designs will suit some topics while others will be better served by qualitative designs. Some researchers will opt firmly for one or other on epistemological grounds or because they feel much more comfortable with one rather than the other, perhaps reflecting their research skills.

In practice, a lot of researchers will employ a mixed quantitative–qualitative approach to gain some of the advantages of both and of triangulation. This has emerged as a common research design in small business research. It combines a quantitative survey (based on face-to-face or telephone interviews or on a mail questionnaire) with a qualitative element such as case studies, focus groups or even participant observation.[24] In effect, the quantitative elements add 'bulk' to the findings, that is, they help support implicit/explicit claims to generalizability that all research makes while the qualitative elements concentrate on 'why' issues: the reasons or causes which might underlie the pattern of findings discovered.

The quantitative elements of the research design reassure those with a strong faith in numbers, particularly policy-makers and politicians. The qualitative elements allow the researchers to go beyond the inferences based on correlations which are all many quantitative designs can strictly claim to have established. It is often easy to show that two or more aspects of behaviour appear related statistically but it is often much more difficult to show convincingly why such relations should hold. There is also a safety factor in mixed research designs of these kinds: collecting data in more than one way helps ensure all the issues relevant to the research are covered even if the researchers are unsure initially about how important each is. Research students in particular find a safety element of this kind comforting.

Constructing Questionnaires

Questionnaires are the most frequently used of all research instruments but their construction is much more difficult than it might first seem. Again, since this is a book on researching the small business, there is no attempt to cover questionnaire construction exhaustively. There are numerous texts that offer detailed treatments.[25] Instead, what follows concentrates on some of the key issues and especially pitfalls in using questionnaires in small business research.

Questionnaires can be placed on a continuum ranging from, at one pole, unstructured to structured at the other. Unstructured questionnaires may be little more than a list of key words or phrases highlighting topics which the interviewer will prompt the respondent to talk about either in a face-to-face or telephone interview. In their most unstructured form, particularly in ethnographic approaches, some would not call them 'questionnaires' at all. At first sight, this approach is attractive because it leaves the interview as open as possible and allows the respondents maximum freedom to offer their views. It is sometimes argued that this strategy means the researcher runs the least risk of imposing his or her own preconceived ideas on respondents. But it should be used only after very careful thought and preparation.

Unstructured approaches to questionnaire construction have three serious potential weaknesses. First, just having to jot down a list of key words or phrases may tempt the researcher to start the fieldwork without having carefully thought through what the research is seeking to explore. A 'flying without wings' approach to research is very risky. Lack of clarity on the aims of the research at this stage can be fatal. Secondly, unstructured interviews are difficult to conduct because they demand a very high level of interviewer skills. As the respondent talks, the interviewer has to analyse what is said in relation to the issues being investigated and, at the same time, frame the next question or prompt to be put. Spotting immediately what is theoretically significant in a respondent's comments requires an exceptional ability to think quickly on the hoof. Thirdly, unless conducted with skill, unstructured interviews may give respondents the impression that the interviewer does not know what he or she is doing: this could cause small business owner respondents to resent what they might see as a waste of their valuable time.

Most small business researchers play safe by combining a structured approach with some unstructured questioning. In other words, the questionnaire 'script' is followed strictly in places but offers freedom to put 'open' questions in others. The extent of the unstructured element will also depend on how the questionnaire is administered. The greatest freedom occurs where the questionnaire is for a face-to-face interview. Here the researcher not only has the respondent's words to help the interview but also the added information from face-to-face interaction. Respondents' facial expressions may express doubt about the meaning of a question or indicate that the question is touching issues the respondents feel reluctant or nervous to discuss. This allows the researcher to adjust the wording of ensuing questions or prompts (without altering their basic meaning) to reassure the respondents.

Telephone interviews may contain unstructured elements but have less freedom for these than face-to-face interviews. The researcher only has the respondent's words and verbal tone for guidance when developing and asking additional questions.[26] Typically, telephone interviews are also much shorter than face-to-face interviews and therefore offer less time to use follow-up questions and probes to add to the detail and meanings associated with first answers. Most limited of all are mail questionnaires where the researcher often never even speaks to the respondent. Mail questionnaires do frequently ask respondents to offer unprompted views – indeed, it is common practice to invite them at the end of a sequence of structured questions or the end of the interview schedule – but this is clearly much less unstructured than would be possible in a telephone and especially, a face-to-face, interview. More typically, mail questionnaires (or similar self-administered research instruments) are the most likely of all to be near the structured pole of the continuum.

Structured questionnaires are usually easier to analyse than unstructured questionnaires (see the next chapter) and this may be a relevant consideration for some kinds of small business research. For instance, research commissioned by commercial sponsors often has tight deadlines with less time for analysis and writing up. The reasons for the relative ease in analysing structured questionnaires are twofold. First, questions are much more likely to be of the kind where answers fall into one or other fixed categories generated in advance so recording data for analysis is easier than for open questions where such categories often have to be generated after the questionnaires have been administered and then sometimes only with some difficulty. Secondly, answers to structured questions can more easily be assigned a numerical value (if they do not already have one) and be analysed fairly quickly with a computer package such as SSPS.

The pressure to opt for structured questionnaires will also be greater for large samples and especially where they are administered by several interviewers/researchers. The obvious reason for this is reducing bias likely to arise from inter-interviewer variations in the way they administer the questionnaire. It is unlikely that a team of interviewers will all have the same approach and high-level interview skills needed to conduct unstructured face-to-face interviews. Inter-interviewer bias can occur in telephone interviews even when the unstructured component is limited. The problems of categorizing, recording and analysing responses is also much more difficult if the data is based on multi-interviewing. These practical considerations therefore reduce the opportunities for maximizing qualitative elements in the research.

Designing questionnaires can be guided by broad principles and experience but much will depend on the topic and aims of the research. Earlier it was suggested that experience indicates that roughly 50 minutes is the maximum length of a face-to-face interview before respondent resistance is likely among small business owners. For a telephone interview the maximum time is likely to be much shorter, say around 15 minutes. A mail questionnaire will also be restricted although here appearance is important. One that seems like it will take a lot of effort and time to complete will end up in the waste bin. The Small Business Research Trust NatWest quarterly small business survey, for example, often contains under a dozen questions, all on one side of A4 paper.[27] One-off mail questionnaires can be longer but will still have to be as short as possible to maximize response. Given enough thought and care, quite substantial amounts of data can be gathered even in a brief mail questionnaire.

Questionnaire Form, Wording and Structure

What the above suggests strongly is that whatever the type of questionnaire, careful thought needs to be given to its construction. New researchers, particularly in their first attempts, often want to cover every possible issue which might be relevant to the topic of investigation just to be safe. Unfortunately (or more probably, fortunately, at least for the respondent) this is not possible for virtually any small business research project. The three maxims that need to be adhered to in constructing a questionnaire can, following Gill and Johnson (1997: 88), be summed up in the words: *focus*, *wording* and *structure*. Each imposes discipline on the researcher but the result is likely to be better research.

Focus refers to making sure that the questions will capture the data needed to test and explore the propositions and issues the research seeks to address. This is much more difficult than it sounds. Every question needs a thorough evaluation to confirm it will actually tap information on the issue it is intended to cover. Any question which is not needed on a strict assessment of its utility in relation to the aims of the project, should be jettisoned. Usually, researchers find that they generate an initial over-long questionnaire and then refine it down. Careful inspection can often show how questions can produce more/better data through better construction.

Wording refers to the way the question is asked. It needs to be clear and the meaning should be unambiguous for the respondent. Will the small business owner or other respondent understand the terminology being used? Can the respondent answer the question at all? A question which asked the owner–managers who state they want to maximize growth what they expected the maximum gearing ratio of the business to be over the next three years would probably be useless. Many small business owners have little or no formal financial management training and would not understand what a 'gearing ratio' was, so could not answer the question (although they might still offer an answer in order not to show their ignorance to the researcher). Secondly, much existing research shows that most small business owners do not plan very far ahead and three years would be a long period for most, often well beyond the planning horizon even of those who very much want to grow.[28] It is a cardinal rule of any research never to ask respondents questions they cannot answer because the resulting 'data' will normally be worthless.[29] In short, questions should be in the language the respondent normally uses and not in words which have a special and restricted use among academics and of a kind that it is reasonable to assume the respondent has the knowledge to answer.[30]

Questions should not 'lead', that is be phrased to elicit one kind of answer rather than another. For example, one survey whose results were subsequently promoted by government, asked: 'How important do you consider the following BURDEN OF GOVERNMENT ON BUSINESS issues are for your business?' (capitals in the original). It then offered respondents the choices of 'cost of compliance', 'employment regulations' and 'VAT regulations'.[31] By phrasing the question in this way, it suggested that all of the choices were, by definition, 'burdens' harmful to business. Yet it is quite possible for a respondent to believe that employment regulations, for instance, were an advantage because they ensured that all employees have the same conditions, thus avoiding unfair competition from unscrupulous employers.

Nor should questions be empty or 'apple pie' questions. Empty questions are those where it is extremely unlikely that any respondent would offer more than one answer. For instance, small business owners might be asked: 'Do you think it is always right to employ the right kind of people for your business?' It is difficult to envisage any respondents answering the question negatively. Moreover, 'right' in this context can mean almost anything. For one respondent 'right' might refer to the cheapest labour while for another it might refer to the most qualified etc. 'Apple pie' questions are those with clear socially acceptable answers in response to which many respondents, if they disagreed, would not wish their viewpoint to be known. For example, 'Do you agree that the interests of customers should always come first?' might produce low disagreement even though, in practice, some business owners might commonly not behave in accordance with the sentiment. Questions of these kinds are a waste of effort and resources and high-quality research avoids them.

Structure refers to the internal ordering of the questionnaire. The introduction should reiterate the guarantee of total confidentiality even though this has been emphasized strongly in the initial contacts. Respondents should also be told that they need not answer any question they do not wish to and simply move on to the next question. The questions proper can then begin. Here four general rules are helpful. First, start with some factual, non-threatening (to the respondent) questions. Some background data will usually be needed whatever the subject of the research – when was the business founded, what are its main products and/or services, how many people does it employ, is it a sole proprietorship, partnership or incorporated, etc.? Even when some of this information is already known, it can be checked for accuracy at the beginning of the interview or mail questionnaire. The reason for this kind of start is that respondents may be nervous, they may assume, for instance, that the researcher is some kind of expert measuring their competence as small business owners. They may also be suspicious of the researcher's motives. An innocuous start helps allay such feelings. Secondly, structure questions from the general to the particular to form a sequence. Multiple questions, that is, questions which are really two or more in one, are very poor practice because they are difficult or impossible to code since it is not always clear which question is being answered in what way. Thirdly, impose a logic on the order of questions and topics covered. A chronological logic is the most obvious with questions starting with the history of the business, moving to current operations and ending with questions about future expectations or plans. Other logics might follow the development of products or services or the process of recruiting employees. Fourthly, beware of straying onto dangerous ground, that is, asking overly personal questions or questions which the respondent may regard as commercially sensitive. For example, questions about personal finance or drawings from the business may be regarded as improper by respondents. They are better not asked unless the ground has been very carefully prepared. Researchers seeking data on turnover have found that offering a 'flash card' containing a series of turnover intervals ('below £5,000, £5,000 but under £7,500, £7,500 but below . . .' etc.) and asking the respondent to indicate which shows the turnover over, say, the last financial year, works well.

Some question structuring requires 'skips'. This occurs where, if respondents answer a question in a particular way, they need not answer the following question(s). For example, an initial question might ask whether the firm is a sole proprietorship, partnership, incorporated as a company or is a co-operative or community business. If the answer is 'sole proprietorship' any following questions on how many other partners, directors, etc. there are do not need to be answered and the respondent needs to skip to the next relevant question for them. In mail questionnaires, instructions to respondents on skipping need to be particularly clear (but even in face-to-face interviews similar indications are helpful to interviewers). Indeed, any question on a mail questionnaire a respondent might find at all ambiguous should have clear instructions attached.

A questionnaire can be too complex, with too many skips, making it difficult for respondents to be interviewed or to navigate their way through a self-administered version. The main reason for this usually is trying to cover too many different types of respondent in a single questionnaire. Where, for instance, the research is interested in owners of different age, gender, educational and ethnic backgrounds, who produce different kinds of products and services, and wants data on each topic, 'routing', that is, guiding the respondent through the questionnaire, may be complex. The solution is either to rethink the coverage of questions or to try to determine in advance what kind of respondent is to be interviewed and use separate questionnaires.

Varying the question form by using flash cards of the kind mentioned above for eliciting data on turnover or cards with statements that respondents can be asked to comment upon or by switching from simple factual questions to questions which ask for opinions or even narrative answers, all help maintain respondent interest. Scale questions offer another variation, although these should only be used after researchers are sure they know how to use this type of question (see Note 2). When the questionnaire switches topic, a brief, neutral, introductory statement helps respondents mentally shift gear to the new topic. In face-to-face interview questionnaires, it is useful to list probe phrases under main questions so interviewers have reminders of all the issues the respondent needs to cover for the data required. Probes, like main questions, should be expressed neutrally. Always thank the respondent at the end. In longitudinal studies the schedule should end by preparing the respondent for any further interview in the programme.

Finally, look at other researchers' questionnaires. Many studies reproduce the questionnaires used in publishing their results. They should not be seen as models necessarily since many contain common faults. But they will suggest forms of questions which have been used previously with the implication (unless the text indicates otherwise) that they have been effective in obtaining the required data. They will also suggest ways in which questionnaires can be structured. Occasionally, it will be possible to use questions from previous studies which permit comparisons to be drawn. For instance, it may be able to show how responses have changed over time or how small businesses in sectors not covered in the original study, differ. Either adds interest to the analysis from the later project as well as a cumulative element to research on the topic. They may also help prevent 'reinventing the wheel', which wastes research effort.

All questionnaires are compromises. Hard choices have to be made to keep the length down to what is practicable for the interviewing format – face-to-face, telephone, self-administered – as well as on kinds of questions. Experienced researchers can draw on their experience on what will and what will not work. But most researchers, and especially research students, should conduct a pilot study to test the questionnaire. Where possible, the respondents should resemble as closely as possible those who will take part in the main project. Testing the questionnaire out on a few friends is not enough. The pilot study will almost always reveal shortcomings on length, questions, form and content, and structure. Curing these at this stage is obviously better than finding out later.

Interviewing and Fieldwork

The central stage in most research projects is the fieldwork, usually interviewing respondents, in one or more ways – face-to-face interviews, telephone interviews, focus groups, case studies, participant observation etc. – individually or in combination. Fieldwork strategies have attracted a huge literature which deals with all of these methods plus others less likely to be used in small business research.[32] Here the focus is on interviewing and fieldwork in small business research.

Interviews

The most common fieldwork strategy in small business research is the interview. Interviews, particularly face-to-face interviews but also telephone interviews, are social encounters of a rather odd kind. They involve people, who have usually never met previously becoming engaged in a complex, sometimes lengthy social encounter. What is especially odd is that most of the information flows one way (from the respondent) and in this sense it is unlike most other interactions between people. Focus groups may appear superficially to be a number of people exchanging views but, again, closer inspection suggests it is a somewhat odd form of group discussion if only because one of those present, the facilitator, attempts to structure the discussion to meet the aim of collecting particular kinds of data.

For both interviewer and respondents, but especially for an inexperienced interviewer, interviewing is hard work and often stressful. Many new interviewers are surprised at just how tiring interviewing can be. One reason for this is that the interviewer has to concentrate hard to ensure the interview is productive especially in unstructured interviews where respondents' answers are difficult to predict and may need to be probed. Focus group facilitators may have to work even harder and find the experience even more stressful where the group are small business owners. Small business owners are often people with strong personalities used to being treated deferentially by employees and others. They often have very strong views on issues linked to running a small business. Interviewers need to be self-confident and well-prepared to handle such determined, strong personalities.

Telephone interviews need to be introduced and the initial statement can be crucial in establishing the quality of the rest of the interaction. Indeed, unless done effectively there may be no interview at all. It has to sell the project and gain the respondent's confidence. Respondents such as busy owner–managers or those who have had a bad day or are anti-research, may be abusive, which can be unpleasant for the novice interviewer. Sometimes skilful, patient interviewers can turn the situation around but a lot will depend on how positive and well-prepared they are. The preparation should include a script for the initial statement. The script need not be followed slavishly but it helps having a prompt in front of you when dealing with reluctant, or even hostile, respondents.

Structured interviews, especially where the data is treated quantitatively, need to stick closely to the questionnaire. Good practice here stresses that all respondents should be asked the questions in the same way so that answers may be treated as equivalents. This is not easy with

strong personalities or people who are expert on the subjects raised in
the interviews. For example, a common problem is respondents answering more than one question at a time, that is, an answer to one question
answers another question later in the interview. Indeed, the response
may answer more than one. Interviewers may feel foolish, if in following
the questionnaire strictly, they have to ask a question the respondent has
apparently already answered.

One temptation where the above happens, is to skip what appears to
be the already answered question. But there is a danger in taking an
answer for granted. Respondents are not always predictable and may
have what appear to be inconsistent views. For example, an owner–
manager asked how prices for the firm's products are fixed, might state
that they are determined by market forces. But asked later if some
customers receive special treatment, the same owner–manager might
state that long-term customers receive more favourable treatment than
new customers (see Jarvis et al. (1996) for this and other examples).

Another problem for structured and unstructured interviews but
especially for the former, is where the respondent does not understand
the question. Repeating the question may not help and departing from
the agreed question means not all respondents have answered the same
question. A skilled interviewer will minimize these effects by asking the
question again in a form as close to the original as possible. Here
the problem is to avoid 'leading' the respondent by inadvertently
indicating a particular answer over the alternatives or assuming that the
respondent will answer in a particular way, based on the answers to
previous questions.

Questionnaires that are unstructured or contain unstructured sections
have their own problems. The key challenge here is wording open
questions or follow-up questions to investigate more deeply answers
already offered. Avoiding 'leading' the respondent is even more difficult
under these conditions and is one of the main reasons why high levels of
interviewer skills are needed. Interviewers also need to be alert to probe
theoretically significant answers and explore them further. Questions
should be relatively brief, concentrating on one issue at a time rather
than raising several subjects simultaneously. Otherwise it is difficult for
the respondent to remember what was asked or lets them wander off the
point too easily.

There are some techniques for constructing probes to follow up initial
questions in interviews to obtain fuller answers. The easiest and one of
the most neutral of all techniques probably is silence. When an interviewer feels a respondent's answer needs amplifying just being silent
can produce the desired result. Most people fill a silence if they perceive
they are expected to say something, if only to be polite. Other neutral
probes are phrases such as, 'That's interesting, could you tell me more
about that?' or 'Why do you think that is the case?' or 'Have you always
had that view?'

Conversely, the interviewer needs to avoid being drawn into a debate with the respondent. Owner–managers with strong views may well believe that they are so obviously right that the interviewer must agree with them while the interviewer may actually disagree strongly. Maintaining neutrality is difficult under these circumstances, even when the interviewer does agree. A vacuous encouraging smile sounds wimpish advice for face-to-face interviews or something along the lines of, 'Well that is a point of view, of course' for a telephone interview. But these may be the only ways to avoid a more leading response which might distort answers to later questions in the interview.

Case Studies

Case studies are particularly popular in small business research mainly because they involve small samples and, in their simplest form, are relatively easy to conduct. The most rudimentary form is the single-firm, single-visit study. This may consist of little more than an interview with the owner–manager and a brief observation of the workplace. Here 'case study' is being stretched beyond what it is taken to mean in other areas of social investigation, particularly sociology and anthropology where the technique was pioneered and where it has produced some of the best-known and most influential theorizing and findings.[33]

More strictly, the case study involves methodological triangulation and multiple visits to one or more firms. The methodological triangulation consists of all or some mix of: interviews (structure and unstructured, single and repeated) with one or more kinds of people in the enterprise; the administration of research instruments, such as personality scales; repeated observation of the firm's everyday activities: respondent diary keeping; the collection of documentary data such as financial records; contacts with the firm's customers, suppliers and providers of support services such as accountants. Inevitably, these involve multiple visits to the firm and others and the case study may last anything from a day (for the simplest single-visit study) to several years. In practice it is rare for a case study to use more than a small proportion of these strategies but they still often last a year or more.

Although single-firm case studies are possible, the ability to generalize from these is limited. More common are multiple or comparative case studies. One of the earlier UK studies in small business research was reported in Stanworth and Curran (1973). This consisted of eight small firms drawn equally from printing and electronics and one firm making wire products. Each firm was visited on average once a month over a three-year period.[34] Most visits were unstructured, although structured/ semi-structured questionnaires were used for investigating specific issues. The main respondents were the firm's owner–managers but others such as employees, were also important sources of data. A more recent example is Holliday (1995) which covered three firms, two in the electronics industry and one making waterproof clothing. This is also an example of participant observation, which is discussed in the next section.

Like other ethnographic research strategies, there is a temptation to simply recruit firms and then visit them, fingers crossed, hoping something interesting will emerge. But preparing for entry by identifying the issues the study will focus upon is essential in using case studies even though new themes and issues should emerge in the fieldwork itself. Preparation, in short, is just as necessary for this strategy as for any other. In comparative case studies, firms will often be selected to reflect the theoretical focus of the research to produce, for instance, theoretically contrasting cases.

Managing fieldwork in case studies, as in other research strategies, has problems which need to be addressed with care. Most obviously, good relations have to be maintained with owners and staff of the firms over an extended period where the approach is being used to its fullest potential. The researcher also needs to avoid getting over-involved in the firm or with the people in it since this runs the risk of losing the outsider's view and the ability to generalize. Equally, the researcher needs to avoid overtly taking sides with people in the business because this will not only make further contacts more difficult but restrict the sources from which useful data can be collected.

Case studies can be a comfortable and very forgiving research strategy: once entry has been negotiated and relations cultivated with people in the firm, the researcher can concentrate on data collection. There is less of a need to keep on recruiting firms and cope with large numbers of new respondents as in the classic face-to-face survey. Case studies are forgiving because if an issue is not covered in an early visit or needs further clarification, it can be covered in a later visit or cleared up in a telephone call. As a theoretical approach is developed, new propositions can be tested in repeat visits. On the other hand, generalization may be difficult. A lot may be learnt about the case study firms but can this knowledge be shown convincingly to be relevant to a wider population of firms? For these reasons, case studies are often combined with surveys or other strategies based on larger samples, as in the study of small business quality management by North et al. (1998).

Focus Groups, Participant Observation and Action Research

Less frequently employed fieldwork strategies in small business research are focus groups and participant observation. *Focus groups*, as remarked earlier, are now more common but there are problems in using them in small business research. Often they are used for testing out the issues salient to a research project in developing the research design. Alternatively, they can be used to test respondents' reactions to interpretations and findings produced by some of the strategies discussed above. Where focus groups are used for these purposes they are not carrying the full weight of the project and may not have very serious consequences if they work less well than hoped.

Those conducting focus groups need many of the skills of interviewers. Like interviewers conducting unstructured interviews, they will have a script or list of issues they need to cover. They also need to be sensitive to others' views, quick to spot issues which deserve further discussion because they seem potentially theoretically interesting.[35] They need to be persuasive in eliciting views from all those present to ensure the full range of opinion emerges and diplomatic in preventing any one person from hogging the discussion or browbeating others who hold different views. In other words, the facilitator is an interviewer but also a moderator and group dynamics manager. Sessions can be tape recorded or videoed to record what occurs and to allow others not present to observe how the discussion developed.

Participant observation again is not greatly used in small business research but can be very effective. Its main weaknesses are that it is extremely time-consuming and recruiting firms may not be easy: not many researchers can afford to spend weeks or months in a single firm and many small business owners are reluctant to allow an outsider free run of the firm over an extended period. It can be seen as an extension of the case study discussed above. A well-known use of the technique was cited earlier (Holliday, 1995). In this study, the researcher spent periods of time in three small businesses working alongside owner–managers and employees although her status as a researcher was known to all in the firms. Covert participation might arguably produce more accurate accounts of what occurs in the firms but ethical considerations might make this unacceptable.

Participant observation can be combined with other strategies such as face-to-face or self-administered interviews and many of those listed above under case studies. Like all research strategies, participant observation has its special problems. For example, a researcher with business skills might easily alter how the firm functions by advising on how the firm or specific tasks could be performed differently.[36] Over involvement may result in the researcher becoming aligned with one faction in the firm (for instance, some of the employees) and being cold shouldered by others (even the owner–manager) jeopardizing the research. At the most extreme, researchers might 'go native', that is, come to identify totally with the owner–manager or employees and thus lose their independent perspective as researchers.[37] Another problem is being in the right place at the right time. Ideally, the participant observer needs always to be where 'the action' is but deciding what 'the action' is in a theoretical sense may not always be easy and nobody can be in two places at once.

What might be seen as a special application of participant observation is *action research* (Gill and Johnson, 1997: 60–76). In this version, intervening in the situation of the firm is seen as desirable and, indeed, necessary to the strategy. Basically, the researcher is conducting a 'before and after' study, that is, the situation of the firm is observed at the start of the project and the researcher (in conjunction with the owner–manager) introduces changes, the results of which are assessed and the action sequence repeated until the project is considered complete (Athayde and Blackburn, 1999). Action research is very close to consultancy and a great deal of activity resembling action research occurs in small firms using consultants. Much of the work of Business Links, enterprise agencies and TECs has been devoted to what could be taken as action research. Unfortunately, little of this is reported in the public domain and hence does not constitute 'research' as defined in this book. Where reports do appear, the quality of theorizing is often very poor (Gill, 1985, is an exception) with the results amounting to little more than description and claims of having changed procedures in the firm(s) in question to achieve better business performance.

In principle, however, action research could resemble participant observation as described above and share much the same problems in terms of initial theorization, generating propositions and conducting fieldwork with the exception that the problems of the involvement of the researcher take a distinctive form. Neutrality, for example, is sacrificed or made very difficult where the researcher deliberately aims to intervene in the functioning of the business. Employees, for instance, may become wary of the activities of the researcher. Generalizing from the results may also be difficult because the focus is so clearly on the firm in the project that the researcher easily loses sight of the wider knowledge aims of their activities.

Recording the Data Collected

Fieldwork produces data – sometimes vast amounts, particularly in qualitative research – and if all the hard work to produce it is not to be wasted, it has to be recorded in some way as a first step towards analysis. This is often seen as another of the boring parts of the research process. It is certainly one of the craft elements of research which needs to be addressed and sound fieldwork data recording strategies are a necessary preparation for good quality results. For several of the research strategies discussed in the previous sections, effective data recording schemes can be difficult to devise and time-consuming.

The easiest, most straightforward and best-developed data recording methods are associated with structured surveys. In the most structured, all questions are 'closed' that is, have a known number of mutually exclusive responses which can be predicted in advance. Respondents' answers are simply allocated to one of the known response categories. For a survey of any size it is usual to construct an SPSS database and the responses of each respondent are coded on to the database for subsequent analysis (Cramer 1994). For telephone surveys, a CATI (Computer Aided Telephone Interview) approach can be used. Here the questionnaire is screen-based so that questions can be read off and responses keyed in directly to an SPSS database which forms part of CATI package. The screen listing of questions can be set to conduct skips automatically as dictated by the responses keyed in. The data is very helpfully ready for analysis at the end of each session of interviewing as required.[38]

However, most questionnaires in small business research usually have at least some questions for which codes cannot be devised in advance because of difficulties in predicting the range and content of possible responses. Here, it may be possible to generate codes after the first few dozen questionnaires have been completed so that later respondents' answers can be treated as closed questions. Care is needed, however, because early respondents may not be representative of later respondents and the coding categories selected must be relevant to the later analysis.[39] In some instances all answers may have to be re-coded because analysis indicates new ways in which they might be fruitfully used. As noted, with care, unstructured questions in telephone surveys using a CATI approach can be dealt with in the same way.

The number of categories should not be so large that it is difficult to make sense of them in the analysis. Nor should they produce distributions in which one or two categories contain virtually all responses while others contain few or none unless the distribution of responses is really so clear cut. Where a team of interviewers code their own questionnaires, checks will be needed to ensure they are consistent in their coding judgements, particularly for open questions. A coding book recording agreed ways to deal with difficult cases is invaluable in ensuring consistency between interviewers. Checks on coding practices need to be conducted from time to time to ensure that the agreed decisions are being upheld.

In face-to-face interviews coding can sometimes be undertaken as the interview proceeds but this is difficult where questions are not straightforward or probes are used because the interviewer is too busy managing the interview to code. Here the solution is tape recording the interview. In practice, all face-to-face interviews should be taped. Not only does this provide a record of the interview but enables interviewer performance to be monitored and coding (and recoding should this be needed) to be undertaken later. Since most interviews contain at least some unstructured questions, these are best coded after the interview anyway.

Keeping up-to-date with coding after each interview requires discipline on the part of the interviewer especially when the fieldwork load is high. One aid to keeping up-to-date is a portable computer on to which interviews can be coded on the train or in the hotel. For the individual researcher, coding as soon after the interview as possible, while the memory is still fresh, produces more accurate coding and also helps assess how the project is developing. It can also make it easier to spot emergent issues which ought to picked up in later interviews.

The more unstructured the questionnaire, the more arduous the above procedures become. At some point, therefore, the systematic recording of responses on an SPSS database becomes non-viable. Where the research is predominantly ethnographic other methods of data recording will be required. These will be more complex than the predefined codes of structured, positivist-based research. Usually also, they require much more skill since they very often involve making difficult judgements on what is significant for the project.

Interview-based interactions in qualitative research can often be tape recorded, transcribed and stored on a computer using NUDIST or a similar package (Richards and Richards, 1994). In approaches using both quantitative and qualitative analytical strategies, face-to-face interviews can be transcribed as well as coded on to SPSS. Respondents' answers are often much more detailed than the quantitative method requires but the additional detail often contains valuable information). However, it is not always necessary to transcribe the whole interview, even in wholly qualitative research. Transcription is very time-consuming and resource-intensive and it is possible that total transcription is not needed for a successful analysis. The stronger the commitment to ethnographic epistemological assumptions, however, the more likely the decision will be that total transcription is required.

The other data recording strategy which is common, particularly for some of the qualitative strategies discussed earlier, such as case studies and participant observation, is some form of note taking. Even where the main data collection strategy is the semi-structured face-to-face interview, notes can be a valuable additional data recording device. Note taking can be of the traditional paper-based kind or computer-based, perhaps using a suitable package which allows different retrieval strategies when the notes are sourced for analysis. Visits to firms can be written up after each occasion either in a free-form style or using an observation sheet with categories or headings. In case studies or participant observation, every interaction and conversation with people, as well as the researcher's observations of what goes on in the firm, are data. Note taking requires skill and practice to ensure that what is recorded is theoretically and analytically relevant. In team projects some agreement on note keeping strategies is desirable.

Qualitative research may prompt other kinds of data recording strategies, some of which can also be used in quantitative research. For instance, documentary evidence can be collected by either. This can consist of financial accounts, manuals such as quality manuals, employment contracts, personnel records which allow turnover etc. to be measured, training and marketing literatures. Layouts of offices and workshops can be drawn, placing people spatially in the enterprise and recording the path followed by a product from the initial order to leaving the firm as a completed product. Services can be treated similarly where the firm is a service provider. Some older members of the firm, owners or employees, may be able to provide oral histories if the firm has been in existence for a long time.

Unobtrusive data can be collected and recorded where this will help. For instance, in one study of a science park, the researcher sat in the common area where people from firms in the science park could obtain food and refreshments, read newspapers and meet each other. He systematically, but unobtrusively, recorded who used the area, how often, and who interacted with whom, over a period of several weeks. This provided a measure of how much people in different firms in the science park interacted with each other and of how much of a tech-nological 'village' the park could be claimed to be. Recording who interacts with whom in an individual firm can often be a measure of how the firm functions as a business. Counting the number of times a tele-phone rings before being answered might be a measure of customer responsiveness in some small firms. In other words, ingenuity might be able to suggest unobtrusive data recording strategies relevant to the aims of a project.

Conclusions

This chapter has been concerned with fieldwork in small business research. Fieldwork, for any project more than the very simplest, is a complex combination of a large number of elements requiring a sound craft approach, interpersonal and technical skills and creative abilities. There is rarely a single best research design for a project. The same set of theoretical and data concerns may be served equally well by a variety of research designs. No research design will be perfect since all involve compromises. For instance, all researchers, particularly individuals working alone, have to accept that their resources are finite. Often researchers admit, *ex post facto*, that if they were starting again, they would amend or even choose a different research design to the one they actually used.

One of the key problems in research designs for small business research is the lack of suitable, high-quality sampling frames from which to recruit small businesses. This problem is all the more serious because of the extreme heterogeneity of the small business population. As the discussion of sampling frames and constructing samples showed, there are solutions to these problems which can produce reasonably satis-factory, if not perfect, results. Some of the common strategies used were described but, of course, others could be devised depending on the ingenuity of the researcher. The emphasis has been on drawing on a diversity of sources to overcome possible biases where only a single source is used. Sample construction requires resourcefulness and hard work but good quality research needs sound preparation.

Another problem stressed was achieving reasonable response rates in studies which need to achieve statistical representativeness. Small business owners, for perfectly understandable reasons, are not always the most willing of respondents. Again, the chapter suggested ways of achieving acceptable levels. Since low response rates will tend to be associated with biases of various kinds, there is a real need to treat this problem seriously if claims of representativeness are to made about the results of the research.

Some small business research does not seek or claim statistical representativeness for its results. But the problem of selecting firms for such projects remains. The discussion suggested some of the issues that need to be kept in mind and some of the strategies which can be used to construct samples for qualitative research. Whatever the research, the issue of generalizability of the findings or interpretation is always present and needs to be addressed. Qualitative researchers need to be especially sensitive to theses issues.

In practice, a high proportion of small business research employs mixed research designs, which include quantitative and qualitative elements. While epistemological purists may find mixed approaches unacceptable, many small business researchers take a more pragmatic approach, depending on the problem they are researching, the skills and preferences of the researcher(s) and the resources available.

Most small business research uses questionnaires of some kind. These range from the highly structured to the unstructured. Each has their merits and weaknesses and, again, what might be deemed most suitable for any given project will depend on the objectives of the project, the research design preferences and skills of the researcher(s), and the resources available. Epistemological considerations will also be relevant. Some researchers will be keen on an ethnographic approach while others will want to adopt a quantitative approach. Others will be happy to employ a mix. Whatever the approach, the discussion suggested that all require careful thought if they are to be effective.

Interviewing strategies in face-to-face and telephone interviews were examined with an emphasis on the skills needed to be an effective interviewer, especially for unstructured and qualitatively based interviews. Other strategies such as case studies, focus groups and participant observation, may include interview elements but will also require other high level skills on the part of the researcher. Not everybody will have these skills and where the project is team-based attention will need to be given to differences in researcher performance if the quality of the data collected is to be maintained.

Finally, this chapter looked at data recording. It examined a number of ways of recording data, ranging from the relatively simple recording of answers to pre-coded, closed questions on an SPSS database, to recording data collected using ethnographic approaches. The latter, it was pointed out, is much more time-consuming and inherently more difficult than using the well-established techniques associated with quantitative research strategies. But just because the latter relies on more standardized approaches does not, of course, mean it is more likely to be effective or produce more interesting results. For some kinds of research problems, only qualitative strategies are likely to be effective and, given a skilled sensitive approach, they have considerable demonstrated strengths.

The research design, fieldwork and data collection stages are preparations for the analysis and constructing of the researchers' answers to the problem they set themselves at the beginning of the research project. In some kinds of research, of course, analysis starts alongside the fieldwork, each interacting with the other as the project proceeds. In grounded theory approaches, for example, this is an essential component in the research process. In practice, most small business research will have an element of grounded theory in the fieldwork but the bulk of the analysis and interpretation of the results will take place after the fieldwork is complete. The next chapter concentrates on these further stages of the research project.

Notes

1 The DTI (1999a: 12) estimated that there were over 14,000 firms in printing and service activities related to printing in the UK, each employing less than 50 people at the start of 1998.

2 See, for example, Cramer (1994) on SPSS or Richards and Richards (1994) on NUDIST. There are numerous texts on statistical techniques for social scientists which are equally applicable to business and social research. Cramer (1994) covers many of the common statistical techniques employed and Bryman and Cramer (1990) offers an alternative. Freund et al. (1993) is a familiar source on statistics for generations of business students and very helpful to those with little knowledge of quantitative analysis. Some of the above also cover attitude scales, but for a more detailed treatment see Kidder and Judd (1986).

3 'Response bias' refers to the probability of respondents with specific characteristics within a selected population being more or less likely to respond. For example, a house-to-house survey of adults aged over 16 conducted in a suburban locality in the evenings might suffer response bias because elderly people may be nervous about opening their doors in the evening and younger people may be more likely to be out socializing.

4 A check of this kind is worth making with any sample to find out what biases, if any, of this kind have occurred. In this case, the benchmark sample could be the DTI estimates of the size distribution of the UK small business population.

5 For a more detailed description of the sampling strategies used and the reasons for the choices made see Curran et al., 1996: Appendix 1. For example, the quotas were not proportionate to the known distributions in the small

business population. This was because the methodological strategy required that all size and activity categories should contain sufficient numbers to permit confidence in the findings for each category. However, a weighting procedure (discussed in the Appendix) was employed to provide indications of what might have been expected if the quotas were proportionate to the distributions in the business population for the size range investigated.

6 Often small business researchers are offered for free what they are confidently assured is a high-quality data set which, on inspection, turns out to be useless. For instance, not all the data may have been entered in to the database. It may also have been collected by a wide variety of 'interviewers' or administrators who did not follow a common procedure when recording the data.

7 It should be noted that the authors excluded the traditional professions such as solicitors and architects who might otherwise have helped increase the representation of those from higher social class backgrounds.

8 For another example of the use of a secondary data set of this kind see Burrows and Ford (1998) which used the data from the *Survey of English Housing 1993–1994*, again conducted officially and based on interviews with about 20,000 households in England, to analyse relations between home ownership and self-employment.

9 Robson et al. (1997) attempted to use *Quarterly Labour Force Survey* data on earnings to estimate the effects of a minimum wage at various levels but found that more data would be a clear advantage. They note that the more obvious data source here, the *New Earnings Survey*, excluded small employers and the low paid, many of whom work for themselves. This suggests that this data set could be improved as a source of information on the small firm.

10 The Business Link Directorate (1999) estimated that although the Business Link network received some 500,000 enquiries a year, this was calculated to be an overall penetration of around 7 per cent.

11 This study also recruited large enterprises and public sector organizations in two of the localities. The selection of these was easier. Like most localities, they contained only small numbers of large enterprises and public bodies. It was relatively easy to construct a list of these and then select a small number representing the private and public sectors and manufacturing and services in the private sector.

12 In fact, the study used data from two separate research projects each with their own sample. In two of the localities only manufacturing firms were recruited while in the other five, only service sector small firms were recruited. However, sample construction and recruiting strategies were almost identical in the two studies. See Curran and Blackburn (1994) for a fuller account.

13 This study also demonstrates that response rates are highly sector dependent. For example, among the owners of computer services small firms the response rate was just under 80 per cent but among owners of small motor vehicle repairers, it was 40 per cent. Curran and Blackburn argue that response rate differences may have been related to a variety of factors. For example, they believe that the educational levels of owner–managers may be an influence: owner–managers with higher educational qualifications may well be more receptive to participating in research than those with no or few qualifications. Owners of businesses such as those engaged in vehicle repairs and servicing, are often very busy throughout the working day completing

work for customers who want their vehicles back as soon as possible. Because of these demands, they can spare little time to be interviewed.

14 Matching for all of these variables might be difficult in practice and it is likely that fewer variables would be chosen in any particular study. Matched samples are a popular research design in business and management research but are difficult to construct in small business research where the base population is highly heterogeneous. However, for an example which worked very effectively see O'Farrell and Hitchens (1989) who compared matched pairs of small manufacturing companies in Scotland and the South of England. The same researchers used a similar approach comparing firms in Scotland and Ireland (O'Farrell and Hitchens, 1988).

15 An exception to the above is where the focus group is used as a means of testing conclusions and interpretations generated earlier in the research. For example, in one of the localities in the study by Curran et al. (1991) a very low level of networking between firms and other local business-relevant bodies such as TECs, was found. The research team brought together respondents from the study, representatives of the local chamber of commerce, TEC and local bankers and accountants, to test the team's explanation for this low level. The focus group supported the explanation. (As it happens, many of the focus group's members had never met because of the low level of networking.)

16 Blackburn and Stokes (in press) report that it took over 100 approaches to business owners to recruit their target of eight willing to participate in a focus group.

17 Curran and Blackburn (1994: 102) reported that among their carefully recruited sample of small firms in eight localities across Britain, only one in four belonged to their local chamber of commerce. They also reported that membership was associated strongly with sector. For example, in one of their sectors, motor vehicle repairs and servicing, only eight per cent belonged but among employment agencies it was almost 45 per cent.

18 Of course, a good deal of small business research has been based on samples where response rates were very much less than 60 per cent. Such research can produce valuable findings, particularly where the study is exploratory. Often later studies, achieving better response rates, simply verify the findings of the earlier studies but without this later support, the findings from the earlier studies can only be treated as tentative.

19 This should be as accurate an estimate as possible based on the pilot try out of the questionnaire. Some interviews will take less time, some more, depending on the owner–manager's business. For example, the business may have a complicated history or be involved in a wide range of activities. Experience shows that busy owner–managers will give up to an hour but requests for longer periods or where the respondent feels the interview will be too time-consuming, will reduce response. Some owner–managers will give much longer, particularly where they have well-developed opinions or enjoy the interview experience, but such generosity cannot be counted upon.

20 As noted earlier (Note 13) response rates are very sector dependent. For low response sectors it may be necessary to do more than one follow-up call or employ other ways of increasing response. For instance, it might be possible to obtain positive coverage in a trade journal or an interview on a local radio station.

21 Some projects did not report response rates or were based on methodological strategies, such as historical secondary data, where response rates were not applicable. Several of those that did report rates had levels below a third.

22 Size is not everything in achieving a representative sample of course. But, as pointed out earlier, low response rates tend to have biases of different kinds, particularly size and sector bias.

23 An alternative is to recruit through trade unions, an approach used by Rainnie (1989) but few small firm employees belong to trade unions. Moreover, approaching them in this way may make it difficult to interview their employers. To fully understand employment issues in small firms, *both* employees and employers need to be interviewed.

24 By 'participant observation' here is meant research strategies in which the researcher actually spends time observing day-to-day practices in the enterprise. It may be covert, that is, the owner–manager and/or employees may be unaware that the researcher is anything other than an employee, or open where the researcher is known by all concerned as a researcher. For an example of the former see Mars and Nicod (1984) and for the latter, Holliday (1995). Covert participant observation, since it involves deception, raises ethical issues.

25 More detailed general treatments are in classic texts such as Oppenheim (1966) while discussions focusing directly on issues relevant to business and management are covered by Gill and Johnson (1997) and Jankowicz (1995; espec. Chapter 12). Scales of one kind or another are sometimes used in small business research in questionnaires and, again, are much more technically sophisticated than many realize. Those contemplating using scales should consult specialist texts but a useful introduction is in Jankowicz (1995: 266–72).

26 Just how much information a lack of face-to-face contact loses can often be experienced when a person only previously known through telephone conversations is met personally. A voice over the telephone conjures a mental picture of the speaker but these are often radically revised at a later face-to-face meeting.

27 The *Small Business Trust NatWest* quarterly small business survey is one of the longest running surveys of small business owners having started in 1984. For an example see SBRT (1999).

28 Those familiar with corporate strategy approaches to planning in larger enterprises are often surprised at the lack of long-term business planning by small business owners, even those with strong ambitions for growth. In fact, this often simply reflects small business owners' realism about their ability to predict or engineer the development of the business over any extended period. For a discussion see Curran (1997).

29 A qualitative researcher, however, may want to use this kind of response as data even though it is recognized that the respondent is not making any knowledge-based assessment. A content analysis of such responses might well offer an interesting insight on how small business owners think but most researchers will wish to treat answers to such questions in a more literal way.

30 Even an apparently simple question such as, 'What profit did the business make in the last financial year?' may be difficult for many small business owners to answer. First, the way in which owners calculate 'profit' may vary greatly and, secondly, many may not actually know what profit they made

since they often wait for their accountant to provide this information on an annual basis. Most small business owners are much more interested in monthly cash flow than annual profit since they regard the former as the best indicator of how well the business is trading (Jarvis et al., 1996).

31 This question is taken from a survey of SMEs conducted in conjunction with the Your Business Matters conferences set up by the Institute of Directors, the CBI, the British Chambers of Commerce, the TEC Councils, the Federation of Small Businesses and the Forum of Private Business following the publication of a 1995 White Paper on competitiveness. The research was organized by the Forum of Private Business. The questionnaire and results were published in *Your Business Matters Report of the Regional Conferences*, London, Institute of Directors, March 1996.

32 Examples of the literature which is helpful in exploring fieldwork strategies generally are: Fontana and Frey (1994) who discuss interviewing in its myriad forms including focus groups; Burgess (1984) who examines not only interviews but other fieldwork strategies including participant observation; and Ackroyd and Hughes (1992) who are sound on interviewing in particular but cover other strategies also.

33 For an overview of the case study research strategy as used generally in the social sciences see Hakim (1987: Chapter 6 *passim*), Yin (1994) and Stake (1995). What these show especially well is how crude and under-exploited the case study research strategy all too often is in business and management research, including small business research.

34 Overall, because some firms were recruited later than others, the fieldwork took over three years to complete. The relations developed with some of the firms were so strong that they continued well after the fieldwork was completed.

35 In market research it is common to use skilled facilitators to conduct focus groups and is sometimes suggested that small business research should use people from a marketing background to conduct focus groups where these are part of the research design. This may be sensible but focus group facilitators also need to be well-briefed in small business research otherwise they may well miss key issues or not allow them to be pursued fully.

36 But see below the discussion of action research where such interventions are integral to the research strategy.

37 For this reason, research texts which discuss participant observation sometimes recommend the researcher has breaks away from the firm regularly. Researchers, for instance, might work one day a week less to give them more time to write up their notes and think about what issues they want to concentrate on when they return to the firm.

38 CATI strategies allow for open questions and therefore some responses will be typed in for later coding and analysis. There may also need to be checks on the quality of coding to ensure the data is 'clean', that is, free from errors.

39 One problem which sometimes occurs is generating too many coding categories because of difficulties in recognizing shared characteristics of responses. This may require categories being collapsed down later to help the analysis. On the whole starting with too many categories is better than starting with too few: it is easier to collapse categories into each other than expand the number because the latter means reviewing all responses to code for the same categories.

4

Analysing Data

As emphasized in Chapter 2, facts (data) do not speak for themselves: *we* have to make them speak through the explanations or interpretations we generate from the data. To achieve this the data has to be analysed. Analysis is no simple or mechanical process although there is some-times a tendency to reduce it to an application of statistical techniques or computer-based manipulation. Good research rarely if ever results from such strategies. Rather, analysis is better seen as an exercise in creativity, whether the approach is quantitative or qualitative. Tech-niques cannot produce new explanations or interpretations, they can only assist.

To many of those who have taken quantitative courses or come from disciplines with a strong quantitative emphasis, the insistence that analysis is, in large part, a creative process may be disconcerting. The creative process is commonly seen as something in which artists rather than business researchers engage. Business and management science, on the other hand, is seen by many as a rational, quantitatively based set of procedures for producing 'objective' explanations. This is a mistaken view. Unless it attempts 'to map the unknown', research is usually little more than corroboration. Qualitative researchers, however, are more likely to accept that their role is to (re)interpret the world of the small business. Techniques for qualitative analysis are much less well-established than those in quantitative research and this forces qualitative researchers to attempt to be adventurous in their interpretations, though success is not easily achieved and the results are sometimes not very exciting.

Of course, not all research will produce startlingly original break-throughs in our understanding of the small business. Not everybody has the intellectual and creative capacity to produce – or the luck to stumble upon – mind-blowing explanations or interpretations. But it should be the aim of all researchers to analyse their data so as to add at least something novel to our present understanding. Even if the end product is very modest in terms of any originality criterion, it is the attempt to conform to the norm of trying to creatively extend understanding which marks the serious and committed researcher. Whatever the approach adopted, analysis and producing satisfying explanations or interpretations is undoubtedly hard work.

The relationship between the techniques of analysis (statistical or interpretative) and the creative processes which results in explanations or interpretations, is somewhat clouded. In practice, the most common pattern is probably what is termed 'a data-theory interaction process'. In other words, there is a continuing 'dialogue' between data (analysed in various ways) and theory (an explanation or interpretation) which eventually results in what the researcher sees as an acceptably robust result.[1] Explanation or interpretation does not result smoothly or easily from the analysis process but has to be struggled for, often with an end product which does not dovetail neatly with all the data collected. Sometimes the researcher often has to be satisfied with a 'best fit' result which is all too clearly provisional. This is the reality of research. Few experienced researchers have no doubts about the explanations or interpretations they present to the world.

In this chapter the main approaches used in the analysis of data are discussed with examples from the small business literature. Both quantitative and qualitative techniques are dealt with critically and the kinds of explanations and interpretations which can result, are highlighted. Because the epistemological problems inherent in producing acceptable results from research of any kind are so intractable, the end product of the researcher's efforts will always be to some degree tentative. What researchers try to do, regardless of the approach they have adopted, is to minimize, as far as they are able, the weaknesses in their work.

Yet the ever present weaknesses in explanations or interpretations have an important role in intellectual inquiry. Just as new research and thinking is often sparked by critical evaluations of previous research, so the results of later research becomes the launch pad for yet further research. This underlines an important element in the research process. The continuity and cumulative aspects of research are integral to the generation of new explanations or interpretations. Research on any aspect of the small business has a context, it is related to what research has gone before even if only indirectly or even if it rejects previous thinking as fundamentally mistaken. To ignore this context in conducting research is to run the very serious risk of producing trivial results or adding little or nothing to what has already been said.

Quantitative Analysis and Explanation Generation

Undoubtedly, until relatively recently quantitative analysis and positivist explanations dominated small business research much as they have in business and management research generally. The obvious reasons for this prominence are threefold.[2] First, has been the conscious modelling, especially in the first half of the twentieth century, of social and business research on nineteenth century natural science approaches. The success of these approaches in the natural sciences led to a belief that they could be applied with equal success to business activities. Secondly, there is the strong cultural appeal of numerically based approaches to understanding such phenomena. If findings and explanations can be expressed quantitatively, they tend to carry enormous significance for audiences of all kinds (and particularly political and policy audiences) compared with alternative types of interpretation. Thirdly, and relatedly, has been the development of statistical techniques which offer a wide variety of ways of handling data in order to generate explanations (Cramer, 1994; Vogt, 1999). The ease of using such techniques has been greatly enhanced by the computer, particularly the PC, and statistical packages such as SPSS.

In one sense, positivist explanations based on quantitative techniques, particularly statistical techniques, have been too tempting as a way of understanding small business phenomena. Because the techniques are relatively easy and quick to use, they invite an almost mechanical approach to analysis. Survey data, for example, can be coded, put on to a computer and subjected to a variety of statistical tests using a powerful package such as SPSS, very easily. The results can then be printed out to be introduced into any report of the project. For some purposes, simply presenting these results together with a brief supporting description and comment, constitutes research. With a little practice, research using this kind of approach can generate reports efficiently and quickly. Well-established examples of this kind of research are the quarterly reports on small business owners' experiences and levels of economic confidence produced by the Small Business Research Trust.

Descriptive analyses of the above kind have their merits. They offer a snapshot of small business owners' experiences and views and how these might be changing over time. They can also offer benchmarks for more specific studies. But whether they offer much in the way of explanation in any rigorous sense is questionable.[3] To be fair, those conducting the surveys do not claim any great explanatory power for their results as witnessed by the often very brief comments accompanying the tabular presentation of results. Commentary is often confined to comparisons with previous quarters' results sometimes coupled with speculation on why any observed differences have occurred. For instance, an increase in the level of reported orders by small business owners may be linked to central government data indicating improved performance of the economy as a whole.

Other small business research adopting a quantitative, positivist-based explanatory framework is much more ambitious. Causal explanations, that is, assertions that the behaviour of 'x' (sometimes called the dependent variable) is determined by 'y' (the independent variable) are more serious attempts at explanation than the kind of speculative relationships mentioned in the above paragraph. Often analyses are consolidated into a more elaborate theorization which aims at generalization to a much larger population of small enterprises.

A very well-known but actually relatively modest example of quantitative small business research of the above kind was the study by Birch (1979). This focused on job generation in the USA. It took as its database, information on 5.6m business establishments covering about 82 per cent of all US private sector employment collected at four different points in time: 1969, 1972, 1974 and 1976. The data was analysed by isolating the so-called 'components of job generation' to show which types of firms contributed most to job creation. The results were reported as showing that small firms, that is, those with 20 or fewer employees, generated 66 per cent of all new jobs created in the USA; that small independent firms generated 52 per cent of the total; and that middle- and large-sized firms, on balance, provided relatively few new jobs (Birch, 1979: 8). These finding were supported by considerable quantitative detail examining possible relations not only by firm size but also by age of firm, region and sector, refining the main conclusions further.

One major reason for the influence of this relatively simple analysis was that Birch explicitly focused on the policy implications of the study at a time when policy-makers, particularly in Britain, were worried about rapidly increasing unemployment. The study was taken as suggesting that encouraging more small firms by 'creating an enterprise society', would help create jobs and reduce unemployment (Storey, 1994: 161 2). Although the findings reported by Birch appear to show a very clear difference in job-creation levels between small and large firms and a clear lesson for policy, the underlying theorization was actually modest. The study did not show *why* small firms were apparently so effective at creating jobs or *why* medium- and large-sized firms were apparently so poor. Of course, later researchers (see Storey, 1994: 161–200) after critically assessing the main thesis offered by Birch, devoted more consideration to explaining the reasons that might be behind the findings. Yet, as argued below, there are severe limits on the extent to which causal explanations can be generated from analyses of the kind exemplified by Birch's work.

Birch's research also illustrates another common problem of quantitative analyses producing positivist explanations. Storey (1994: 161–73) in his very detailed review of Birch's work and a comparison of similar research in the UK, showed that studies employing this kind of approach very easily get bogged down in discussions of the adequacies of the quantitative techniques employed, detracting attention from the more important explanatory element of the research. This is not to say that care does not need to be taken in ensuring that data is as accurate as possible and that the analytical procedures adopted are as powerful as possible. But, at the end of the day, it is the explanation or theorization that counts. As Storey (1994: 201–2) demonstrated, the result of a great deal of research effort in the USA and the UK attempting to measure the job creating propensities of small firms and to compare them with medium and large firms, was that it appeared clear that small firms were indeed able to create jobs at a faster rate than larger firms and that small firms were less affected by the ups and downs of macro economic conditions in doing so than large firms. *Why* this should be the case, however, was still far from clear.

Moreover, as Storey also pointed out, quantitatively based studies of job creation based on large data sets of the kind used by Birch[4] and others who have employed the same approach, tell us very little about other key aspects of the jobs created by small firms. For example, the *quality* of the jobs generated measured in terms of productivity, training levels and employment relations, are all neglected. In other words, it is quite possible that the jobs created by small firms are less productive, accompanied by poorer levels of formal training and are more poorly managed than those created by larger enterprises. Jobs created by small firms, in short, may not really be adequate replacements for the jobs lost by disappearing or downsizing large organizations. To determine whether this is the case demands much more research, much of it based on approaches which differ fundamentally from the quantitatively based approach employed by Birch and most other contributors to the small firm job generation literature.[5]

Some quantitatively based small business research is much more complex, with more complex analyses, than the examples discussed above. An excellent example is the study by Barkham et al. (1996) of small business growth. This was a sophisticated, ambitious attempt to explain growth processes in small businesses (those with under 50 employees) in manufacturing in four UK regions over the period 1986–90. The authors argue that small firm growth is likely to reflect three groups of influences: the nature of the firm (such as size, product markets and location); the characteristics of owner–managers (age, education, experience etc.); and the business strategies of owner–managers (the extent of forward planning, use of marketing strategies etc.). The project collected a wide range of data on variables related to the three sets of influences and then used quantitative analysis to isolate the relative importance of, and interactions between, the variables.

The data was collected using semi-structured, face-to-face interviews with the principal decision-makers (usually the owner–managers) of 172 carefully selected firms from the four regions. The data from the 53 questions put to respondents was coded to produce 240 variables which were subjected to a regression analysis generated by a step wise process.[6] This still produced rather unmanageable results and the authors felt the need to generate what are called 'reduced form models'; which contain the strongest variables that appeared to be related to growth using this approach.

The bulk of the analyses consists of the presentation of the results of the regressions in relation to business growth and region. The findings are very carefully presented, with detailed qualifications on their applicability or contribution to an explanation of small business growth. However, several variables stood out as of some importance. For example, undertaking formal market research appeared to be positively related to growth, whereas age of the owner–manager appeared negatively related. But it would be unfair to the subtlety of the analysis, and the presentation of the findings, to suggest that specific variables are offered in this way as the key to understanding small business growth.

The treatment of the regional dimensions illustrates well the complexity of the analysis presented. Although Barkham et al. examined a wide range of differences between the four regions, they argued that such differences had little importance in explaining growth patterns in the small firms. The reason for this, they suggested, was that although each region had advantages in some key variables linked to growth, they also all had disadvantages in others so that, overall, the results were self-cancelling. On the other hand, the results did tend to show that firms in Northern Ireland (one of the four regions) outperformed firms in the others. This appeared, however, to be the result not so much of the way the firms themselves were run but of mainly exogenous variables such as the highly proactive UK government policies (in particular, the extensive economic support provided to counter the adverse local political situation in the period covered) and the very active local support agencies, also largely funded by central government.

In terms of the central focus of this chapter, the authors were very explicit in excluding what they obviously saw as 'soft' data, particularly owner–manager motivations. They felt that it would be difficult to quantify this kind of data and rather than attempt to do so, decided to disregard it altogether. Epistemologically and methodologically this was rather curious. Epistemologically, the researchers' decision appears to reflect a fear of trying to incorporate the psychological and motivational dimensions of small business management. Methodologically, they argue that motivational variables, defined psychologically, are difficult to measure and that, therefore, they should be excluded. Even if this is true, it would still be a curious decision.[7] Given the key importance of owner–managers in the decision-making processes of the small firm, it seems odd to exclude data on their motivations from a study of small firm growth. In fact, the authors found it necessary (see Barkham et al., 1996: 73–6) to examine the personal objectives of the owner–managers or principal decision-makers in some detail. Inevitably, this alluded to their motivations for holding particular objectives.

What this sophisticated quantitatively based study shows in terms of the examination of analyses and explanation generation – the subject of this chapter – is that despite the well developed techniques applied in such approaches there are considerable problems.[8] Basically, the main problem is that while the studies produce a great deal of quantitative data expressed as findings of one kind or another about which it is possible to be confident at some level in a statistical sense, they are often short on answers to 'why' questions. Probability statements, the quintessence of statistical analyses, however sophisticated, are not causal explanations. For example, quantitative treatments of small business growth do not really offer explanations but statistical associations. That is they show that at some level of statistical confidence variable 'x' is likely to be linked to variable 'y' so that this pairing occurs more frequently than would be expected by chance.[9]

For instance, one common finding in research on small business growth is that small business owners who are willing to allow external equity participation in their businesses are more likely to experience growth than those who do not (Storey, 1994: 146). But this cannot be taken to mean that we can say that where the owner is willing to accept external equity participation this results in rapid growth or that businesses which do not accept external investment cannot experience fast and successful growth. Strictly, explanations established on the basis of statistical associations tell us nothing about what any *individual* business will experience since such associations only apply to *populations* of firms: any particular firm in the population may or may not reflect the association.

Moreover, as proponents of such approaches such as Barkham et al. (1996) make abundantly clear, there are no single indicators or even easily identifiable clusters of indicators which could be used as predictors of business performance. As they suggest, small business growth is, at the very least, influenced by a wide range of factors including owner–managers' skill and strategies, the organizational structure of the business, the characteristics of the sector in which the firm trades, the performance of the wider economy, and government economic and other policies. This is one reason why even well-conducted quantitatively based research is often not much use to, say, the clearing bank decision-maker who is attempting to assess whether the business should be granted a long-term loan.[10]

Assessing the Power and Limitations of Quantitative Analyses

One of the most refined reviews of the explanative value of quantitatively based analyses of social and, by extension, business and management phenomena, is offered by Sayer (1992: Chapter 6 *passim*). The fundamental distinction between association in the statistical sense and causality, has already been made: the probability or relative frequency of an event occurring, however well-established or described, is not an explanation of *why* it occurs. But he makes a number of further points which are equally important when transposed to small business research. For instance, he notes that a good deal of quantification assumes that what is being measured (such as job creation or small business growth) is what he terms 'qualitatively invariant', that is, the phenomena in question:

> . . . can be split up and combined without changing their nature. We can measure them at different times or places in different conditions and know that we are not measuring different things. (Sayer, 1992: 177)

Sayer points out, however, that some of the phenomena we are most interested in are very far from 'qualitatively invariant'. In small business research, take owner–manager attitudes to growth, for example. As is fairly easily established, these are context dependent, that is, they are conditioned by a wide variety of influences such as the skill levels and prior experiences of the owner–manager, market conditions such as interest rate levels, technological change and government policies on, for instance, capital investment allowances. Some such as owner–manager skills and experiences, are irreversible processes subject to continuous qualitative change producing emergent properties which materialize, dissolve and combine and recombine in all kinds of ways as time passes. Others are dependent on context in the sense that they are related to wider social structures and their emergent properties. In neither case, therefore, can they be treated as invariant for statistical purposes.

A more uncompromising epistemological position is that positivist models of causality or explanations are inappropriate to human and social phenomena. This offers an additional powerful reason for rejecting statistical and quantitative analyses in small business research. If the 'logics' in which human and social phenomena are embedded are not of the linear or other kinds embodied in mathematical models, then the attempt to fit such phenomena to the latter is doomed. However, it is possible (and common, as shown below) to adopt a rather less black and white position epistemologically than abandoning all quantitative analyses as inherently useless for understanding the small business and its role in the economy.

Finally, it is worth re-emphasizing one of the key reasons discussed at length in the opening chapter on why quantitative analyses of small business phenomena have to be treated so cautiously, that is, the extreme heterogeneity of the small business population. This makes it very difficult to adopt the usual assumption required for quantitative analyses, namely that all those designated as belonging to a named category share sufficiently similar characteristics so that we may confidently discuss them as being 'the same' for the purposes of analysis and explanation. Where a field of research is characterized with extreme heterogeneity this assumption is undermined and the value of statistically based analyses substantially reduced.

The above assessment of the value of quantitative analyses in small business research appears almost overwhelmingly damning. 'The main verdict on statistical methods must therefore be that despite their logical rigour they are primitive tools as far as explanation is concerned' (Sayer, 1992: 198). But we need not throw the baby out with the bath water. As much of the previous discussion in both this and earlier chapters has suggested, quantitatively based small business research has a constructive role in establishing knowledge on how small firms function in relation to the wider economy. First of all, quantitative approaches are valuable at the descriptive level. We *do* need accurate quantitative estimates of the numbers and kinds of small enterprises in the UK economy for example.[11] It *is* valuable to have an age distribution broken down by gender, etc., of owners of small businesses. We *do* find it helpful to have quantitative estimates of the job-creating propensies of small enterprises as compared with larger firms.

Secondly, all social and business research is difficult because of the inherent complexities of the phenomena in question. Where explanations are difficult to generate because of poor-quality data or because causality is hard to establish, it is nevertheless worth the attempt. Researchers worth their salt rarely accept that any issue is impossible to research. Descriptive quantitative treatments leading on to more refined quantitative analyses can be key steps in the process of constructing satisfying explanations. Further, even when the attitudes and behaviour of owner–managers or the ways in which small firms function in the wider economy are well-established in a genuinely causal sense, quantitative analyses are very helpful in providing information on the numerical dimensions of the processes known to occur. For example, the reasons why owner–managers adopt particular kinds of training strategies in relation to their employees may well be established but quantitative data (updated from time to time) on the incidence of particular forms of employee training is invaluable (see, for example, Cosh and Hughes, 1998: Chapter 2).

One way of assessing the value of quantitative analyses of small business phenomena, therefore, is to argue that they are not only worthwhile in their own right for the kinds of reasons listed above but they help fill gaps in our understanding when more powerful forms of explanation are not available. As a better understanding of the causalities and contingencies underlying small business phenomena is established, the role of quantitative analyses of the statistical variety inevitably declines. Association is helpful but real understanding is more. For some researchers real understanding can only come from qualitative or interpretative approaches.

Qualitative Analyses of Small Business Phenomena

The advance of qualitative and non-positivist approaches to studying the small business has lagged behind their advance in social research in general. In one sense this is a little surprising because it might have been supposed that qualitative research would have been especially appealing in an area where a main focus is on the activities of small groups of people. After all, owner–managers with between one and four employees make up 70 per cent of all businesses with employees in the UK (DTI, 1999a: 7). Yet, in practice, there has been a tendency to follow the model of the quantitative approaches which have dominated research on larger enterprises and macro-economic activities.[12] More recently, however, non-positivist analyses have become much more common.

It is not as easy to discuss approaches to qualitative analysis compared with those in quantitative analysis. One reason is that the former have had less long to develop so guides to qualitative analyses techniques have been much more difficult to find (Huberman and Miles, 1994: 428). Another reason is that there are a wide range of approaches to qualitative research, some of which do not share common epistemological or methodological assumptions. Some, indeed, are reluctant to separate analysis from the other elements which make up the research process on the grounds that data collection and analysis are so closely interwoven that it is spurious to discuss them separately (Bryman and Burgess, 1994: 217–18).

Nevertheless, for the purposes of examining ways of handling qualitative data in small business research as well as consistency, the analysis in qualitative research is dealt with here separately. Certainly, the relative absence of well-established, widely used techniques for qualitative analysis creates problems for researchers.

For example, as anybody who has used a qualitative approach will readily attest, one result is that analysis is much more difficult and time-consuming than in quantitative research.[13] These problems are magnified greatly because qualitative research often produces huge amounts of difficult-to-categorize data from even quite small samples. Qualitative researchers have to forgo the 'magic machine' approach of coding the data on to a computer using a package such as SSPS and then 'number crunching' out some results. Although computers are now regularly used in qualitative analysis (see below) they do not produce neat, ready-digested end results which can be fed into a report or thesis.

On the other hand, the absence of well-established analysis practices in qualitative research reduces the temptation to embrace the kind of cookbook approach sometimes found in quantitative research. Instead, it forces the researcher to think harder and, hopefully, to be more creative when generating interpretations. This is not easy and not all qualitative research rises to the challenge. Indeed, the banality of the results is often much more obvious than in similarly unimaginative research based on quantitative approaches where triteness can be hidden behind the sophistication of the statistical treatments used.

Descriptive Qualitative Analyses

The simplest use of qualitative research strategies produces the equivalent of descriptive statistics in quantitative research. Often this is based on similar motivation, that is, to carry out an initial exploration of an area not previously researched.[14] The level of analysis will be relatively low and the extent of theorizing limited. The prime aim will be to delineate the universe of meanings, attitudes and values of a group of respondents such as the owner–managers of a particular kind of economic enterprise. The result is an analysis often illustrated with quotations from respondents expressing their views in their own words, which attempts to let the reader enter the world of the respondents and see it from their point of view.

The term 'descriptive' in this context should not be taken as disparaging to this kind of research. Some commentators refer to this kind of qualitative research as 'thick description' to emphasize that it is more than just a simple, literary account (Hammersley, 1990: 19; Gill and Johnson, 1997: 120). To make this point even more firmly, ethnographic analyses of these kinds may also be labelled as 'analytic' or 'theoretical' descriptions to denote that even though the researcher's aim is to offer a relatively straightforward analysis, there will frequently be the beginnings of a more theorized treatment in the form of possible analytical categories and propositions suggesting links between elements in the phenomena, which can be tested in further research.

In descriptive ethnography of the above kind, the researcher tries to offer an account that avoids moral judgements on the views or behaviour of the respondents. As with quantitative descriptive statistics, the selection of respondents needs to be undertaken with care to ensure credibility. Respondents, for example, may be selected employing some kind of theoretical sampling strategy. For instance, the firms may be chosen to represent small and larger firms within whatever size limits adopted or firms may be selected to represent those in prosperous and less prosperous markets etc. While the main emphasis may be ethnographic, some quantification may be included to add flesh to the account offered.

An excellent example of descriptive ethnography is the study by Werbner (1984) of Pakistani owner–managers in the Manchester garment trade. This sought to show how the cultural worlds and business strategies of these ethnic entrepreneurs were intimately linked. Werbner argued that being in British society but – as outsiders – not of it, these Pakistani immigrants were unfettered by the constraints of the host culture and so were able to develop a distinctive entrepreneurial style. Their understanding of trading originated in the bazaars of South Asia but was applied to garment manufacture, an inherently labour-intensive form of enterprise needing relatively little capital, which was already well-established in Manchester. As a typically fragmented form of economic activity, garment making is mediated through agents, sub-contractors and homeworkers. This pattern mapped easily on to the community linkages, family labour resources and, especially, the potential for trust relations in the ethnic minority.

Culturally, Werbner argued, the entrepreneurial behaviour of these Pakistanis was fed by deeply held beliefs about work as a source of self-respect and commitment to the value of economic independence compared to working as an employee. Credit granting was normal among minority members, helping stretch the often meagre capital they were able to accumulate. The existence of ready made economic forms – garment manufacture and retailing – in the locality offered suitable outlets for these aspirations, though not all members of the community were able to express themselves entrepreneurially or were successful when they did.

Pakistani culture and behaviour offered a base from which links were forged with the host society and economy. Bonds of kinship, ritual and community were accommodated to the potentially contradictory capitalist, competitive market ethos. Werbner is careful not to romanticize the cultural patterns and behaviour of these immigrants. Trust was not automatically given to another member of the community simply because they were a member. Children were placed under a heavy obligation to their parents for the sacrifices the latter felt were being made for the children's futures. New entrepreneurs from the community were often resented for undercutting established entrepreneurs and competition between established business owners could be fierce. Employers from the community frequently paid lower wages than equivalent non-community employers. Relations between those of unequal economic success were viewed in the community as problematic.

In other words, while the cultural and community resources of these Pakistani entrepreneurs were very positive advantages in their economic activities, tensions and contradictions remained and surfaced frequently in day-to-day relations. Links with the host society and economy were also often difficult. Nor, it might be added, could the patterns reported be assumed to be permanent. As the histories of other immigrant groups have shown, as one generation succeeds another and young people become exposed to the host culture, new tensions and contradictions are likely to arise to change economic relations and small business ownership patterns.

The above account does not do full justice to Werbner's analysis but the study illustrates very well what can be achieved by a well-conducted qualitative study in terms of the richness of the results. While it is essentially descriptive rather than theory-generating, it is valuable in adding to the understanding of a particular variety of small enterprise and offers a strong basis for comparisons with other research on other small businesses, including indigenous kinds. Moreover, other researchers can draw on the analysis as a source of ideas and as a starting point for their projects, particularly on other groups of immigrant entre-preneurs. What is also worth highlighting is that it is very unlikely that any quantitatively based research could have achieved the same fruitful results or achieved them so parsimoniously.

Analytic Induction and Grounded Theory Approaches

Like quantitative research, most qualitative research seeks to go beyond the descriptive to generate a new theorized understanding of the phe-nomena under study. In qualitative research the most frequently chosen strategy for this purpose is some variety of analytic induction, par-ticularly the kind discussed briefly in Chapter 2, called grounded theory. This popularity is reflected in the large literature devoted to discussing the pros and cons of analytic induction both at the epistemological level and as a practical approach to research, analysing the results and gener-ating interpretations.[15] Here, as elsewhere in this book, the emphasis is on the role of analytic induction as an aid in small business research.

Following the frequently cited schema originally offered by Denzin (1970: 195) the bones of analytic induction can be seen as embodied in the following six steps:

1   A rough definition of the phenomenon to be explained is formulated.
2   A theory/interpretation of the phenomenon is formed as a tenta-tive, first approximation to be revised as observation and analysis proceeds.
3   One case is investigated or set of observations made with the aim of determining how well (or poorly) the initial theory/interpretation is supported.
4   If the theory/interpretation is not supported either it is reformulated to produce a better fit or the definition of the phenomenon being studied is adjusted to make observations and phenomena as con-sistent with each other as possible.
5   Confidence in the analysis and interpretation increases as the number of cases or observations which support it increases. However, the discovery of negative cases or inconsistent observations necessitates further reformulation. This process may continue through several iterations.
6   The above continue until an acceptable level of fit between a detailed theory/interpretation and sufficient number of cases or observations has been completed. What is 'acceptable' is a matter for the judge-ment of the researcher and the audiences to which the results are presented.

As will be quickly recognized, this format has been mentioned earlier (see Chapter 2). Here it is reintroduced to emphasize the analytical aspect of the procedures but this reintroduction underlines the point made by qualitative researchers that concept formation, propositions, analysis and interpretation (what they commonly term 'the data-theory interaction process') are closely integrated with each other in their approach.

The proponents of analytic induction in qualitative analysis argue that the results, in the form of a theory or interpretation, isolate causal connections much in the same way as positivist approaches attempt to do since both are based on careful observation and testing to produce an end result where all observations are accounted for causally.[16] For qualitative accounts, no statistical support is required though quantitative support may be helpful at the descriptive level to add to the interpretation or theory. But the focus of analytic induction in qualitative analysis is very different to that in quantitative approaches. Whereas the latter often concentrates, sometimes exclusively, on behaviour and directly observable aspects of the phenomena, qualitative research aims to reveal the subjective influences and respondent motivations and rationales underpinning and shaping their actions in the small enterprise and its relations with the wider economic and social environments.

Grounded theory, the best known version of analytic induction, was made famous by Glaser and Strauss (1967) in several empirical studies[17] and refinements to the methodological and analytical approach it embodies. However, despite the frequent claims by later researchers (and even more commonly, by research students) that their work was inspired by grounded theory, there are few examples in small business research which clearly show, stage by stage, the approach at work and how the final theoretical result emerged from the analytical strategy. This is probably due to grounded theory as propounded in Glaser and Strauss (1967) and later methodological texts, clashing with the untidy realities of the research process. Analysis often tends to be a much more haphazard process than is admitted by either researchers or in books on research methods.

On the other hand, it is possible to illustrate how grounded theory analysis works by reinterpreting research which has been reported in a form which suggests an approximation of the approach could be used to produce the interpretations offered. A good example is the study by Holliday (1995) mentioned earlier.[18] This, it will be remembered, was based on case studies of three small firms. Participant observation in the form of part-time working in the firms over a substantial period was used to collect the data and develop the wide range of interpretations offered. These covered managerial strategies, organizational structures, recruiting and training, and social relations within the firms.

Of particular interest in discussing the analytical strategies adopted by Holliday, was her previous academic background before embarking on the research reported in *Investigating Small Firms, Nice Work?* Her first degree was in production management, a quantitatively based approach to developing efficient production strategies, particularly in

large firms. She therefore did not begin with the kinds of presupposi-
tions which someone from, say, a sociological background might have
brought to the project. The interpretations she developed required a
good deal of rethinking of her previous understanding of how economic
activities were managed in the typical enterprise. Rather than the
rational, well-ordered procedures offered in production management
texts, she found complex, firm-specific cultures, elaborate patterns of
social relations and the outcomes of owner–managers' often idiosyn-
cratic personal strategies. Her interpretations suggested that the production patterns, organizational structures and managerial outcomes
observed, as well as the firm's relations with the wider environment,
were largely contingent on these cultural, social and management
strategy influences.

Holliday's account of the production process at 'Wellmaid Clothing',[19]
a small manufacturer (seven employees) of wax jackets of the kind used
in country leisure activities, offers an example of how a grounded theory
analysis can be made. She begins with a descriptive account of the firm,
its products, employees and markets. The examination of the scheduling
of orders is described and the analysis begins to uncover some of the
constraints and firm-specific 'logics' governing production. For instance,
ideally garments would be made for stock in quiet periods to meet
future demand but the firm had too little working capital to allow this.
Instead, overtime working was used even though this cost more than
stock piling, that is the constraints under which the firm operated meant
that to an outsider it might seem to have less than optimal production
methods.

Taking account of additional data offered, an alternative analysis can
be offered of the production process in 'Wellmaid' which could show it
was more 'rational' than it appeared. After the garments were cut out
they were distributed to the machinists. One initially puzzling finding
was the seemingly almost random path of the work around the
production room. In part, this could be explained by limitations of space
but much more important was the recruiting and retention of staff:

> . . . a new machinist must find a sewing machine somewhere amongst the
> existing vacant machines. As these machinists are likely to be recruited by
> friends or family members then the most obvious place for them to sit was next
> to their recruiter. Thus, instead of workstations being laid out in terms of their
> sequence in the production system, they are *ad hoc* and placed in terms of their
> social preference. (Holliday, 1995: 117)

While the above layout was clearly 'irrational' in terms of a textbook
production layout, it did reflect the constraints which arose from the
labour market situation of the firm. Holliday reports (1995: 42–3) that the
firm had huge problems in recruiting suitable staff due to local shortages
of skilled machinists and the availability of alternative jobs locally.

Moreover, making wax coats required special skills not used in making other kinds of clothing and many newcomers had to acquire these and get their work up to speed to optimize their earnings. Training was provided mainly by the other machinists, particularly the machinist who had helped recruit the newcomer. Although there was a core of employees who had been with the firm a long time, among the rest turnover was high and absenteeism was high among all, even long-term, workers. Recruiting and retaining employees, therefore, might well have been supported by the bonds arising out of the socially determined production layout while a more textbook production layout could have made this more difficult, thus actually reducing efficiency.

Again, qualitative analysis of the above kind offers results which would be difficult or impossible to arrive at using positivist, quantitative approaches. It is also possible to see the thinking behind the analysis as a grounded theory strategy. The initial hypothesis or proposition might have been that the production layout would conform to the rational criteria advocated in production management texts. The data clearly did not support this. A number of alternative hypotheses or propositions might have been examined to attempt a better fit with the data. For instance, it might have been suggested that the 'irrational' production layout was the result of management incompetence. Some data would fit this proposition but an even better fit would be obtained with an analysis along the above lines, which brings more influences into the account and also shows the constraints on management's ability to rationalize the production layout.

Variations on Analytical Strategies in Qualitative Research

Grounded theory approaches are not, of course, the only analytical strategies employed in small business research. In practice, researchers use a variety of approaches to arrive at theorized qualitative interpretations. One common strategy is well-illustrated by the classic, much cited study of small business owners by Scase and Goffee (1982).[20] Here the starting point was the sociological analysis of class in industrial society in the late 1970s. A range of initial propositions were derived from sociological theory and research on small business owners, the *petit bourgeoisie* class, as they are known in sociology. Most of this previous thinking was, in fact, based on little or no detailed empirical observation of either small business owners or their enterprises.[21]

Scase and Goffee undertook an intensive study of 100 owner–managers in the building industry, selected to cover four types classified in relation to the kind of business they ran. These were the:

1 *self-employed* without any employees;
2 *small employers* who worked alongside their employees;

3   *owner–controllers* – those whose enterprise was large enough for the
    owner to be solely concerned with managing the business;
4   *owner–directors* who controlled their businesses through developed
    structures based on some delegation of managerial functions.

Respondents were interviewed using a semi-structured questionnaire
with each interview lasting typically between one and three hours.
In addition wives of a number of the owner–managers were also
interviewed.

By modern standards, the sample size would be considered large for
intensive qualitative research. Some contemporary qualitative researchers would argue that 100-plus respondents is much too many to gain an
in-depth understanding of their motivations, world views and social
relations with others. Moreover, a fuller understanding of the social and
organizational workings of the enterprise would require contact with
other actors in the enterprise. However, at the time the study was conducted, qualitative research was much less well-understood, or accepted,
than it is now in small business studies.[22]

The analysis of the transcripts of the interviews was carried out by both
researchers. They were mined for respondents' observations on the
central themes of the research derived from sociological thinking on the
petit bourgeoisie. A good deal of the analysis concentrated on internal social
relations in the firms and how owner–managers maintained control, as
well as the wider issues of the social processes underlying the formation
and growth of the small business. The analysis is illustrated by quotes
from the interviews and the researchers anticipated the frequent objection
(discussed further below) that qualitative researchers may be tempted to
select only those quotations which support their interpretation. The
methodological appendix (Scase and Goffee, 1982: 200–1) reports that
every respondent is represented in the quotations, only three respondents
were quoted more than five times and the broadly equal distribution
between the four types listed above is shown in tabular form.

Here the analysis is, in effect, a mix of deductive and inductive
approaches. It is deductive in as far as the data collected is used to test
previous sociological thinking on small business owners, particularly
their role in the class system. It is inductive both in generating an
alternative theorization of the latter role to fit the data collected and
in suggesting some of the processes which might help generate a more
detailed, qualitative understanding of the way the small business functions internally. It shows that a revealing, innovative qualitative analysis
need not be hampered by taking previous, relatively well-developed
theory and propositions as a starting point. In this, it counters those
advocates of grounded theory who argue that each new project should
begin with as few prior suppositions as possible or run the risk of being
unable to break away from previous thinking to generate new understanding.

In Chapter 2 one source of ideas for projects was drawing on analogies with thinking in other areas of social or even non-social phenomena. A good example of the use of analogy in this way is provided by Holliday and Letherby (1993).[23] One of the most common analogies in discussing social relations in small firms is the family. In one sense of the label, 'the family business', the meaning is literal in that it refers to the fact that the firm is run by or (more rarely) made up wholly or mainly of people related by blood or marriage. Alternatively, the phrase is used more loosely as an analogy, that is, employee–employer and intra-employee relations are likened to those in a family. Unlike large firms where relations are characterized as impersonal and bureaucratic often with high levels of conflict, relations in the small firm, it is alleged, are friendly, co-operative and free of serious conflict. Employees in small firms, for example, are often reported as being recruited by word of mouth through family or friend-ship linkages so that relations in the firm become an extension of relations outside the firm. Asked about relations in the firm, owner–managers are often quoted as saying, 'it's just like a family' to convey their quality. One frequent way of describing management style of small business owners is to label it 'paternalistic' – echoing again a family analogy.

Of course, there has been plenty of research on small firms that has questioned the family analogy in describing employment relations (see, for example, Curran and Stanworth, 1981a; Rainnie, 1989; Scott et al., 1989) but it has been highly popular among all kinds of commentators particularly in emphasizing how small firms differ from larger enter-prises. Holliday and Letherby used qualitative data to test how good a fit the analogy is with observed employment relations in small firms. They record that much early thinking on the family in sociology saw it in idealized, highly positive terms as the secure foundation of all social life. Contemporary popular and political views often offer similar ideal-izations. Media commentators, for example, often lament the 'loss' or 'collapse' of the family, seen in highly idealized terms, while the Con-servative Party of the 1980s and 1990s portrayed itself frequently as 'the party of the family'.

Later sociological thinking, argued Holliday and Letherby (1993: 57–8), offered a much less idealized characterization of the family, highlighting the tensions and instabilities of family life as well as the more positive aspects. Making a link between this more modern view and what goes on in small firms, the authors argued that the family analogy could still be employed and that, indeed, it might well offer a sound model of employ-ment relations. People do often get on very well in small firms with close, emotionally rewarding and supportive relations but there are also squabbles, favouritism, tensions, parting of the ways, exploitation, gender inequalities and painful emotional pressures that are often found in families. The result, they argue, is a superior account of small firm employment relations which distinguishes them from relations in the large enterprise but also escapes the weaknesses of previous rosy idealizations.

Some Analytical Techniques and Strategies

Imposing order on the data and constructing interpretations in qualitative research is, as noted earlier, more difficult in many ways than in positivist, quantitatively based research. One chronic risk in qualitative research is being swamped by the data. As remarked previously, even quite modest projects can produce huge amounts of data which rapidly become unwieldy or difficult to fully exploit. Contradictions in the data are also common – particularly where different actors offer contradictory accounts of how they relate to each other – yet these have to be resolved in some way if anything like a coherent account is to be developed. There are, however, some techniques which can be employed to help counter these problems.

Grounded theory proponents argue that their strategy of continuously developing and refining interpretations and testing them in an ongoing process of observation and data collection, avoids the qualitative researcher being swamped by the data. In practice, life is often not that simple. For instance, in small business research data collection cannot always be an ongoing process, with frequent entry and re-entry into the field, simply because small business owners do not have the time or are unwilling to permit constant incursions by the researcher because they feel it will disrupt the operation of the business. Data collection may well run ahead of theory building because the sheer rate of accumulation offers too many possible alternative interpretations which need to be explored before researchers can produce an interpretation with which they are satisfied.

Computer packages such as NUDIST or Ethnograph (Glesne and Pershkin, 1992: 141–5; Dey, 1993: Chapter 4 *passim*; Miles and Huberman, 1994; QSR NUDIST, 2000) mentioned briefly in Chapter 3, are extremely useful for storing qualitative data. They can even go further and help researchers to make links between elements in the data. However, their usefulness in theory building is limited. They are also very time-consuming to use where the main form of data is interviews with small business owners, employees or others connected with the firm. Transcribing interviews, especially long interviews, fully onto the selected computer package can take a lot of time. Usually also, some kind of tagging or index marking of the transcription will be needed so that the package can be used in its most common form, that is, as a 'code and retrieve' system.

The advantages of computer packages of the above kind are that all data, no matter how large the volume, can be recorded so that, given appropriate retrieval strategies, no data is ever forgotten or mislaid as it otherwise might be. Code and retrieve procedures are undoubtedly the most popular way of using computer packages in qualitative research but advocates such as Richards and Richards point out, they also always involve an element of theorization (1994: 47). The reason for this is that the tagging or coding categories selected are, in effect, implicit in theory building. The categories are not chosen randomly but are either based on existing categorizations or theory or, at the very least, researcher intuitions on what is likely to be theoretically significant when developing a full interpretation.

It is even possible to go beyond 'code and retrieval' in using computer packages to analyse qualitative data with computer-based formal logic systems or graphical representations of conceptual data and linkages (Richards and Richards, 1994). But these appear to have been rarely, if ever, used in small business research. If they were to become more popular they might add to the usefulness of computers in qualitative research. But they would also pose some obvious risks. Formal logic-based analyses of qualitative data, for example, would run counter to the argument made by many qualitative researchers that the 'logics' which human agents generate to underpin their thinking and actions do not resemble formal logic and cannot be reduced to the latter. There might also be a tendency to use such approaches mechanically – much in the same way that some uses of statistical techniques in positivist, quantitatively based approaches have been criticized. This, it could be argued, would undermine the essentially imaginative and creative processes required to produce novel breakthroughs in understanding the small business and its functioning.

One issue that often baffles those new to qualitative research, and which has a direct relevance to analysis in this kind of research, is posed by the question: whose account counts – that of the subject or that of the researcher? Qualitative researchers aim to enter 'inside the minds' of those they study to understand the values, meanings, motivational repertoires and logics which govern the actions of the small business owners and others who create, sustain and interact in some way with the small enterprise. This is the essence of ethnographic research. But should the resulting interpretations simply mirror the subjects' world views, reproducing them as accurately as possible or should they be the researchers' interpretations of the actors and their situations? If the researcher offers their own interpretation does this not deny the validity of the subject's reality and simply substitute that of the researcher?

As remarked earlier in discussing Scase and Goffee's (1982) research on small business owners, some critics of qualitative research are unhappy about the use of direct quotations from transcripts to support the analysis. They suspect that the quotations may be selected to fit the interpretation rather than the reverse, that is, the interpretation emerging from the accounts offered by respondents. Scase and Goffee, it will be remembered, sought to anticipate this criticism by showing quantitatively that the quotations they included were representative of the views of all respondents interviewed. Yet, equally clearly, the interpretation offered by Scase and Goffee also came from their own theoretical position which, in turn, derived from sociological thinking on class relations in market-based societies. So the question might be put: what was the status of the respondents' accounts in relation to the overall interpretation offered? In other words, Scase and Goffee's work offers a concrete example of the epistemological dilemmas in the previous paragraph.

The answers to the above questions are difficult at the philosophical level but for the practical accomplishment of small business research these issues can be dealt with reasonably succinctly.[24] Basically, the key answer is (as might be expected for any questions touching closely on the philosophical) that all accounts matter but not in the same ways. Actors' accounts are crucial in that they represent the basic data of qualitative investigation. They deserve the greatest respect and closest of attention in their own terms. But the researchers' account is also significant as well as totally unavoidable. Any report on human actors and their situations is inevitably selective. Further, from all the data collected (which is likely to include not only actors' accounts but other contextual data such as documentary and other data not from, or perhaps even known to, the actors) the researcher attempts to produce a coherent interpretation. In short, the process of analysis generation inevitably involves the imposition of an external framework on the data so that respondents' contributions can only be a part, albeit a key part, of the final interpretation. But whatever the final theorization, it always follows the uncovering of the meanings, values and logics of the respondents.

Typologies as Popular Examples of Analytical Tools

In making sense of the data, researchers need constructs to help organize the data into forms which highlight what, in the researcher's account, are key points and findings. One very common organizing strategy is the typology. This consists of grouping categories and data into cases or 'boxes' according to some common criterion or criteria. One has already been presented in this chapter, that is, the small business owner typology generated by Scase and Goffee to categorize relationships between owner–managers and others in the enterprise. Here the criterion used was the relationship between owner–manager and lowest level employee ranging from no relationship (the self-employed without employees) to the most organizationally complex (owner–directors whose relations with employees are mediated entirely though a bureaucratic structure of delegated managerial functions).

Another example of the use of typologies is that of Goss (1991) who generated four types of small business owner labour control strategies based on two criteria: the dependence of the employer on employees and the capacity of employees to individually or collectively resist the exercise of owner–manager power. The four types were:

1   *Fraternalism*, which occurs where there is a high-level of employer dependence on employees who provide skills and experience crucial

to the survival and success of the business. Goss offered the example of the small building firm where the owner–manager was often *primus inter pares* working alongside employees whose skills differ from those of the owner–manager but are just as essential to the successful completion of the work taken on by the firm.

2 *Paternalism* occurs where the employers' dependence on employees is less than under fraternalism but where employee power is also low. Differentiation between employer and employee is marked but there is often an overt employee identification with the employers' values and goals. Here an example might be agricultural employment relations, particularly in isolated rural areas.

3 *Benevolent autocracy* is where the employers' power is based on simple positional power, that is, their role as employer as defined by law and custom in a market economy. Employers are not powerful enough to practise paternalism but neither are employees so dependent that they cannot effectively assert their interests to some extent. Goss sees this as probably the most common employer–employee relationship in a modern advanced economy.

4 *Sweating* occurs where the employer has dominant power and employee power is weak so that employers can easily replace employees and employees have little access to more attractive employment alternatives. The classic sweatshop industry in the UK has been seen as clothing manufacture.

Goss's typology has spawned critical discussion (see, for example, Curran, 1991: 204–6) but has undoubtedly been useful as a construct to analyse employer–employee relations in small firms. Many other examples of the use of typologies in the analysis of qualitative data could be cited[25] but the above shows how the strategy can be used in analyses in qualitative research. (It is also used just as commonly in positivist, quantitatively based research.) It is important, however, to be clear on the explanatory status of typologies. They are no magic key to an accurate representation of data. Typologies are neither true nor false but merely useful or useless in generating meaningful interpretations. In other words, at best, they help researchers organize data in order to generate plausible accounts but have no special claims otherwise. For these reasons, despite all their usefulness, they are just as likely as any other construct to be criticized by later researchers for their inadequacies in helping produce acceptable interpretations.

Researchers' Interpretations vs Actors' Interpretations

Sometimes, the interpretations offered by researchers may even appear to contradict the accounts offered by the actors whose situations are being investigated. As emphasized above, qualitative researchers have an epistemological and ethical duty to small business owners, small business employees and others from whom they collect data, to listen carefully to, and respect, the views offered. They have no special prerogative as researchers which allows them to impose their own values or political views, take sides with one kind of respondent against another or misrepresent the accounts offered by respondents. On the other hand, there is no duty to accept uncritically the accounts offered by respondents as truth beyond question. A principle that underlies qualitative research is that no account – whether that of the actor or the researcher – is privileged in any absolute sense.

The generation of interpretations by qualitative researchers may therefore meet all the epistemological and ethical criteria listed above but still depart substantially from, or even contradict, the accounts offered by the actors under investigation. An example of how this might occur is offered by the findings on small business owner–manager views on employment legislation and its impact on their freedom to manage their employees and create jobs. There is a large literature from the late 1970s onwards which reported consistently that small employers found employment legislation a major burden (see discussions in Curran, 1991; Kitching, 1997; for a direct example of small employers' complaints, Institute of Directors, 1996).

What is interesting about this very consistent repetition of owner–manager views is that it appears not to tally very closely with their actual experiences in running their businesses. In report after report the proportions of small employers stating that they personally have found employment legislation a serious burden in recruiting and managing their employees is low, particularly in firms with under 10 employees, that is, the great majority of small firms (Kitching, 1997). Similarly, the proportion who have had direct experience of an employee complaining, or threatening to complain, to an industrial tribunal is also typically low (Curran et al., 1993b). Even more significantly, their knowledge of employment law and how it could impact on their firm is often very poor (Ford et al., 1984; McLennan, 1986; Kitching, 1997).[26] This is supported by the lack of formal employment procedures which might be expected to be used by employers to minimize the impact of employment laws. Moreover, the employment rights of employees, particularly in small firms, were significantly reduced after 1980 (Goss, 1994), which might have been expected to go with a reduction in employers' perceptions of the problems the law makes for their businesses.

What the reports cited above do show, on the other hand, is a continuing, widespread, generalized worry about the *possible* adverse impact of employment law among small firm employers. Up to half of small employers are frequently shown to feel that the legislation might affect the firm or claim that it caused them to be more cautious in employment decisions. But a generalized worry which rarely manifests itself in direct negative experiences is not really consistent with the notion that employment law is a *major* constraint on employer–employee relations or job creation in small enterprises.

A qualitative interpretation of the above findings and seeming inconsistency between employers' worries about employment legislation and their actual experiences, might see these generalized worries as symbolic rather than real. Employing people in any business (small or large) is a major headache, as employers' accounts constantly reiterate. For a wide variety of reasons, human beings are always difficult to manage (Kitching, 1997: 62–78). The problem is also a permanent one: everyday employees have to be persuaded, encouraged, supervised and sometimes sanctioned, to ensure they achieve what employers see as an adequate performance.[27] It might be, therefore, that the consistently negative views of owner–managers on employment legislation are symbolic of the problematics of the employment relationship rather than a reflection of their everyday experiences.[28] In other words, they signify the very real difficulties inherent in employing people in any business which would not be eliminated even if all such legislation was abolished. As it is, the employment laws are a convenient lightening conductor for owner–manager frustrations with managing employees.

An interpretation of the above kind illustrates how researchers' interpretations can be detached from, and even contradict, those of actors. As long as the distinction between the respondents' account and that of the researcher is made clear, either or some mix of the two can be offered as an interpretation but with no automatic privileging of one over the other. In practice, researchers' interpretations are usually a mix drawing on respondents' accounts, the additional data collected by the researcher (some of which may not be known to the respondents) and the categories and analytic structures generated by the researchers. The latter will often include terms, constructs and theorizations which the respondents might find difficult to agree with or perhaps even fully understand. In principle like any other theorization, qualitative interpretations are always provisional, always open to challenge and always likely to be refuted or refined by later researchers.

Validity in Qualitative Interpretations

One worry which many new to qualitative research have is whether those reading their interpretations will question the validity of what they have produced. This is a problem that quantitative researchers are far less likely to face because of the strong, 'faith in numbers' characteristic of Anglo-Saxon cultures. Thick descriptions, for example, are often regarded as little more than superficial, literary accounts rather than 'proper' research. More theorized interpretations may fare better but the suspicion that they are in some sense or another 'soft', is widespread.[29] Qualitative researchers therefore have to anticipate these doubts when presenting their work to various audiences. They should have no illusions that all potential audiences can be satisfied.

Small business research has a wide range of potential audiences and here, retaining the emphasis on *doing* research rather than philosophizing about it, it is possible to discuss validity in relation only to some of these. A main audience are fellow researchers but others include policy-makers and research users, such as the staff of support agencies. One point to be kept in mind is that the researcher cannot force any audience to accept an interpretation. All the researcher can do is influence how an audience is likely to receive any interpretation by how it is presented. It should be stressed that this applies equally to quantitative and qualitative and positivist and non-positivist research.

An initial key first point is that all 'explanations', whether quantitative or qualitative, positivist or non-positivist, should be regarded as *interpretations* in a strict sense. As argued in Chapter 2, there is no way of achieving direct access to whatever we define as 'out there': all theorizations are just that, that is, they are constructed using definitions, categories and the assumptions of the producer in their generation. The researcher supports them by whatever measures, indicators, data and forms of presentation are deemed to strengthen the persuasiveness of the interpretation.

Naive positivists, of course, object to the above by arguing that it is possible to have direct knowledge of the world 'out there' through positivist procedures of one kind or another.[30] The position adopted here is that for social and business phenomena this is not possible. It is only possible to view phenomena through the mediating prism of the ways of thinking we employ to make sense of 'out there' for that is also how 'out there' is constructed, that is, it is originated out of the meanings and actions shared with other human beings which create structures such as 'the market', 'the small enterprise', etc.

Having stated the above, the maxims for establishing the validity of qualitative interpretations do not differ greatly from those which may be applied to any kind of research on social and business topics.

First, the *statement of the problem* the research aims to address needs to be expressed clearly and precisely. Failure to achieve this is damning since all that follows will be undermined by this initial failure.

Secondly, all *key concepts and assumptions* need to be stated clearly and precisely. As noted in Chapter 2, this may not be easy. If, for example, a small business research project seeks to study 'the normative values central to ethnic entrepreneurial cultures', the problems of adequately conceptualizing 'normative values' and 'ethnic entrepreneurial cultures' may be severe and success in overcoming these will be one of the critical validity tests for a project of this kind.

Thirdly, validity also rests on *methodological adequacy*, that is, the ways in which data have been collected. While size of sample is not crucial as it would be in quantitative research, the theoretical justification for the kinds of respondents or case study situations selected, needs to show evidence of careful thought and to be persuasive. Similarly, the theoretical representativeness of respondents and case studies are important: do they provide indicative data for the whole range of instances the interpretation claims to cover? Are they an eccentric selection from which generalization will be questionable? How the data were collected is also important. The strategies used, for example, in interviewing respondents or in participant observation, need to be described clearly. A key test of methodological adequacy is the extent of any data triangulation, that is, is the interpretation supported by a range of data collected using different kinds of data collection strategies? To the extent such triangulation occurs, this normally leads to greater confidence.

Fourthly, validity is also dependent on *analytical adequacy*, that is, are the elements in the interpretation clearly stated and is the logic linking them equally clearly presented? Are the stages in the generation of the interpretation shown clearly? For example, one of the attractions of grounded theory is that its analytical procedures, based on the notion of successive refinements of an interpretation employing a continuing data theory interaction process, offer a convincing basis for establishing (though not, of course, guaranteeing) analytical validity. Finally, is the 'internal logic of the situation', the interplay between the definitions and actions of the actors in the research situation, disclosed clearly? This is the heart of any qualitative interpretation. To be analytically adequate it should also be convincing in the sense that alternative interpretations are shown to be less plausible in the light of the data.

Fifthly, is the *interpretation* situated clearly in the context of previous research and does it anticipate (and counter convincingly) the objections an informed reader might make? Here this will depend to some extent on the audience for whom the interpretation has been generated. Superior interpretations are indicated by being able to convince a wide range of audiences but the most important are the researcher's peers where the interpretation seeks to be assessed *qua* research.

Sixthly, what form do the *claims made* by the interpretation take? Are they qualified to refer to a specific range of situations or are they universal claims? All research makes claims but qualitative research tends, rightly, to be reluctant to make universal claims. Modesty is usually an indicator of strength though wider claims offered clearly on a speculative basis are acceptable and even helpful pointers to future researchers. What suggestions are made for further research? While replication in the form advocated in the positivist paradigm is not a requirement (or even thought possible in any strict sense) in qualitative research, the development of an interpretation through further case studies etc., is desirable. Qualitative research is a social process involving a shared striving to construct interpretations of social and business activities: qualitative researchers are always involved in a dialogue (even if only implicitly) with other researchers and other audiences.

Seventh, where the research has *implications for policy and practice* do these receive sufficient attention? Meeting the needs of policy-makers and practitioners is often not the prime aim of small business research. It is entirely legitimate for researchers to define their main aim as advancing understanding of the phenomena studied and the validity of any research does not depend on meeting the needs of all potential audiences. Many research students, for example, will concentrate on satisfying the requirements for the award of a research degree. But virtually all projects have some implications for policy-maker and prac-titioner audiences and bridging the gulf that so often exists between researchers and non-researchers is eminently desirable.

One particular kind of validation often seen as specific to qualitative research is respondent validation (Hammersley and Atkinson, 1983: 195–8).[31] Given that the respondent actors are so central to qualitative research, it is sometimes argued that they should also play a central role in validation. Who better to assess whether the researcher has captured the definitions, world views and their logics of action than those studied? In small business research, reporting back to those studied can even be a means of ensuring continuing co-operation by showing respondents that the time they have given to the research has an end product which they might find interesting and relevant to their needs.

Presenting interpretations to respondents is certainly a check on their validity and one relatively easy to use in small business research. Owner–managers, for example, can be sent draft reports (perhaps edited to take into account that they are busy people) or invited to participate in focus groups where interpretations are presented for their comments (see, for example, Curran and Blackburn, 1994: 104). Feedback may not only increase confidence in the interpretation but may produce additional data from respondents to strengthen and develop it further. But respondent assessment is not a guarantee of validity. Researchers may have used data not available to the respondents. Respondents' beliefs about their motives may be self-serving: most people like to see themselves in as favourable light as possible. Small business owners may see an interpretation as critical of their skills or motivations and reject it on these grounds. Finally, making respondents final arbiters of the interpretations of their motivations and actions privileges them over others, which not only restricts the interpretations that researchers might offer but contradicts a key epistemological principle of qualitative research that no account has an automatic claim over all others.

Assessing the Advantages of Qualitative Research Approaches

The principal claims which can be made on behalf of qualitative approaches to small business research are twofold. First, is the epi-stemological claim that it is especially advantaged for investigating human and social phenomena compared with positivist approaches. This claim has now been well-rehearsed in the literature and consists mainly of arguing that because human beings are conscious, purposeful entities, their activities can only be understood by accessing the meanings and logics through which they shape their lived realities. Secondly, and relatedly, social research like all research, attempts to establish why things occur, that is, what causal linkages explain particular kinds of social arrangements and activities. Qualitative research does this in a way denied to positivist approaches because the latter seeks to explain what is observed in terms of quantitative regularities of one kind or another. In this it is typically reductionist often to the point of dismissal, in its treatment of the special internal worlds of human actors. In qualitative research, on the other hand, causality is intrinsic to the internal world of meanings, motives and logics of the human actors and can only be established by research approaches which focus directly on these.

While qualitative research approaches have gained considerable ground in small business research in recent years, particularly among younger researchers, they have their weaknesses. No research paradigm solves all the epistemological questions about how we can acquire a credible and complete understanding of the small business, owner–managers, employees and all those other institutions and actors whose activities sustain and constrain their endeavours. In other words, whatever the undoubted strengths of qualitative approaches to studying the small business, there are also shortcomings which need to be recognized.

The great strength of qualitative approaches is their ability to focus on the micro level, the level of everyday lived activities. The small business owners' decision-making strategies, the way people (employees, customers, suppliers, bank representatives, accountants, etc.) are managed (or not) are highly amenable to qualitative strategies. In contrast, quantitative approaches, particularly employing relatively insensitive strategies such as postal and telephone surveys, can only very imperfectly capture this level of lived reality. Even face-to-face interviews based on open approaches have problems in matching the power of, for instance, participant observation as a means of investigating at this level.

On the other hand, the weakness of qualitative approaches shows up in the inability to focus effectively on the macro level, the wider economic and social structures that are relevant to understanding the small business and social life generally. There is an 'out there' which is made up of relatively fixed structures and institutions. The EU, national government, the legal system, the banking system, market structures, etc., all exist and affect life at the micro level. Actors at the micro level may not even be aware of some parts of these structures or lesser structures such as local power networks or may not understand how they function. Just because actors are unaware or declare a lack of interest in structures such as political parties or Parliament, does not mean they have no impact on their lives or their activities. Research which concentrates on the micro level of the small business is ill-suited to integrating the micro and macro levels of social and business activities.

Small businesses play a role in the economy as a whole, a role that small business research needs to investigate to gain a full understanding of its significance as an economic and social phenomenon. The share of small businesses in output and sales in particular sectors, trends in small firms' share of total employment over time, the inter-relations with trading markets such as the EU, the take-up of new technologies by small firms and the impact of changes in fiscal policies on small firm performance, are all examples of macro level phenomena which qualitative approaches cannot really investigate effectively. Here quantitative approaches employing agreed standardized methods score well and their behaviourally based explanations are invaluable. Qualitative approaches, for example, abhor standardized approaches and quantification: social phenomena for qualitative researchers cannot be split up into convenient, standard 'bits' to be measured and manipulated statistically. Conversely, the weaknesses of positivist approaches in accessing the internal world of the actor are not a decisive barrier to contributions to the understanding of macro level phenomena.[32]

A further weakness of qualitative approaches is their typically limited scale, which weakens their generalizability. Because they are so labour intensive and so dependent on the skills of the individual researcher, they often lack authoritativeness for many audiences, particularly policy-makers who feel much more comfortable with the results – expressed quantitatively – of large-scale studies which can make claims to generalizability simply because they have investigated the issues using large samples. This weakness is, however, tempered in the case of small business research by the characteristics of the phenomena studied. One, in particular, reduces this weakness; that is, of course, the extreme heterogeneity of the small business population and all those linked to small-enterprise activities. The claims to generalizability made by quantitative research, which often professes to be talking about *the* small business, that is, the whole UK small business population, are usually facile because they fail to acknowledge this heterogeneity. Nevertheless, there is a role for large-scale small business research (provided it is sensitive to these problems) and this means it has strengths qualitative research cannot match.

Qualitative research is, as pointed out earlier, much more difficult to conduct than quantitative, positivist research. First, the lack of standardized methodological and analytical techniques means that the craft element is much less well-developed. Secondly, the lack of standardized strategies also means that there is a much greater burden on the researcher to demonstrate creative and innovative approaches to research strategies and especially analyses, if significant and interesting results are to be generated. This is not, of course, an argument against qualitative research but rather a caveat. Qualitative research is difficult and highly challenging, which is the main reason why qualitative research can frequently produce shallow results that hardly go beyond re-stating the obvious.

Overall, therefore, qualitative research has tremendous potential for small business research, as some of the research cited above shows. But it also has limitations which need to be acknowledged. For those who have adopted an extreme epistemological position which asserts that all positivist approaches are irretrievably and fundamentally mistaken as a basis for understanding any kind of social phenomena, the above will be troubling. But for most of those engaged in small business research, the debate on the philosophy of social and business research has shifted to a more pluralist position in recent years. It is increasingly accepted that different research problems are amenable to different approaches and adopting extreme positions is simply unreasonably restricting the tools at the researcher's disposal.

Pluralism as a Solution to the Debate Between the Two Paradigms

In practice, small business researchers are often pluralist in the sense of a 'mix and match' approach to research and analytical strategies which crosses the divide between the quantitative and the qualitative and the positivist and the non-positivist. This is often a rather crude belt-and-braces approach but is popular because of its promise to exploit the strengths of quantitative *and* qualitative research paradigms while, at the same time, countering the weaknesses of each. A large-scale survey, for example, might be conducted to map the quantitative dimensions of the issues being investigated. But a qualitative strategy in the form of case studies will be employed to establish what is 'behind the numbers' and especially to try to isolate causalities. North et al. (1998) used this approach in their study of quality management strategies in small firms, for example, and many other examples could be cited.

Epistemological and methodological pluralism of the above kind does not, however, square the circle, eliminating the split between the two approaches to small business research. At the philosophical level the division remains as fundamental as ever and it is not solved simply by a crude mixing of the two. Even at the practical level of accomplishing research, the problems of each paradigm remain. All the problems of, for example, constructing a representative sample of small firms, achieving an acceptable response rate and devising suitable research instruments remain in quantitative research. Equally, accessing the lived realities of small business owners, their employees and all those whose activities impinge on the small enterprise, is just as difficult. In some ways constructing explanations/interpretations which combine the results of the two paradigms fruitfully is more difficult than where only a single paradigm is employed. What should be given the greatest significance in putting together an overall account, the impact of macro-level structural influences or the meanings and world views of small business owners?

Co-existing with the pluralism of the above kind is the pluralism which takes the form of the proponents of each paradigm happily carrying on conducting research within the approach with which they feel most comfortable. Nor, it might be argued, is there much wrong in each seeking to maximize the knowledge gains from their chosen approach. But this might equally be seen as too complacent. The increase in the importance of qualitative approaches in small business research is a real addition to expanding the understanding of how the small business functions as an economic and social phenomenon. For those steeped in the longer established positivist, quantitative approach, simply accepting co-existence is not a sufficient response. There is a need to engage more positively with the epistemological principles underlying qualitative research and to consider the implications for their own research.

If quantitatively based positivist researchers do not seriously attempt to understand and respond to the carefully developed alternative research approach of qualitative researchers, their work is likely to stagnate. The volume of quantitative, positivist small business research is now large. Many of the key issues, such as small business growth, have been visited and revisited again and again. The limits of what is achievable by a purely quantitative, positivist approach in many of these areas have been reached and further research in the same tradition is at best replication or records some of the changes reflecting economic and political restructuring. As argued earlier in the chapter, a major limit of quantitative-positivist approaches is that while they can establish associations, often measured very subtly, establishing causality is much more difficult. This is especially the case when establishing the role of owner-decisions and actions or the actions of others (employees, customers, suppliers, credit providers, competitors etc.) in explaining the associations discovered.

In other words, the evolving relationships between the different approaches to small business research are not halted because of the emergence of a live-and-let-live ethic among researchers which allows each to practise their approach without fear of being condemned as 'not research'. Each needs to engage with the other much more if the power of their approaches is to be harnessed to expanding understanding of the small enterprise. The discussion in this chapter has attempted to show how each might contribute by showing both the strengths and weaknesses of each as well as stressing the need for them to work together more closely.

Conclusions

This chapter has concentrated on the how and why of analytical strategies in small business research. It has devoted attention to both quantitative and qualitative research, isolating and contrasting the different kinds of analytical strategies each employs. For each, the advantages and the disadvantages have been examined. The position maintained in previous chapters, that both can contribute significantly to our understanding of the small business and its role in the economy, has been upheld.

The longer established quantitative-positive paradigm has dominated small business research until relatively recently. In analytical terms, the chapter demonstrated that while it has its strengths, it also has considerable weaknesses, particularly in establishing causalities and in coping with what was termed the variant qualities and heterogeneity of the phenomena associated with the small business. Nevertheless, in describing aspects of the small enterprise and its operation, quantitative assessments are useful, particularly for initial explorations of topics. Even when more adequate explanations and interpretations have been generated, numerical information on the incidence and extent of key dimensions in these explanations/interpretations is also valuable, particularly for meeting the needs of some audiences such as policy-makers.

Qualitative analyses of small business phenomena have increased greatly in popularity in recent years. Many researchers are convinced they have powerful epistemological advantages in accessing the lived realities of small business ownership, employment and the involvement of others linked to small firms. Further, ethnographic approaches stress that because the small business is a social construction which arises out of the world views, meanings, motivations and actions of human beings, qualitative analyses are superior in uncovering causalities whose basis is the rationales of the actors who make the enterprise. These, it is asserted, are fundamental to any proper understanding of the way the small firm functions. Quantitative, positivist-based analyses, on the other hand, whatever their other merits, find it difficult or even impossible to enter the internal human world of the small business from which so much of the observable data – the essence of quantitative analysis – comes.

However, the chapter argued that qualitative analytical approaches are difficult to employ. They cannot be technique-driven in the way that is possible in quantitative analyses. There is no equivalent to the ready made analytical techniques freely available to quantitative researchers. One result is that qualitative analysis demands a much more imaginative, creative approach than quantitative analysis if it is to go beyond the banal. In quantitative research banality is common but can often be hidden behind flashy techniques which all too easily mislead less statistically sophisticated audiences.

The chapter showed that there are different levels of analysis in both quantitative and qualitative research. In both the easiest is the descriptive. Exploratory research, in either positivist or non-positivist paradigms, often exploits descriptive analytical strategies. In quantitative research, numerically based descriptions are helpful for establishing the significance and incidence of phenomena. In qualitative research, description, particularly in the form of 'thick description', is an equally useful first stage in charting an area of enquiry. Both are more than description in any simple sense, however, since both inevitably contain implicit categorizations, and even initial theoretical propositions simply by how they are fashioned.

More complex forms of analysis in both quantitative, positivist-based research and qualitative, non-positivist research obviously seek to achieve much more than description in the above sense. They aim to offer answers to 'why' questions. In quantitative research, however, too often statistical association is easily mistaken for causal explanation. Establishing causality, however, goes beyond statistical association and requires reasoning which is epistemologically quite separate from the analytical techniques of positivist research. The result of this separation is that, logically, any positivist explanations can only ever be a provisional interpretation, to be treated as such.

What the above also suggests is that positivist analyses produce results which, at their most developed, are the equivalent of the qualitative interpretation, that is, a provisional account which seeks to offer an answer to a 'why' question. The most common approach to producing such answers in qualitative research is some variety of analytic induction with grounded theory being the most popular. Grounded theory differs from the kinds of analytical techniques employed in quantitative–positivist research because analysis and theory generation are said to run together with proposition formation, testing, analysing and generating interpretations completely integrated throughout the research process. In this way the 'why' question is constantly being addressed.

On the other hand, while analytic induction and especially grounded theory versions are constantly proclaimed as the foundation of much of the qualitative research published on the small business, explicit examples of the method at work are not all that common. It is actually difficult to practise the textbook form when confronted with the messy realities of everyday research. Even with the help of computers in storing data in a readily accessible form, the sheer volume and complexity of the data can make analysis difficult and the opportunities to test and retest interpretations may not always be easily come by. Moreover, the requirement to generate ever more encompassing interpretations as the data-theory process continues puts considerable demands on the intellectual and creative abilities of the researcher.

Grounded theory, despite the considerable literature devoted to it, is only one approach to analysis in qualitative research. There are a very large number of alternatives, most of which have not been discussed in this chapter because they are not much used in small business research. But the chapter did discuss the use of typologies which are common in all kinds of research, non-positivist and positivist, and the use of analogies as analytical templates for generating interpretations. It is very likely that other approaches in qualitative research – such as discourse analysis[33] – will become very much more popular in small business research than they have been up to the present.

The relationship between respondents' accounts and researchers' interpretations raises problems for qualitative research. Respondents' accounts are the key resource of the qualitative researcher and need to be treated as central to any interpretation. On the other hand, all interpretations are necessarily the researcher's. First, it is the researchers who construct the interpretations which offer answers to 'why' questions – questions which they posed in setting up the research project initially. Secondly, researchers often access data not available to the respondent which also contribute to the interpretation. Thirdly, the researchers' account may use categories or combine data in ways which respondents would not recognize or possibly agree with. No account, whether that of the respondent or the researcher, is privileged in any absolute sense. But this poses a dilemma for qualitative research which is not easy to solve. At the end of the day, what needs to be emphasized is that all interpretations are provisional.

The issue of validity, particularly in relation to quantitative research, was examined more closely later in the chapter. Validity is, of course, a problem for all kinds of small business research but quantitative–positivist approaches receive an easier ride. A seven-criteria model for assessing the validity of qualitative interpretations was offered but, further, it was argued that, in principle, these were the same criteria which should be applied to *any* kind of small business research, regardless of the research paradigm adopted.

One reason why all interpretations are provisional and open to challenge is that, in one way or another, they all also reveal the weaknesses of their paradigm as a means of gaining access to the world 'out there'. The weaknesses of the quantitative–positivist paradigm have received an enormous amount of attention. But qualitative research, despite its popularity, is not a complete answer to generating interpretations of the small business, its social relations or its relations with the wider environment. For instance, it is weak as a way of exploring the links between the small firm and the macro level, the social, political and economic structures which impinge on the firm, its owners, employees and others whose activities directly influence its functioning.

In practice, much small business research employs a 'mix-and-match' approach, that is, it combines quantitative–positivist elements with qualitative-non-positivist elements. For many researchers, this helps ensure that their approach will have the principal benefits of each while, at the same time, avoiding their main weaknesses. It was pointed out that simply combining the two approaches in this way does not really achieve these aims in any strong epistemological sense. On the other hand, in terms of the practical accomplishment of small business research, combined approaches are useful and produce worthwhile results.

Other researchers continue to plough a path firmly in one or other paradigm on a live-and-let-live basis. This is perfectly viable and suits their preferences. But given the relatively recent rise of qualitative research strategies in small business research, there remain enormous opportunities for expanding our understanding of the small enterprise employing this paradigm. There are also weaknesses in adopting the epistemological pluralism position. The potential for quantitative–positivist explanations to reveal more about the small firm in any radical, far-reaching sense, appears limited. At the moment, it is the qualitative paradigm, perhaps with some quantitative support, which has the greatest potential and the most work to do.

Analysis is, in a sense, 'the middle game' of the research process. What follows is just as crucially important; that is, the presentation of the results and interpretations to fellow researchers, policy-makers, those providing services and support to the small firm, customers and suppliers and small business owners themselves. Doing good research is not enough if the results never reach, or fail to persuade, fellow researchers or any of these other potential audiences. The next chapter addresses the issues of presentation and creating a dialogue with these audiences for the results of small business research.

Notes

1 In attempting to capture the dynamics of this interaction, 'dialectic' (as derived from Marxist discourse) might be a better term than 'dialogue'. It brings out more clearly the reciprocity and especially the tensions involved in creatively relating data and theory to each other to produce a final acceptable, albeit always provisional, result.

2 The discussion of these emphases on positivist and quantitatively based explanations in the development of business and management research has produced a huge literature. Towards the end of the twentieth century, a great deal of the discussion had become very critical on a wide variety of grounds, some of which are highlighted later in the chapter. For a more detailed discussion of these issues see Gill and Johnson (1997: especially Chapters 9 and 10).

3 For example, methodologically, doubts can be raised about whether such surveys actually measure, in any strict sense, changes in small business owners' views, experiences and confidence levels over time since each survey contacts a different sample of respondents. To be more valid, it can be argued, they should contact the same sample of owners each quarter. Response rates

are also often low – often below 25 per cent – so there may also be doubts about the representativeness of the respondents who reply, particularly for such a highly heterogenous population as small business owners.

4 Interestingly, given the discussion of the problems of sampling frames for research on small firms in Chapter 3, Birch's original data was taken from the files of the business information specialists, Dun and Bradstreet. The same firm's UK database was also used for several parallel studies of small businesses and job creation in the UK (see, for example, Daly et al., 1991). The data is in the form of a selection of basic quantitative indicators of the firm's characteristics and performance over the relevant time period but say little or nothing about management or other processes inside the firm.

5 Some of this further research has already been conducted. See, for example, on the quality of the jobs in terms of employment relations, Scott et al. (1989) Holliday (1995) and Kitching (1997), and on training, Curran et al. (1996). Each of these also offers further references on these issues. While some of these studies have a clear quantitative component, most also employ qualitative approaches with the authors arguing that only the latter can adequately capture the complexities of small enterprise employment.

6 For more detailed explanations of what the statistical manipulation involves, see Barkham et al. (1996; Chapter 3) on how the approach was used in this study and for a more general discussion, Cramer (1994: Chapter 11, *passim*).

7 While such variables are indeed difficult to measure, so are many of the other variables routinely addressed in the analysis of small business growth such as profit levels, innovation behaviour and marketing performance. Each of these presents formidable problems in conceptualization and measurement but this does not prevent researchers (including Barkham et al., 1996) from employing them routinely in their analyses.

8 It should be stressed that the studies discussed in this chapter are simply examples. Other similarly sophisticated attempts at generating quantitatively based models of small business behaviour include the study of small business success and failure by Storey et al. (1987) discussed in Chapter 2; the study by Reid et al. (1993) listed in Table 1.2, Chapter 1; the study of mature manufacturing SMEs by Smallbone et al. (1993); and the study of start-ups by Reynolds and White, 1997).

9 As Sayer (1992: 179) notes, the common practice of designating one variable in a mathematical model as the 'independent' variable and another as the 'dependent variable' does not mean in any strict sense that causality has been established since any imputation of causality must be based on non-mathematical criteria. Mathematics is a formal language which does not refer directly to the world 'out there' since whatever the latter is taken to be, it is logically independent of any formal language in terms of which it may be accounted for. In practice, the variable designated as 'independent' is often chosen on some intuitive basis, that is, the researcher has a *belief* that it is the prime causal agent or, even more prosaically, it is the one for which reasonable quality data is most easily available.

10 Of course, this does not remove the need for clearing bank decision-makers or others involved in assessing individual small firms' performances, from attempting appraisals as a foundation for their decisions. Often such appraisals will be largely quantitatively based. After all, such decisions cannot be made randomly but must appear to be arrived at on some rational basis. But

most people involved in making such decisions are often only too aware that their 'objective' appraisal procedures are not always accurate and often need a substantial input of subjective judgement (Deakins and Hussain, 1994; Fletcher, 1996).

11 Although, as made clear in Chapter 1 and later chapters, such estimates will be dependent on acceptable solutions to the problems of conceptualizing what should be treated as a 'small business'. In other words, there is nothing mechanical about such approaches.

12 There is also a 'guru literature' on the management, organization and employees of the large firm known though the writings of, for example, Drucker (1964 and, especially, 1985 on topics relevant to small business research) in the US and Handy (1992 and 1995) in the UK. This is very largely qualitative but is based on little systematically conducted, clearly reported research. While this literature is influential in business education and sells well, it is not regarded as serious research by many business and management academics.

13 As a rule of thumb based on experience, it can be suggested that in constructing a timetable for a research project the time allowed for analysis and writing up should be four to six times longer than would be needed for a quantitative project of similar scope.

14 Indeed, it is now common practice in quantitative research to conduct a preliminary exploration of the topic using a qualitative approach. For example, focus groups or unstructured interviews with relevant respondents, may be used to isolate issues to be explored in the main quantitative study.

15 A selection might include Denzin (1970) who offers a much cited early formulation, and Hammersley and Atkinson (1983) who offer a detailed exegesis and critique. Each lists additional sources discussing the issues raised by both proponents and critics. Both Denzin and Hammersley and Atkinson and the further sources they review, discuss analytic induction mainly in relation to the concerns of sociology, the discipline which has the most developed body of research employing approaches of this kind. Gill and Johnson (1997: 120–5) examine analytic induction in the context of business and management research.

16 However, they point out that their use of analytic induction would be a very time-consuming method of establishing causalities of a positivist kind. For example, the detailed study of a large number of cases is very labour-intensive and time-consuming and collecting all relevant data to ensure that a theory accounts for every relevant aspect of the phenomenon is very difficult employing conventional survey approaches. Positivist researchers themselves, of course, are usually satisfied if they can account for a proportion rather than all possible observations, employing statistical procedures to increase the confidence that can be given to the partial account offered.

17 Probably the best known and most impressive empirical study by Glaser and Strauss is of a terminal cancer ward in *Awareness of Dying* (1965). Further discussions of grounded theory by Glaser and associates are given in Glaser (1978), Strauss (1987) and Strauss and Corbin (1998).

18 Holliday is very explicit in discussing her qualitative research approach and more quantitative alternatives. The opening two chapters of her book, particularly Chapter 2, offer a personal and thoughtful account of her initial experiences as a research student embarking on her first project.

19 As in virtually all small business research and particularly in qualitative research, Holliday uses fictitious names to preserve the anonymity of her respondents. However, it is made clear that 'Wellmaid' is not one of the big names in this kind of clothing.

20 Scase and Goffee also published another detailed qualitative analysis (Scase and Goffee, 1980) based on the same data as in this study, which is rather closer to 'thick description'. The focus is more on the small business owner, the small enterprise and its role in the economy than the sociological concerns of the better known, *The Entrepreneurial Middle Class*.

21 A notable exception was Bechhofer et al. who carried out a number of studies of small business owners in Scotland in the 1960s and 1970s. An excellent introduction to their work, which includes a number of papers on small business owners in other countries in Europe (Bechhofer and Elliott, 1981), has been cited earlier.

22 The researchers' concerns about how their research would be received by others, including other sociologists, is indicated in their methodological appendix where they state that the representativeness of their claims would need testing quantitatively (Scase and Goffee, 1982: 200). Few qualitative researchers would make such a concession to quantitative explanatory approaches today.

23 The ideas examined in the article by Holliday and Letherby (1993) are also discussed in detail in Holliday (1995: Chapter 8 *passim*) and the latter may be taken as an alternative source.

24 For those who wish to investigate these issues in greater depth the following will be found useful: Hammersley (1990) and Altheide and Johnson (1994). However, there are plenty of further sources, many of which are listed in the above.

25 Other examples may be found in: Stanworth and Curran (1976); Goffee and Scase (1985); Rainnie (1989) and Chell et al. (1991). These, it should be stressed, are only a selection of studies employing this popular organizing strategy in qualitative (and quantitative, positivist) small business research.

26 Interestingly, as Curran et al. (1993b) and Kitching (1997) also show, employees in small firms appear to have little knowledge or interest in the rights conferred on them by employment legislation. This again suggests that these laws have little relevance to employer–employee relations in most small firms. If neither employers nor employees report a knowledge of, or interest in, the content of employment legislation or that it enters much into day-to-day relations with each other, it is reasonable to conclude that it is not central to those relations.

27 Indeed, some research (see, for example Scase and Goffee, 1980: 55) suggests that 'one person businesses' may never expand to employ others because the owners want to avoid what they see as the problems of managing employees. Others sometimes prefer to use self-employed labour rather than directly employed workers because they believe this reduces labour management problems.

28 The introduction of a National Minimum Wage in 1999 offered a similar example. Prior to its introduction, there was much speculation by small firm lobby groups and others that it would hurt small firms greatly, destroying large numbers of jobs. The evidence, however, suggests it has been less detrimental than these Jeremiahs predicted especially when set against other

day-to-day issues faced by small business owners (British Chambers of Commerce, 1999).

29 Implicitly or even sometimes explicitly, 'soft' in this context is often being contrasted derogatorily with 'hard' or 'proper' research which, it is assumed, must be quantitatively based and grounded in positivist models of causality.

30 There are many 'naive positivists' who are unaware this label might be attached to their epistemological position. These sometimes include politicians, policy-makers, small business support advisors, media represen-tatives as well as small business owners themselves. They often feel continuously frustrated at researchers' refusals to offer unqualified conclu-sions and their stress that their findings are provisional. This frustration is increased where researchers appear to disagree or later appear to reverse a previous position claiming that new research has caused them to revise their views. Worse, researchers are seen to be quite content with, and even to revel in, what has been called 'the endlessly contestable character' of social and business research.

31 In fact, there is no reason in principle why respondent validation should not be used in quantitatively based positivist research though the significance it might be accorded would differ from the role it plays in qualitative research.

32 However, much macro-level, positivist research on the small business is weakened, often substantially, by its refusal or reluctance to take into account actors' responses. For instance, research on training policies for small businesses has often been ineffective because of this deficiency (see Curran et al., 1996).

33 Examples of discourse analysis and similar approaches are appearing in small business research showing well their potential strengths as Downing (1997 and 1998) and Lightfoot (1998) illustrate.

5

Presentation – the Last Link in the Research Chain

At the beginning of Chapter 4, the point was repeated that 'facts do not speak for themselves' – we make them speak through the interpretations and explanations we generate. In the last chapter 'speak' referred to the analytical processes involved in generating explanations and interpretations. In this chapter, it refers to the presentation of the results in word and graphical form. Researchers communicate routinely with a wide range of audiences including fellow researchers, policy-makers, support agency staff and small business owners themselves. The ways in which researchers communicate – the word structures and visual forms in which these are composed – need careful consideration. What is suitable for one audience is not for another. A means of communication has to enable interpretations and explanations to reach their targets effectively. There is little point in research if the results never reach an audience in a form that wins them a fair hearing.

Until relatively recently, most methodology texts skipped the issue of presenting the results of research. Historically, writing on research tended to see presenting findings and interpretations as unproblematic:

> . . . the world of writing has been divided into two separate kinds: literary and scientific. Literature from the seventeenth century onward, was associated with fiction, rhetoric, and subjectivity, whereas science was associated with fact, 'plain language', and objectivity. . . . Fiction was 'false' because it invented reality, unlike science, which was 'true', because it simply 'reported' 'objective' reality in a single unambiguous voice. (Richardson, 1994: 518)

Such a division is no longer tenable. The idea that reporting research consists simply of presenting the findings in some allegedly neutral, objective language, is now seen as an illusion. The conscious reflexivity of modern social and business research has led to an awareness of the literary and linguistic devices, conventions and rhetorical practices researchers use to communicate with their audiences.[1]

At a more basic level, little attention has also been given to issues such as writing styles. Perhaps it is assumed that researchers are literate enough to present their findings and interpretations without such advice. After all, they have usually been educated to higher level than most of the population and therefore should be able to write clearly and effectively enough to present their results without further help. Lamentably, as most of us are only too aware, writing is actually difficult to do well and a lot of research reporting is not all that effective. The results are often interpretations/explanations which make much less of an impact than they might.

This chapter explores how findings and interpretations/explanations can be communicated to different kinds of audiences effectively and suggests good practice for this final stage of the research process. Particular emphasis is given to two kinds of vehicles for communicating research: the research degree thesis and the report to non-academic audiences such as policy-makers. But other means of reaching audiences such as the learned journal article and newspapers also receive attention. As in previous chapters, examples from small business research are used as illustrations.

In suggesting good practice in the presentation of small business research, there is no intention to offer a 'one best way' of organizing any kind of report. Writing up research is not only a craft but also, like research itself, a creative process. There is no one best way to structure and present a thesis, report, learned journal article or other way of communicating research. Being creative can mean new ways of presenting data and interpretations, especially to non-academic audiences. On the other hand, writing up practices in business and social research have conventions which it is well to consider before trying radical alternatives. Some conventions or good practice principles are common because they are effective even if others are somewhat ritualistic. However, even ritualism can have rhetorical power: some readers, for example, give credibility to the academic mode of presentation *because* it displays the conventions of language and structure peculiar to that form.

Modes of Presentation

Small business researchers have a wide range of audiences whose receptiveness and needs differ greatly. The learned journal article, for instance, is primarily addressed to peers. They will be interested professionally in the way in which the research was conducted, how it follows on from previous research and the novelty of the interpretation or explanation offered. Any byproducts such as implications for policy may also be addressed but unless the central point of the article is converting research into policy, the latter will be secondary. Many researchers writing for academic journals will not see themselves as having a duty to always discuss policy implications.[2] Indeed, the length constraints imposed by journals may force researchers to concentrate on only one or other aspect of their research with others reserved for alternative forms of presentation.

Policy-makers, on the other hand, tend to receive information in the form of a report. They want well-conducted, well-argued research but they are also keenly interested in the recommendations to be derived from research. For them, nothing is more irritating than working their way though a report only to find that the author has not explicitly linked the results to policy. Researchers who see their role as being academically neutral, believing it is for the audience to derive any policy implications, are not seen as helpful by this audience. Equally, support agency staff want the implications for day-to-day practice spelt out. They see anything that is 'purely academic' as useless to them as busy practitioners who are trying to help small businesses.

What the above suggests therefore, is that no single mode of presentation serves the needs of *all* the audiences for small business research. Attempts to produce all-purpose reports almost inevitably fail. In small business research this can be an acute problem, for instance, where the write-up is for an undergraduate or post-graduate Master's level dissertation. Course requirements often insist dissertations should reach high academic standards and yet also concentrate on the practical needs of business. Students often find it difficult or impossible to balance these two needs. For instance, the linguistic and structural conventions appropriate for each often conflict so that discussion tends to switch uneasily from one to the other, doing neither well.

The Research Degree Thesis

One of the most difficult vehicles for the presentation of research is the traditional research degree thesis. The PhD thesis is the main requirement for what is normally regarded as the highest academic qualification. It involves producing a lengthy document (usually around 80,000 words) offering a sustained, well-developed, coherent account of the background, methods of investigation, findings, analysis and a novel addition to the understanding and/or solution of the selected research problem. Its junior cousin, the MPhil, is usually shorter (around 40,000 words) and less demanding. Typically, the MPhil candidate is expected to meet similar objectives and standards to those of the PhD, but does not have to meet the novelty criterion other than perhaps indicating how this might be met.[3]

In addition, a thesis will normally have an *abstract, acknowledgements* (to the respondents and others who helped or supported the research and supervisors) and a list of *references* or *bibliography*. Material not in the

- *Introduction*
- *Literature review*
- *Research methodology*
- *Substantive chapters*   Two or more chapters presenting findings and analysis usually in the form of a continuing data-theory interaction. Each of these chapters is a 'building block' in constructing an integration of findings, analysis and theorization.
- *Conclusion*   This presents the overall theorization, bringing together the findings and analysis presented in the earlier chapters. In the PhD especially, this should not simply be a summary but a conclusion which takes the argument beyond the analysis presented earlier to produce something 'greater than the sum of the parts', adding a new way to the understanding of the phenomenon researched.

Figure 5.1   *An example of a presentation format for a research degree*

main body of the thesis such as unpublished documentary sources, questionnaires, data not presented earlier but deemed helpful to the reader in fully understanding the research etc., may be presented in an *appendix* or *appendices*. Material in appendices does not usually count towards any stipulated word total. The relevant university regulations may also prescribe other content and stylistic rules such as those governing the use and position of notes.

It is not the task of this book to offer comprehensive advice on completing a research degree. So much depends on the topic, the candidate and the supervisory team.[4] Although, as earlier chapters have stressed, small business research has special characteristics, research degrees on small business topics are suited to the conventional format in writing up the PhD/MPhil thesis. While a thesis may adopt an innovative structure to present its results, the conventional format (Figure 5.1) has a sound track-record as a vehicle for successfully presenting research for a research degree.

One point worth remembering is that it is possible to obtain any thesis submitted to a UK university through the British Lending Library.[5] This means that any research project which has been successfully submitted as a thesis can be consulted. Although much of the most influential research on the small business is best known through books or journals, it often originated as a thesis.[6] Going directly to the original thesis is often better for a literature search and is also very helpful in two other ways. First, it gives an idea of the standard needed to achieve a PhD. Secondly, it also demonstrates the way in which a successful PhD has been presented. Most, it will be seen, have followed more or less closely the format shown in Figure 5.1.

The version of a thesis obtainable through the British Lending Library, it should be remembered, is the *final* version. As the song might have put it, 'writing up is hard to do'. Nobody gets it right first time and the final version is usually the outcome of several drafts painstakingly trying out different ways of presenting the findings and analysis. This occurs whether it is a positivist, quantitatively based or a qualitative/ interpretative thesis but most of the sweat and tears involved in arriving at the final polished version will not be apparent so the result may look easier to achieve than it is. Richardson argues writing up is itself 'a method of enquiry' (1994). In other words, it is a continuation of the analysis stage, adding further to the interpretations/explanations arrived at using the analytical procedures discussed in Chapter 4. Experienced researchers often remark that findings and their interpretation are not fully understood until they have been expressed on paper. As the writing up progresses, new insights and ways of interpreting findings and links between them and other research, emerge almost spontaneously. For similar reasons, writing, seen in this way, can be used all through the research process. The literature review, for instance, normally undertaken at the beginning of a project, is also 'a method of enquiry' to develop a secure understanding of what previous research and theorizing have achieved. Writing papers and provisional statements on findings and initial theories throughout the project, in short, uses writing as a research tool as well as making the final write-up much easier.[7]

The key problem of the final write-up stage can be simply stated yet often takes a lot of experiment to solve: it is finding an overall logic or rationale for the findings reported. Simply reporting the findings as they emerge from the analysis does not produce a proper theorization. This is particularly difficult for quantitative researchers employing a positivist paradigm. The temptation is to number-crunch the data and write-up the results hoping that, with luck, they will add up to some larger result. This rarely happens: findings are not explanations. *Why* a particular pattern of findings resulted calls for a theorization which offers an overall rationale in which findings are related to each other in a coherent fashion, that is, they become something much more than just findings.

Qualitative researchers, however, do not escape the above problem even if it presents itself rather differently. The main problem for those adopting a qualitative paradigm, is going beyond the obvious. Successfully accessing respondents' motivations, logics of action, aims and strategies is crucial but, even added together, they do not provide an overall interpretation with the originality or novelty required for a successful research degree. As the previous chapter made clear, the qualitative researcher usually needs to incorporate other kinds of ideas and data (derived from sources other than the focal respondents) and researcher-originated constructs, to produce an overall interpretation of the actors' relationships with their businesses and social situations. Generating this overall construction is not easy but is the acid test for a qualitatively based thesis.

A final point worth stressing is the importance of readability. Just because a thesis deals with complex issues or has striven for analytical rigour, does not mean that it cannot be written in clear, readable English. Writing up in an opaque, dense style is not usually an indication of

intellectual quality. It may be the opposite. It may be an attempt at
hiding weaknesses in analysis and theory building. Some would insist
that if an argument cannot be expressed clearly and precisely, it probably
indicates that the writer does not really understand what he or she is
trying to say or has not clearly thought through the ideas. The term
'PhD-ese' is often used to describe a particularly wooden, verbose
writing style full of long sentences with multiple subclauses and the
extensive use of foot/endnotes. Publishers, for example, usually refuse
to accept a thesis or part of a thesis in its original form because they
believe readers will be deterred by the style of the typical thesis.

The Research Report

It is much more difficult in some ways to write about the research report
than the research degree thesis. First, the conventions for presenting
research in report form are much less well-established than for the
research thesis. Secondly, the variety of audiences for research reports –
from policy-makers to small business owners themselves – means that no
single format is likely to be effective in reaching all audiences. Thirdly,
some audiences are, at the least, sceptical of research as an activity. In
part, this reflects an anti-intellectualism which sees 'theory' and
academics as divorced from 'the real world', believes that 'anything can
be proved by statistics', and that only direct experience of running a small
business produces a legitimate understanding of this economic activity.

Some audiences want 'research without the research' in the sense that
they want reports to be as brief as possible, concentrating on the 'bottom
line'. They are not all that interested in the detailed background of the
research, how it was conducted and the usual cautious, tentative, heavily
qualified conclusions characteristic of academic outputs. Instead, they
want reports which state unequivocally and succinctly, firm conclusions
and recommendations which can be acted upon. In the extreme form,
they may claim they are busy people and they do not have the time to
read any report 'longer than two sides of A4'.

Yet, despite the above problems, research reports are important for
communicating with those outside the small business research community. The impact of research will be limited if these other audiences
are not reached and persuaded. More mundanely, much of the financial
and other support for small business research comes from sources outside academia and the research councils. Reporting research is therefore,
inevitably, a marketing exercise as well. But producing attractive, convincing research reports for non-academic audiences is never easy.

One solution to the above problems is what might be termed 'empa-
thetic targeting'. Researchers need to produce reports designed for
specific audiences rather than all-purpose reports which never quite
engage any audience successfully. This involves, firstly, an almost ethnographic approach to determine what a specific audience wants from

research and how the report could become part of the audience members' way of viewing the small business. In other words, ideally, the report is persuasive enough to be incorporated into their world views but without any sacrifice in the researcher's commitment to academic standards or 'telling it like it is'.

Of course, the above is a tall order in relation to some audiences. Small business owner lobby groups, for example, are often suspicious of research which they see as all too often critical of small business owner–managers or which suggests restrictions on their ability to run their businesses as they see fit. They see the proper role of research as providing unequivocal support for their members: anything else should be rejected. For example, in Chapter 4 it was argued that research on the impact of employment legislation on small businesses suggested that small business pressure groups consistently overstate its negative effects. Research which reiterates these findings, however empathetically presented, is likely to be rejected strongly by this kind of audience.

Other audiences such as policy-makers, support agency staff and the staff of larger organizations such as the clearing banks interested in small businesses as a market for products and services, are likely to be receptive to research but wary. There is a fine line between reporting the counter-intuitive and telling the audience what they think they already know. Counter-intuitive findings say something that is new on how the small firm functions but may also challenge the audience's beliefs and prejudices and, as a result, may well be distrusted or even rejected. For instance, a study of soft loan schemes[8] (Curran et al., 1994) to help small business start-ups, reported that such schemes could be viable economically and that failure rates among businesses began in this way appeared no higher than for conventional small business start-ups.

The above findings were counter-intuitive for the main audience for the report, senior executives of the major high-street bank which sponsored the research. As bankers, they might be expected to believe that their professional judgements on loan applications, based on their experience as providers of finance for business, would be sound. Soft loans, on the other hand, violated sound lending principles by definition and implied that the assessment procedures they normally employed mistakenly refused loans to start-ups that would otherwise survive and prosper at least as well as the businesses for which they did give loans.

In presenting their findings and conclusions, the researchers tried to counter any scepticism by pointing out that, as part of the soft loan awarding process, applicants received professional support in developing sensible business plans. The results were then very carefully assessed by an expert panel (often including a bank manager) and often modified further as a result. After start-up, the owner–managers received mentoring to help them through the difficult initial period. This meant that even if the original business idea was not well thought out (and therefore rightly rejected for a conventional loan initially) by the time the business was launched, it was much better prepared. From being a marginal proposition it was converted into a more viable enterprise with similar chances of survival to those of a conventional start-up. In contrast, people starting conventional small businesses usually receive no support or training and often find running a business much more difficult than they had imagined. Moreover, if they provide most of their finance from their own sources and ample security for any additional finance from, say, a bank, lenders may take a greater chance on their success because, even if they fail, the loan is secured.

Reporting findings which support the audience's beliefs, on the other hand, may be dismissed because 'we knew that already'. For example, one of the most investigated of all topics is why small businesses fail (see Keasey and Watson, 1993: Chapter 6 *passim*; Storey, 1994: Chapter 4 *passim*). Yet despite all this research, the ability to predict failure – of enormous value to audiences ranging from bankers to policy-makers attempting to 'pick winners' – remains very low. The research shows that failure is a complex process since any or a mix of a wide range of factors, may be precipitators. Quantitative research has been the favoured approach but this has almost invariably focused on a narrow range of factors for which quantitative data is available. This tends to take the form of information on cash flows, liquid asset levels, debt levels and other financial indicators for the period before ceasing to trade. The result is that study after study tends to conclude somewhat tritely that small businesses fail because they get into financial difficulties. Practitioner audiences, as might be expected, tend to respond with, 'we knew that already'.

Another problem, of course, is that most of the above research is at the aggregate level. The conclusions refer to *populations* of firms and their utility for predicting behaviour at the level of the individual firm is quite limited. As Keasey and Watson (1993: 128–34) also point out, a wider range of variables needs to be taken into account than financial data. These include factors external to the firm (such as the state of the local and national economy) and, most especially, owner–managers' decision-making strategies. The latter, as argued in previous chapters, are best investigated qualitatively but are unlikely to produce precise quantitative indicators of the future failure of individual firms. This is the kind of research topic, therefore, where results are always likely to elicit a 'we knew that already' response from non-academic audiences.

On the other hand, not all research need receive such sceptical receptions from user audiences. A mix, weaving together counter-intuitive and findings confirming existing beliefs, presented well, may give the counter-intuitive findings as well as the report as a whole, credibility and persuasiveness. This can be increased if the key recommendations offer a positive, practical strategy to the audience. What the effective report seeks to do, in other words, is to persuade the audience to accept ownership of the findings and analysis (including those they initially doubt). This requires rethinking on their part but they will do so if they see it will further their goals.

Another example of attempting to change attitudes over time might be taken from research (see, for example, Curran and Blackburn, 1994; Storey 1994) which has tried to wean policy-makers and practitioners away from seeing the small business as a single homogenous population for which 'one size fits all' policies and services can be created. As Chapter 1 made clear, this view of '*the* small business' is inadequate given the extreme heterogeneity of small-scale enterprise in the UK.

The message from much small business research has been that the extreme heterogeneity of the small business population means that policies and services designed to meet the needs of some hypothetical typical small firm, are likely to fail. The situations and needs of small firms are too varied to be met in this over-arching, over-simple way. Indeed, that is one of the reasons why so many of the small business polices since the early 1980s have had so little impact (Storey, 1994; Gibb, 1998; Curran, in press).

Often policy is coupled with a strong belief in a local economy made up largely of small firms whose needs could be served by support agencies run mainly by local business people who would best know the needs of local enterprise. The importance of the local economy as a distinct unit has declined as the UK has become more integrated and centralized. Small firms are increasingly just as likely to be linked to the wider economy as they are to the economy of the area in which they are located. This will become even more apparent as more and more small businesses become e-commerce-based. The small firm-based local economy, in other words, is declining and bodies providing support based on this unit are likely to be less and less effective (Curran and Blackburn, 1994).

Policy-makers and support agency personnel find many of the above arguments counter-intuitive and are resistant to them. The idea of a small business community which can be seen as a powerful contributor to local economies, is very appealing to policy-makers. Offering support to the small business population as a whole is also administratively attractive and likely to cost less than a mix of policies. The local economy is also often seen as a part of 'the local community' in a wider sense and the latter has a strong ideological appeal to many in politics and policy-making even though other evidence suggests that community in this sense is losing salience in contemporary Britain.

One positive alternative which research offers as a more fruitful way of viewing the small business and its support, is based on the notion of sector. The heterogeneity of the small business population, it is argued, can be recognized and harnessed to provide more effective policy-based support. Targeting support is increasingly fashionable in other areas of government intervention as an effective use of resources so why not target support for the small business in the same way? This already happens in some sectors, such as electronics (Storey, 1994: 270–1), and the approach could be extended. Equally, if the importance of the local economy is played down in favour of concentrating resources on supporting small businesses through sector-based strategies, this does not mean that locally based agencies have no role. There will always have to be local deliverers of support but they could be orientated much more to sector needs, albeit retaining a local emphasis where sector and locality coincide as happens for some older economic activities and, to a lesser extent, in some of the newer knowledge-based activities.

The positive implications for policy of the counter-intuitive findings and analyses outlined above are far from accepted as yet. But they illustrate the strategies which researchers can employ to reach non-academic audiences with messages which the latter do not find immediately acceptable. There is never any guarantee that they will succeed of course. The adage 'truth will out' is both epistemologically and politically naive. Policy-makers, support providers and those seeking to sell products and services to small firms, have their own agendas. They are also often subject to lobby group demands and market forces. Small business researchers and their messages are only one influence and are unlikely to be a major one. Persuading audiences to accept research conclusions may, in other words, depend on many more other things than the quality of the research or the way it is reported.

The Research Report Format

Despite the above it is possible to suggest some common elements of a format for the research report. The structure and style of reports for non-academic audiences has been developed mainly by commercial sources such as market research agencies and consultants. For academics, it is very much a matter of adapting the format to their needs. For most academics, the report format is constraining since it imposes severe limitations on how far the analysis and argument can be developed and, inevitably, there is a risk of superficiality and presenting the message in overly black and white terms.

Different audiences will be susceptible to variations on the format but Figure 5.2 summarizes the basic features of reports for audiences such as government departments, support agencies and commercial sponsors such as the high-street banks. For commercial audiences, the emphasis on positive recommendations may need to be stronger, giving less space for other elements. For policy audiences, recommendations need to be aware of what is politically acceptable as well as resourcing and administrative costs.

Simplicity and clarity of presentation are essential to all reports. For all of these audiences, the writing needs to be in short, punchy paragraphs with clear graphics and layout using subheadings and white space effectively. These good-practice points are important in ensuring the

♦ *Executive Summary*   Usually presented in bullet point form to cover: a statement of the problem or issue upon which the report focuses saying why it is important to the audience; how the research was conducted (stated very briefly); principal findings; and, finally, conclusions often in the form of clear recommendations for action. Ideally the summary should be no longer than two sides of A4 and it should be free standing, that is, it should be possible to detach it from the main report for separate circulation.

♦ *Introduction*   A statement of the problem/issue addressed by the report. This might include any brief provided by the sponsor. Brevity is again desirable.

♦ *Methodology*   Brief details of how the research was conducted. In some cases the methodology may be better included in an appendix.

♦ *Findings*   Main findings presented in a succinct, logical sequence with tabular or graphical illustrations where appropriate. Findings may be presented in one or more brief 'chapters' or sections. If the findings and analysis are at all complex, each chapter or section should conclude with a summary of findings/conclusions in bullet point form.

♦ *Conclusions/recommendations*   The heading for this section may be just the latter term or the two may be reversed. For some audiences the term 'policy' may be used. The stress should be on the *action points* which follow from the findings. The tone should be positive rather than tentative or defensive.

♦ *Appendix or appendices*   To present additional detail from the findings or other background data which might be useful to the audience. It may also contain a description of the methodological strategies or more detail on these.

♦ *References*   The report should use references sparingly so that the final list is short.

Overall, paragraphs should be brief, the presentation should include plenty of headings, some variation in fonts or typeface and plenty of white space. An uncluttered, reader-friendly appearance should be the aim. The report should be concise: some suggest a fifteen page maximum though this depends on the kind of subject, level of sponsorship, size of project and audience preferences.

Figure 5.2   *The format of the research report*

report is read: too many reports end up gathering dust on shelves having been read by too few of the target audience to have any real impact.

Some academics will cringe at writing up their research to fit this format. Presenting key findings and conclusions in bullet point form will, in their view, be too close to a superficial, 'soundbite' treatment of research. They may believe that it will lack depth and leave out the qualifications which should be attached to their conclusions and recommendations. No action or policy recommendations, however well-supported by research, are free from disadvantages, they will point out. A sound approach will always highlight the 'no free lunch' aspect inherent in all policy and support recommendations.

Others will object to talking down to the audience. Arguments in bullet point form may be suited to those with an 'attention deficiency disorder' but serious research deserves to be treated seriously. Part of the role of the researcher, as they see it, is maintaining and raising standards of debate by educating audiences rather than a 'dumbing down' discussion of the small firm. Small firms and small-scale enterprises may be small but this does not mean they are simple. The way the small firm functions in different sectors and the way it articulates with the wider economy and society are as complex and difficult to unravel as for any other kind of economic enterprise.

Many of the above points have force. There is a debate on levels of discussion of business and economic activities in our society. Much of the writing on management and business in the UK and the US is superficial, encouraging over-simple analyses and quick fix solutions. Nonetheless, researchers have to reach the audiences who are the customers for their work. This, in the same way as reaching customers for any other knowledge product, is not best achieved by telling them that what they want is wrong and that they have to accept what we say, and the way we say it, as good for them. On the other hand, as producers of other kinds of services have demonstrated, it is possible to both meet consumers' perceived demands and educate them to adopt more sophisticated approaches to what they consume.[9] That should be the goal – admittedly not an easy one – of the researcher seeking to reach and influence non-academic audiences.

Graphical Representation in Research

A picture is worth a thousand words says the maxim and graphics can be a powerful aid in presenting research, particularly to non-academic audiences. On the whole, graphical presentation is under-used in small business research. Where it is used, it tends to be in the traditional form of the statistical table even though this is by no means the only effective way of using graphics. But, like other presentational devices, graphics can have disadvantages and can fail in conveying findings and ideas efficiently and clearly to readers.

Graphical presentation has two main forms. The first and most common is *numerical graphics*: the presentation of numerical data in different ways with the statistical table containing data in columns and rows, as probably the most common. The second is *analytical graphics*: the presentation of ideas in diagrammatic or schematic form. This is often used to present a model of the relationships between variables. Analytical graphics may have numerical content but their main aim is to offer a 'map' of the links between elements in the model. The power of both forms, but especially that of numerical graphics, has been greatly enhanced by PC packages which can produce complex and attractive results not easily produced otherwise.

Examples of numerical graphics are common in small business research but some are more effective than others. Although tables or charts are generally a more succinct and clear way of presenting numerical data than in text form, not everybody is graphically literate. 'Reading' a table or other representation of numerical data to get the most information out of it takes skill and experience. One principle in constructing these forms of presentation is to avoid cramming too much information into a single table or chart. This may be particularly important in research reports for non-academic audiences where over-complex presentation may simply contribute to the report being unread. Percentages are usually easier to read than raw numbers. Most tables do not need both except that the base number should always be given so that percentages can be converted if the reader feels the need. Alternatively, bar, pie and line charts may be superior in conveying numerical information than a table of numbers.[10]

Another good practice principle for presenting numerical data is to keep the presentation uncluttered. For instance, it is not really necessary to use lines to separate columns and rows in most tables since the white space between them is usually sufficient to separate the data clearly and provides a less cluttered appearance. Some computer packages offer ways of generating 3D tables and charts which many see as a sophisticated form of presentation. But often the result is cluttered, difficult to read, contains no more information than the conventional 'flat' presentation and may actually obscure some of the data. This can occur, for instance, when a column in a 3D table is shorter than the one 'in front' so that readers cannot see the precise height of the shorter column.

The decision to use simpler or more complex forms of graphical presentation depends on whichever is most effective in conveying information to the particular audience. Does it need a '3D' form? Would the data be more clearly presented in simpler, clearer graphics? Colour can be an aid, particularly in presenting findings to non-academic audiences, though, again, over-exuberant use is likely to be counter-productive.

Analytical graphics serve essentially the same purpose as numerical graphics, that is, presenting a message more succinctly and clearly than would be possible in text form. An example in small business research is provided by Atkinson and Meager (1994) and in Storey (1994: 197); this seeks to show the range of influences which impinge on small business employment practices (see Figure 5.3). The graphic also distinguishes between influences which are assumed to be fixed for any given small firm and those which are variable. Arrows are used to show the direction and strength of relations between the variables displayed.[11] Another example, provided by Oakey (1991: 131) (see Figure 5.4), offers a life cycle model of product development by high technology firms showing the financial impact on the firm throughout the entire product cycle from initial decision to obsolescence.

Simpler graphical presentations take the form of lists of variables thought to be relevant to the analysis being undertaken. There may be some indication of the assumed or indicated (from the research findings) relative strength of the variables. Kitching (1997: 217 and 224) used this approach to list the main components of employment cultures in three

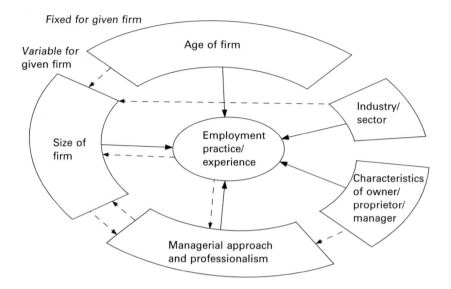

Figure 5.3   *Influences on small business employment practices*

Source: Atkinson, J. and Meager, N. in Storey (1994: 197)

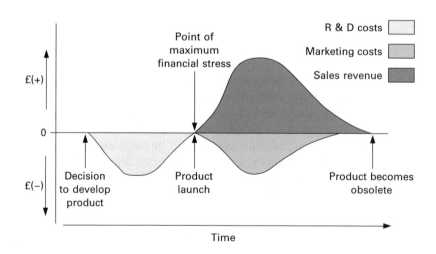

Figure 5.4   *A life-cycle model of product development*

Source: Oakey, R. (1991: 131)

Characteristics of employment cultures 1			
	Computer services	Employment and secretarial services	Free houses and restaurants
Pay	+	++	+
Social rewards	+	−	++
Work intrinsic rewards	++	+/−	+/−

Characteristics of employment cultures 2			
	Computer services	Employment and secretarial services	Free houses and restaurants
Pay	+	++	+
Social rewards	+	−	++
Work intrinsic rewards	++	+/−	+/−
Influence of *personal* relations between owner–managers and employees			

Figure 5.5   *Characteristics of employment cultures 1 and 2*

Source: Kitching, J. (1997: 215 and 224)

types of firms in his analysis of employment in small service firms (Figure 5.5). The relative strength of each component in the employment cultures of firms of each type was indicated by '+' and '−' signs, a useful device where data does not permit precise quantitative assessments but only 'more' or 'less' estimates.

Another common technique in graphical representation is the 'cross' or 'four box diagram'. This consists essentially of two axes crossing each other at right angles to form four quadrants. Each axis can represent a variable and its relative strength and firms or any other subject, can be located in the four quadrants to show the relative values of the two variables for that subject. A simple example is Ward's representation of the business participation rates of different ethnic groups in the UK (see Figure 5.6). More complex examples have quantitative indications along each axis to provide more precise measures of the positions of the subjects distributed across the quadrants.

Converting data and ideas into graphical form also has other advantages. For instance, it may be a form of enquiry in itself in the sense that tabular representations of numerical data may suggest relations which have not been seen in earlier analyses. Even more useful can be the

		Business participation rate	
		High	*Low*
Unemployment rate	*High*	Pakistanis/ Bangladeshis	Afro-Caribbeans
	Low	Indians	Whites

Figure 5.6   *Business participation and unemployment rates for selected ethnic groups in the UK*

Source: Ward, R. (1991: 59)

graphical representation of ideas. Putting a model down on paper can often indicate missing links or relationships which need to be given more attention in the model building and analysis. It may even suggest propositions that might be tested. At the least, such representations help ensure that the ideas and rationale upon which it is based have been clearly thought through. Note also that analytical graphics can be used in both quantitative, positivist-based *and* qualitative, interpretative research.

The Journal Article

In academic status terms, the learned journal article scores high in business and management research, higher generally than a book although there are exceptions and much depends on the status of the journal in which the article is published. The main reason for the high status of learned journal articles is that articles submitted are peer reviewed anonymously. They are sent to one or more reviewers selected for their expertise on the subject of the article who make recommendations on whether the article is of a high enough standard to be published.[12] Most journals reject, at least initially, a high proportion of the articles submitted as unsuitable. Authors usually receive a copy of reviewer's comments (anonymously again) and may be invited to resubmit after revising the article to take account of the comments. Normally, neither the author nor reviewers are paid so there are no monetary influences on the decision of whether to publish.

Individual journals have conventions on style and length which need to be observed. Indeed, becoming familiar with the house style of a journal and ensuring the article emulates it reasonably closely, can help greatly in achieving publication.[13] The length of the typical journal article is around 6,000 words and authors can find this restrictive sometimes. On the other hand, this forces writers to focus clearly on their chosen topic and make their arguments as concisely and effectively as they can – a benefit to readers. Although most journals have a waiting list for publication of articles already accepted (the lag is sometimes over a year) it is usually quicker to publish in this form than in book form. It is also likely to reach a wider audience more quickly than if published as a book.

There are four broad classes of learned journal in which small business research might be published:

1   Specialist journals concentrating on small business research, such as the *International Small Business Journal* in the UK or the *Journal of Business Venturing* in the USA.
2   Single-discipline journals which, in principle, will publish research on any topic provided it makes a contribution to the discipline. In the UK, the sociological journal *Work, Employment and Society*, in the USA, economics journals such as the *American Economic Review* or in geography, journals such as *Regional Studies*, are examples which have all published articles on the small firm.
3   General learned journals covering business and management issues such as the *Journal of Management Studies* and the *Strategic Management Journal*.
4   Journals which concentrate on broad, non-business subject areas such as *Urban Studies* or *Local Government Studies* and will publish articles on small scale enterprise where they contribute to understanding in the area.

Generally, it is easier to publish articles in specialist small business journals than in the other kinds. One obvious reason for this is that there is less competition since small business research is a narrower, more specialist area compared with the areas covered by other types of learned journal. Another reason is that small business research has lower status academically than social science disciplines such as economics and therefore does not have the attractions of researching and publishing in a main disciplinary area. In business and management research generally, theory and research linked to the concerns of larger enterprises and the functions held to be central to their operation such as business strategy, finance and marketing, has higher status than small business research. Hence journals which concentrate on these topics and functions tend to have higher status.

The above are very broad generalizations and plenty of exceptions can be found. There are outstanding academics in the small business area publishing high-quality theory and research. Some single-discipline journals have relatively low standards compared with the leading journals in their disciplinary area. Some of the general business and management journals are also of poor quality. But for any researcher in the small business area wanting to publish in a learned journal, the considerations in the previous paragraph are worth taking on board. On the whole, most small business researchers publish too much in specialist journals and too little in the main disciplinary and high-status business and management journals.

Newspapers and Other Popular Outlets

Small business research is not just for other researchers, policy-makers, support agency staff, larger organizations selling to small firms or even small business owners. As Chapter 1 demonstrated, the small business is central to economic activities and employment in the UK. Yet the mass media and the general public often have highly inaccurate views of the role of the small firm and how small firms function. In part, this is due to the ideological halo enveloping 'enterprise' which small businesses are often assumed to embody in its purest form (Rainnie, 1989: 1–2; Goss, 1991: 8–14; Ritchie, 1991). But it also reflects a general tendency to underestimate the importance of small-scale economic activities in modern economies (Curran, 1999: 1–3).

It might be argued, therefore, that one responsibility of small business researchers is to bring the results of their work to the wider public to correct misleading views of the small firm. Despite the media's stereotypical views of the small firm, it is still receptive to popular accounts of small business research. Writing for newspapers and other general-interest publications requires an approach and writing style different to those discussed earlier. Nevertheless, there are tips on publishing in this medium which increase the chances of publication and, unlike most of the formats discussed above, authors usually get paid, albeit not very generously.

Newspaper articles and articles in other popular media are usually short, often 500 words or less and rarely more than 1,500, so the article has to get up to speed quickly. Key findings or, even better, a 'hook', that is, a theme or novel way of expressing research results or a link with current economic and political issues, need to be at the beginning to grab the reader's (and editor's) attention. The article can then unwrap the hook, providing more detail in a lively, concise style. A human-interest aspect helps enormously. Findings, for example, can be couched in stories centred on individual owners, for example, rather than expressed statistically. Statistics, unless used sparingly, are likely to be seen as boring.

One way of being invited to write for the popular media is ensuring that editors know about your research. A press release (perhaps based on an executive summary but highlighting a hook) sent to editors and specialist business journalists, will sometimes produce an invitation. More likely it will simply result in a telephone call from a journalist who will use the researcher's work for his or her own piece: journalists do have to show their boss they are working! If a link can be made with a current issue in the media, a telephone call to the relevant journalist might similarly earn an invitation or at least a mention of the research. The local media – newspapers, radio and television – are usually more accessible than the national media. Press releases making a local or regional link with the research findings help here. Even a brief mention in a news report is worthwhile since it produces publicity for the researcher and the research.

Too close a link with the popular media can be seductive. Being quoted in newspapers or popular magazines or even better, writing for them and appearing on TV or radio, are wonderful boosts to the ego. But they are only sidelines for the serious researcher. They are very useful in helping journalists and the general public understand the small business but real research still needs to be aimed at peers and specialists. Peer respect tells a researcher that what they are doing is worthwhile but it is earned through the unglamorous grind of research based on carefully conducted fieldwork, time-consuming analysis and writing up in a form which will be judged a genuine addition to understanding the small business.

Conclusions

This chapter has focused on the rather neglected topic of writing up and presenting small business research. Some of the media discussed, such as the research degree thesis and the learned journal article, are common to all social science and business research but small business research is distinctive in needing to reach an exceptionally wide range of audiences. Besides their peers, small business researchers routinely write to reach policy-makers, support agency personnel, professionals such as account-ants, representatives of larger businesses who offer small businesses their products and services, as well as the general public.

Writing up research has arguably become more difficult in recent years. Earlier, it was assumed that all that was required was a straight-forward reporting of 'the facts' in a neutral, objective way. But as researchers have become more conscious of the reflexivity of research accounts, their construction has become much more of an issue. In a sense, rather than offering neutral, objective accounts it might be more fruitful to go to the opposite extreme and accept that all of us are, to some extent, 'spin doctors' when we write up a research project.

Two modes of presentation were given special attention: the research degree thesis and the research report, particularly for non-academic audiences. The research degree thesis aims for a high academic qualification. It demands high standards in constructing a sustained, detailed, coherently presented account of a research project. The account has to set the topic selected in its intellectual and research context, evaluate the methodological strategies employed, report and analyse the findings and, finally, for the PhD especially, offer an overall theorization which proposes a novel understanding of the issues investigated. The style and presentation conventions for the thesis are relatively inflexible but guidance is available and a standard format which would be suited to most small business research for the PhD or MPhil degrees, was discussed.

The research report, normally produced for non-academic audiences, is more difficult to generalize about. First, the conventions for producing research reports are less well-defined and the audiences for such reports are immensely varied. Secondly, the structure and style of this vehicle for presenting research has been determined largely by commercial consultancy and marketing agencies. Academics often find writing up research in this form restrictive. For instance, the bullet point form of presentation favoured for this kind of report sometimes makes it difficult to avoid superficiality. Meeting the demand for clear, positive conclusions and recommendations often goes against the provisional character of much research.

On the other hand, small business researchers have to communicate with non-academic audiences. To fail to do so means research fails to reach some of those most in need of the knowledge or most able to use it to help the small firm. Moreover, government departments, small business support agencies and commercial sources are important patrons of small business research. The chapter examined the problems in writing this kind of report and suggested strategies for overcoming them. It was noted, however, that not all the difficulties can be easily overcome if researchers are to sustain their research integrity.

Despite the difficulties in constructing an effective, persuasive research report, a format for reports to non-academic audiences was offered. It was stressed that this would have to be adapted considerably for some audiences if the results were to be effective communication. The point was made that the various audiences for small business research were best seen as 'customers', that is, that their wants and needs as they perceived them, should be given high priority in constructing and presenting the report. While small business researchers need to educate others about the way the small enterprise functions and its role in the economy, this has to be accomplished with subtlety rather than over-didactically.

Somewhat unusually, the chapter discussed the graphical representation of research. Presenting numerical findings in graphical form (especially in the standard columns and rows table) is very common and might not be thought worth much discussion. But the section argued that because it was so common it was often done less effectively than it might be. For example, there is a tendency towards cluttered, unclear presentation which needs to be resisted particularly in presenting numerical data to non-academic audiences. The graphical presentation of numerical data has important aesthetic as well as clarity dimensions and good practice gives proper attention to these to ensure effective communication.

Analytical graphics receive even less attention that the numerical kind. They are concerned with presenting ideas and relationships as clearly as possible and can complement text discussions powerfully. They are particularly useful in presenting theoretical models. Although they can be used in any kind of research report including the research degree thesis, they are especially useful in presenting ideas to non-academic audiences. Several examples were offered of how this form of graphical representation has been used in small business research. They are not without drawbacks, of course. For instance, graphically presented models can imply a more static, less dynamic set of relations than actually occurs as small firms develop and interact with the wider environment.

The chapter also discussed the learned journal article as an outlet for small business research. It was noted that this carries high status in academia because of the principle of peer review and the rigorous criteria journals apply in deciding whether to publish. On the whole, it was suggested that publishing in specialist small business research journals was probably easier than publishing in single-discipline, business and management and general learned journals. On the other hand, it was argued that small business researchers need to publish more in the latter than they tend to do now to raise the status of small business research and educate others on the increasing importance of small-scale enterprise.

Finally, publishing small business research in newspaper and popular outlets was discussed. Although reaching the wider public is important and some tips were offered, these kinds of outlets are secondary to the academic and special interest audiences for small business research. They help in educating the wider public on the small business and may even improve the image of academia but, on the whole, will never be a key audience for the hard, time-consuming substantive work of small business research.

Presentation represents the last stage in the research process from originating the research topic to planing the fieldwork, analysing the results and fashioning them into an enhanced understanding of the functioning of the small firm and its role in the economy. The reason why a whole chapter has been devoted to presentation is that its importance is too often neglected. It is almost as if research was supposed to write itself up or that all researchers are naturally gifted, effective reporters of their work. In reality, writing up is a skilled, difficult task with problems almost as exacting as those in earlier stages of the research process.

Presentation is the final link in the research chain and it has to be as strong as the other links if the hard work, time and creativity demanded by small business research, is to be rewarded.

Notes

1 This reflexivity now extends to the outputs of natural scientists who also often make the same claims of objectivity and neutrality. They are now seen, no less than business and social researchers, as presenting their theories and conclusions in forms which have clear linguistic conventions and strategies that incorporate all kinds of rhetorical devices with the effect (often intentional) of increasing the persuasiveness of the results for their peers and the general public.

2 Here they part company sharply with some audiences for small business research such as some lobby groups and support agency staff who believe the only justification for research is to help the small business be more successful and that one of the major shortcomings of academic researchers is the negative, critical and overall unhelpful stance of much of their work.

3 Each university has its own rules for the award of research degrees so the criteria mentioned here are only approximate. Increasingly also, mixed-mode doctorates are being introduced which, for example, involve a structured element such as taught courses combined with a shorter thesis than the traditional PhD or comprise several shorter, discrete research projects written up to be the equivalent of the traditional thesis or several previously published articles or other materials with a commentary. These alternatives are not discussed here since the traditional thesis is still the most common form of the PhD and remains the exemplar for the award of a doctorate. However, most of the suggestions below apply to the newer formats also.

4 There are guides to undertaking research degrees such as Phillips and Pugh (1987). Gill and Johnson (1997) recommend a US source, Rudestam and Newton (1992), as particularly helpful. Some universities also produce guides for students which can be useful. All have their own rules for awarding research degrees and anybody embarking on a research degree should consult those of the institutions at which they think they might register.

5 It is also possible, although more difficult, to obtain copies of theses submitted to American universities. However, since the American economy and society is different to that of the UK, care needs to be taken in using American findings and research approaches in the UK.

6 For example, see some of the following: Ingham (1968), a very clear, elegantly argued thesis, albeit criticized by later research, on employment experiences in the small firm; Batstone (1969) which, again, although submitted almost 30 years ago, offers a good example of a well-presented, well-argued thesis; Goss (1986) which like that of Kitching (see below) is concerned with work experiences in the small firm; Holliday (1993) whose research was discussed in some of the previous chapters, is an example of a thesis with a very strong qualitative approach; Kitching (1997) an example of a recent thesis demonstrating a concern with contemporary epistemological issues affecting small

business research as well as reporting substantive research; and Lightfoot (1998) who offers another example of a thesis based on qualitative research.

7   At a research degree supervisors' workshop, a strong consensus emerged on the importance of writing throughout the whole research degree process. It was agreed unanimously that 'write, write, write' should be emphasized to research students as indispensable. Not only was it seen as a way of clarifying ideas and preparing for the final write-up but it also provided psychological rewards. For instance, presenting a paper or publishing an article is a boost to confidence and a reward on the often very long haul to final submission. For many research students, this 'write, write, write' emphasis also helps develop writing skills in ways the secondary school and the typical undergraduate or masters degree, fail to do as well to raise them to the standard needed for a research degree.

8   'Soft loans' are capital made available to a borrower, in this instance those wishing to start a small business, either interest free or at an interest rate and/ or under other conditions more favourable than the recipient could obtain in the market. For a further discussion see Curran et al., 1994: Chapter 1 *passim*.

9   A good example, is the way pressure groups such as the Soil Association have promoted the benefits of organic produce in recent years. Consumption of organic produce has risen despite being more expensive than non-organic produce and UK consumers' keenness on low food prices.

10 A helpful discussion of the presentation of numerical data with examples is provided by Hussey and Hussey (1997: 295–306) and there are a number of computer packages including SPSS, Excel, Nvivo and Decision Explored which offer a variety of ways of presenting the same data. Sage's research methodology catalogues offer references to these. Examples of good practice in presenting numerical data graphically are provided by Storey (1994).

11 Interestingly, this graphic is very similar to an earlier one by the same authors (Atkinson, 1984) which offered a model of what was labelled 'the dual economy'. *Inter alia*, this offered a view of the role of the small firm in the UK economy as a whole in the restructuring alleged to be emerging from the mid-1980s onwards. Again, the graphic was very effective in terms of the wide citation and influence on discussion it achieved. For a critique of this characterization of the position of the small firm in the wider economy see Curran (1990: 127).

12 In practice, two or more reviewers are the norm. If, in the editor's judgement, the reviews diverge greatly, further advice may be sought. Sometimes authors protest that the reviewers have not properly understood the argument or were not the most competent and the editor may be persuaded to review an assessment. It might be sent, for instance, to a further reviewer to provide additional comment for the editor to make a final decision.

13 This is particularly important where the house style is very distinctive. Journal editors quickly recognize the 'all purpose' article submitted to several journals and tend to treat it less seriously. (Sometimes the dog-eared appearance of the manuscript shows it has been submitted to (and rejected by) several journals.) There is a strict convention (which most journals make a condition of acceptance for consideration) that an article should only be submitted to one journal at a time. Being accepted for publication in more than one journal wastes editors' and reviewers' time (given for free) because it has to be withdrawn by one or more of them.

6

Conclusions

Small business research in its present form is now over a quarter of a century old. In the UK the starting date for most commentators was the Bolton Report, published in 1971. As always, dating any human endeavour historically is somewhat arbitrary. As Chapter One pointed out, significant contributions to understanding the small firm in the UK were published before 1971, such as the studies by the Acton Society Trust (1953 and 1956) and the study of social and employment relations in small firms published just before the Bolton Report by Ingham (1970).[1] But the real take-off post-dated 1971.

As the earlier chapters have shown in the examples discussed (a selection only it should be remembered) small business research has undoubtedly expanded greatly in the last 30-plus years. Yet there remain indications that full maturity has still to be achieved. The 'map' of small business research remains fragmentary. New researchers, for instance, often complain of the difficulties in locating relevant previous research. It is common to read new contributions to the literature written by people clearly unaware of previous work on their chosen topic. One result is that even where authors are familiar with some of the previous work, there is still often a lack of a sense of continuity or of the cumulative character of small business research.

On the other hand, there are some significant reasons for the slow progress to maturity. Some are related to the character of the area itself and the ways in which researchers have sought to uncover and interpret the circumstances of the small enterprise. Others have to do with the time period in which most of the research has taken place. For instance, where several disciplines are involved in research in an area, as in small business research, barriers between disciplines help sustain a fragmentary character. The late arrival of small business research also occurred against the background of the epistemological splintering of research approaches which developed from the early 1970s onwards. This has questioned ideas of continuity in research or the possibility of cumulative developments in knowledge.

In this final chapter, the aim is to examine some of the problems faced by contemporary small business research and to place it in the context of social and business and management research generally. Small business research clearly has a very distinct character as a variety of business and management research and in the way it draws on the social sciences generally. But it is also part of the wider unfolding of business and management research, sharing many of the hopes and problems which excite and worry researchers in this area. Its coming of age, therefore, is as full of optimism, or as problematic, as different observers want to make it. The results of over a quarter of a century of research on the small firm can be seen as an evolving development of understanding of the small firm and its role in the economy, but others may see it more as resembling what they see as the fragmentary, directionless character of much modern business and social research. The position argued here is that it is closer to the former.

Enemies of Integration in Small Business Research

Small business research will always face problems in becoming a coherent field of inquiry. First, it is genuinely cross-disciplinary which, while highly laudable in principle, does not help in gaining coherence. Arguments for breaking down the barriers between social science disciplines (and between these disciplines and business practice) have been around a long time and have extra force in areas such as business and management research where no one discipline can claim overall sovereignty. But in the research from which much of what is taught on business and management courses originates, disciplinary frontiers remain remarkably intact. In business and management education, for example, despite frequent claims to offer 'an integrated approach', clear divisions remain. This means that much small business research never crosses such barriers, making it difficult to fuse it into a single approach to the small enterprise.

Secondly, small business research is predominantly an applied area of research. 'Applied' here has two meanings. Commonly it refers to research which strives to resolve practical problems such as those connected, for example, with business start-up, growth and innovation in small firms. Small business research is 'applied' in this sense although, as previous chapters have demonstrated, it also encompasses much research which seeks to extend knowledge for its own sake. But a second, research-linked meaning of 'applied', refers to any area of inquiry which does not belong to a single discipline. The small business is of interest to all the social sciences from economics to anthropology and all areas of business and management practice from accountancy to marketing. One characteristic of applied research in this sense (as well as in the first sense) is that it lives a great deal off of ideas and approaches developed in the core social sciences and areas of professional practice. Small business research, in other words, is mainly a follower rather than a leader intellectually. This drawing of research ideas and approaches from such diverse sources also undermines coherence: few even of full-time small business researchers can claim to have a complete, across-the-board knowledge of what is happening in the whole area.

Thirdly, the neglect of the small business as an important area of academic business and research inquiry by the major business schools in the UK, robs it of a research and intellectual prominence that would promote coherence. Leaving aside exceptions such as the Warwick University Business School, most of the top-rated UK business schools (as measured by research assessment exercises) devote little research effort to the small enterprise. Small business research has been concentrated in the new universities who lack the prestige of the likes of the London Business School. For any area of business and management research to be seen as of major significance requires championing from this kind of institution, regardless of the quality of research emanating from researchers at other, less prestigious institutions.[2]

Besides the above barriers to integration in contemporary small business research, its relatively late emergence as a significant area of inquiry has probably made it more susceptible than most to the upheavals following post-modernist critiques of intellectual activities.[3] References, for example, were made in previous chapters to the reflexivity now widely accepted as inevitably associated with the research process whatever the subject investigated. This has undermined traditional notions of objectivity in research by emphasizing that researchers need to take account of, and reflect upon, the assumptions, models and analytical devices they use at all stages from the statement of the topic to final interpretation/explanation. Understanding, in other words, is relative to, and a function of, the paradigmatic positions adopted by researchers. These views of the research process have developed powerfully in some of the key feeder disciplines of small business research and, hence, affect small business research. The result is a fragmentation of approaches and research methods which, again, works against coherence in small business research.

In this book the position adopted has been to try to move beyond debates about the quantitative–positivist versus qualitative–interpretative division which so electrified some, especially younger, researchers in the 1980s and early 1990s. Each paradigm, it has been argued, has a role to play in the practical accomplishment of small business research. Each can be part of the toolkit for tackling topics selected by researchers or suggested by sponsors. But, again, it has to be acknowledged that an eclectic position of this kind does not help produce coherence in small business research.

Similarly, the position adopted here in relation to post-modernist debates is that small business research needs to avoid getting bogged down in these disputes which seem, in their extreme versions, to deny the basic utility of research as a way of gaining an understanding of the phenomena we choose to study. While small business researchers should accept the necessity to be reflexive in relation to the methodological practices and strategies they adopt, this does not entail abandoning their commitment to 'telling it like it is'. The *raison d'etre* for research with all its attendant uncertainties, hard work and need for sustained commitment, is the age-old urge to learn about 'the world out there'. To cheat in that aim by ignoring epistemological and methodological problems is of course self-defeating, whatever the political or rhetorical objectives it might seek to serve. What the recent debates emphasize strongly is that the results of research will necessarily be different ways of 'telling it like it is', depending on the paradigm adopted. But this is nothing new really: all inquiry produces competing accounts.

In embracing the insights emerging from the above debates, the price exacted is an addition to the forces undermining coherence in small business research. It seems, therefore, that one result of these forces is that progress towards a single, consolidated small business research approach, equivalent to something like a discipline, is likely to be a chimera. One slightly comforting thought perhaps, is that other areas of inquiry whether discipline- or practice-based, are suffering the same disintegrating effects from one or more of the above forces. In other words, disciplinary and practice coherence may be less and less the norm anyway, whatever kind of inquiry in which researchers engage.

The Future of Small Business Research: Grounds for Optimism?

Whatever pessimism the above section induces can be set against some more positive prospects for the future of small business research in the UK. First, as Chapter One demonstrated, the economic importance of the small firm has grown considerably since the early 1970s. It is now responsible for a very substantial proportion of the gross national product and employment. Some might argue that this is a temporary blip in the longer historical decline in small-scale economic activities which will be reversed by increased concentration in the developing global economy. But there are plenty of reasons for supposing that the importance of the small enterprise will continue to grow (Blackburn, 1996; Curran, 1999). Even if this optimism were to prove somewhat over-optimistic, small business researchers are unlikely to run out of subjects.

Intellectual responses to the revival of small-scale enterprise from the mid-1970s onwards still lag behind the resulting changes in the economy. Like politicians, the social sciences generally and business and management research in particular (as well as business and management education) have found it difficult to adjust to the revival and new importance of small-scale economic activities.[4] Small businesses are still treated largely as marginal or peripheral to the mainstream economy in many disciplines and in much policy-making.[5] The processes of adjustment and catching up with these changes will include, *inter alia*, a need to have a more secure knowledge of the internal workings and role of the small firm in the economy. Some of this knowledge will come from mainstream social science disciplines and areas of professional practice, thus making small-scale enterprise more central to their activities, but much will need to come from those working in a mixed-disciplinary small business research. All this offers optimism for the future of small business research.

One problem in small business research has been its inability to attract able research recruits. For example, small business research, even more than business and management research generally, has had difficulties in attracting able research students. This may now be changing. Although there are no statistics on the numbers of research students whose topics are directly related to the small firm, there are indications of an increase. For example, the annual UK Small Firms Policy and Research Conference, held every year since 1977, introduced a one day, pre-conference doctoral workshop in 1997 for the first time. It attracted over 30 research students, most of whom were just starting out on their research. The workshop has continued in subsequent years. Research students are now also coming from older universities such as Cambridge rather than, as previously, mainly from the newer universities – another indicator of increased interest. This is exactly the kind of upsurge in young researcher interest that any area needs to assure the future and expansion of its work.

The last chapter discussed the publication of research on the small business. The argument was made that although there were now several established specialist journals (most of which, like the oldest in the UK, the *International Small Business Journal* (ISBJ), have emerged in parallel with the growth of small business research since 1980) their status was lower than the main disciplinary and top-rated business and management learned journals. But standards are rising and gaining acceptance is getting more difficult according to the Editor of the ISBJ.[6] More generally, articles with a small enterprise focus also now seem more common in other mainstream business and management journals as well. Again, all this points to a coming of age and a more secure future for small business research.

Being More Adventurous in Small Business Research

One aspect of early small business research was its conservatism in theorizing and research methodologies. In part, this paralleled the conservatism of much business and management research in the period generally. But it arguably also stemmed from the lack of confidence in a new area of research. Theorizing was often very second hand and research methods were largely based on the standard quantitative survey, usually in the form of the mail survey. This still continues, of course, with new researchers sometimes believing that all they have to do is to borrow from the latest fashionable thinking on large enterprises for their project on small firms, number crunch the results and write them up. This is now becoming less common as researchers realize that small firms are not large firms scaled down but distinct economic entities in their own right, requiring an approach which recognizes this distinction. Yet, as the examples of small business research used to illustrate the discussion in this book show, little of the influential research in the area has been highly innovative methodologically.

There are plenty of ways in which small business research could be more adventurous methodologically and in the selection of topics. For instance, like most business and management research, small business research has been very ahistorical. True, there have been exceptions such as research by Bechhofer et al. (1974) on small shopkeepers and Foreman-Peck (1985) examining the rise of small firms in the 1930s and relating it to the more recent revival, but these have been rare. The revitalization and expansion of the small business in the UK has now continued for over a generation. But how the experiences of the earliest owners and their employees compare with their more recent counterparts, has received little attention. Gauging how small firms in particular sectors have changed might be examined historically, for example, to offer insights on how small firms cope with change generally and how they play their roles in a changing economy.[7]

Although as previous chapters have shown, qualitative approaches in small business research are now well-established, there has been little use of some of the more difficult or innovative strategies such as discourse or narrative analysis.[8] Perhaps this reflects real difficulties in utilizing these approaches but, *a priori*, methodologies allowing investigation of the fine detail of relations in the small enterprise, appear to have considerable potential. What actually happens day-to-day, hour-by-hour in the small firm remains a considerable hole in our understanding of how it functions. Most of the data on management strategies and relations within the enterprise, for example, consists of *ex post facto* reporting by those involved, which is now widely accepted as subject to distortion for a wide variety of reasons.[9]

Women are involved in small-scale enterprise as owners, employees and as partners or family members of those who run and work in small enterprises. For example, there has been a good deal of research on women as owner–managers (see, for example, Goffee and Scase, 1985; Carter and Cannon, 1988) but little of this has been grounded in a feminist methodology (Olesen, 1994). There is, of course, a debate on the epistemological status of feminist research approaches (Gill and Johnson,

1997: 150) but one test for this approach is surely exploring the role of the female entrepreneur and, in turn, discovering how such an exploration helps in understanding the role of the *male* small business owner as well as how small business activities are embedded in social and community activities generally.

It is to be hoped that an expansion of theoretical and methodological inventiveness in small business research will occur over the next few years. The potential is clearly present and all it needs is a commitment to pushing the envelope of current approaches beyond its present limits. Researchers have, on the whole, shown more imagination in widening the range of topics investigated than the theoretical and methodological strategies by which they are investigated. But just as it is difficult to see any end to the questions which can be asked about the internal workings of the small firm and its articulation with the wider economy and society, it is equally difficult to see any inherent restrictions on the investigative strategies which might be employed.

Small Business Research and Policy-Making

Small business research has long been associated with policy-making. Indeed, the Bolton Report, which kindled much of the revival in the small business and small business research, was primarily policy-centred. Since then there has been a steady stream of published work linking policy and research (see, for example, Beesley and Wilson, 1981; Storey, 1981; Bannock and Albach, 1991; Storey, 1994; Blackburn et al., 1999; Curran et al., 1999; Hart and Gudgin, 1999; Kitching and Blackburn, 1999b; Curran, 2000). Much of this, however, has been commentary linking policy and research, discussing the effectiveness of the wide range of policies introduced since 1980. Some has concentrated more on evaluations of specific policies (see, for example, Gray and Stanworth, 1986; Harrison and Mason, 1986 and 1991; Hart et al., 1993; Bennett and Robson, 1999) with a substantial proportion being undertaken by consultants rather than academics (see, for example, Segal Quince Wickstead, 1988; Leslie Hays Consultants 1990; Graham Bannock & Partners, 1994; PA Cambridge Economic Consultants, 1995).

Despite the close association between policy-making and the expansion in research on small businesses, the relationship has not been entirely happy. One reason is that much of the policy has been ideologically or politically driven, that is, governments, Labour and Conservative, have had strong views on the role of the small firm (Goss, 1991: 8–14; DTI, 1998). Researchers tend to assess the results of policy against the ideological objectives declared by governments. Often their assessments have been critical, pointing out the shortfalls of the policies as measured against declared objectives (Curran, 1993; Storey, 1994: 263–301; Curran, 2000). One result of critical appraisals of these kinds was that the research has, on the whole, not been as well received or as influential on policy-making as it might have been.

Consultants' research has tended to be closer to policy in the sense that a good deal of their government-sponsored evaluations have often stressed the positive achievements in helping small business start-ups, growth and employment creation etc. Government has often used such consultancy reports selectively to suggest policies have been largely successful (see, for example, the Small Firms in Britain reports published between 1991 and 1996 by the Employment Department and the DTI). All this is, of course, what might be expected from governments who will naturally claim success in order to vindicate their policies and win voter support.

There will always be a gulf between the academic researcher seeking to advance knowledge on social and economic activities for its own sake and politicians in a democratic political system who have to operate in an essentially adversarial way to try to show the weaknesses of their opponents' ideas and the quality of their own promises and policies. All parties will try to use research and researchers for their own advantage. Researchers themselves have values and views which may make them more sympathetic to one party than to others, even though they remain committed to being as honest as they can be in conducting their research. Any idea of purely objective research, linked closely to rationally based, evidence-driven policy-making and implementation, is unlikely in any modern society.

However, there is a clear potential for small business research to have more influence on policy-making. If, as argued above, the importance of the small business in the UK economy is increasingly recognized, then there is also likely to be a clearer recognition for the need for more research to support effective policies and avoid the waste of public resources. Moreover, policy-makers may well become more sophisticated consumers of research, more aware of the possibilities offered by different approaches and of how to interpret the results.[10] Some of the increase, if it occurs, will no doubt come from the individual social science disciplines and more will be carried out by private sector consultants. But also more will hopefully come from dedicated specialists who have a strong background knowledge of previous research and have developed the skills and experience needed to overcome the formidable problems in researching the small business.

Challenges and Rewards

To paraphrase Dr Johnson, for the committed small business researcher, the person who is tired of small business research is tired of life. It is difficult to imagine ever running out of topics connected to the small business that are worth researching. Intellectually, the small business is a crossroads where almost every discipline and every issue can meet. It is almost possible to write 'the small business and . . .', filling the blank with virtually any word or phrase that comes to mind, and come up with a researchable issue. Few other areas of research can make such claims or such a promise. Moreover, small business research is, in a sense, an ever renewable resource. New topics emerge continually as illustrated in the range of topics now engaging small business researchers that did not exist 30 years ago. Small firms and information and communications technologies, small firms and the Single European Market, small firms and owner–manager stress, small firms and knowledge management and small firms and green issues, are just five examples of newer topics which have attracted small business researchers.

In this book, the focus has been on the special character and problems of small business research. All social, business and management research produces topics and research problems which are individual in the intellectual puzzles they pose and the kinds of research methods best suited to solving them. This book has concentrated on the methodological challenges in investigating the small business. It has also discussed some wider issues such as recent debates on epistemological issues, doing a research degree and carrying out research for non-academic sponsors as well as communicating research results to different audiences. All these have been discussed in relation to researching the small business and its role in the economy and all have been directed to the practical accomplishment of research.

The attractions of small business research are, of course, very similar to the attractions of research in the social sciences and business and management research generally. Posing problems, finding answers, adding to understanding how the world 'out there' functions, helping others solve practical problems and informing the wider debate on what kind of society and economy can be fashioned within the constraints of political and market forces, are the rewards of all kinds of research.

In addition to the above, however, small business research offers some less easily come by rewards. For instance, there are the opportunities to have close contacts with enterprises and people in ways in which many other areas cannot match. Much of social and business and management research involves little close contact with businesses and those who make them happen: the units of analysis ('human resources', 'corporate performance' etc.) are often people-less. The researcher will rarely or never meet or know the people who make up these abstractions. In other instances, the researcher's contacts are with fragments of what are large, even world-level organizations which it is difficult for an individual observer to envision as a whole. Small business research, in other words, is much more research on a human scale and research with a human face.

As this chapter has emphasized, it is not just the stream of small business research topics which is expanding but the ways in which small business research itself is conducted. Both are becoming more exciting and the challenge to the intellectual imagination on both counts, is almost limitless. The coming of age of small business research is evidenced by the increase in volume, the range of topics, the research strategies employed and the increasingly public profile of its subject matter. All increase the challenges for small business researchers just as they increase the rewards. Our hope is that this book helps meet those challenges and stimulates the seeking of those rewards.

Notes

1 There was also a small and very influential literature in the United States prior to 1971 (see, for example, McClelland, 1961; Collins et al., 1964; and Smith 1967). But even in the US, the main growth of small business research came after the early 1970s.

2 One heartening development was the establishment of a small business research centre at Cambridge University as part of the Economic and Social Research Council's large-scale Small Business Research Initiative which ran from 1989 to 1992. Following the end of the Initiative, the Council established a Centre for Business Research at Cambridge containing several of the key researchers involved in the Research Initiative. This fostering of small business research by one of the UK's most prestigious universities should help small business research more generally.

3 The wider debate and large literature on post-modernism and intellectual inquiry is well beyond the scope of this book but a summary of much of the literature, particularly in the way it applies to qualitative/ethnographic research, is provided by Marcus (1994) who also provides many references. See also Gill and Johnson (1997: 144–9).

4 True, politicians now seem acutely concerned with 'enterprise' and 'entre-preneurship' and especially the links between the latter and e-commerce. Equally, they often couple these with the small business but it remains doubtful whether their knowledge of these notions is really very deep. Rather they appear to serve ideological visions of some future economy which the real economy will only ever approximate to, if at all.

5 Despite the increase in policies designed to support the small firm since 1980 (see, for example, Storey 1994: Chapter 8 *passim*; DTI, 1998) a closer inspection suggests that much of it centres on encouraging more 'enterprise' rather than on recognizing the real importance of the small business. In the UK the relatively low status of the Minister responsible for small business affairs (who is also responsible for a number of non-small business activities) is another indicator.

6 The authors have been active members of the editorial team of the ISBJ for several years and their experience agrees with the assessment of the Editor on the rising standards.

7 An interesting and innovative approach is demonstrated in Guedalla et al. (1997). This used the idea of the street saturation survey to track the history and changes of 116 offices and shops trading in Marylebone High Street in central London. The study started in 1994 but the authors use historical

sources to trace the history of the street since the early 1800s to provide a context for their ongoing study of businesses in the street. The results discuss issues as diverse as the status of family businesses, employee recruitment strategies, the use of information technology and, of course, business survival.

8 In previous chapters, the research of Downing (1997) and Lightfoot (1998) was cited as examples of how innovative approaches can be used. Downing, for instance, tries to show how owner–managers 'talk' their relations with others and how this helps build the 'social architecture' of enterprises.

9 'Distortion' here should not be inferred to mean that respondents deliberately do not tell the truth as they understand it but to stress that, for a wide variety of reasons, people offer different accounts of their relations with others or particular incidents due to memory lapses, the understandable wish to be seen in a favourable light and gaps in their knowledge due to no fault on their part. More fundamentally, all accounts are accounts, that is, as previous chapters have reiterated, there are fundamental epistemological objections to the notion that there is one 'true' account of what happened in any social encounter or situation.

10 As remarked earlier, up until relatively recently, policy-makers have been wedded closely to the quantitative–positivist paradigm believing that 'real' knowledge can only be expressed numerically in models based on nineteenth century natural science approaches but there are now indications (shown, for instance, in the increasing use of qualitative approaches such as focus groups) that other research paradigms and strategies may come to be recognized as having value in policy formation and evaluation.

References

Ackroyd, S. and Hughes, J. (1992) *Data Collection in Context*. London: Longman, second edition.

Acton Society Trust (1953) *Size and Morale: a Preliminary Study of Attendance at Work in Large and Small Units*. London: Acton Society Trust.

Acton Society Trust (1956) *Size and Morale Part II: a Further Study of Attendance at Work in Large and Small Units*. London: Acton Society Trust.

Advisory Council on Science and Technology (1990) *The Enterprise Challenge: Overcoming Barriers to Growth in Small Firms*. London: HMSO.

Altheide, D. and Johnson, J.M. (1994) 'Criteria for Assessing Interpretative Validity in Qualitative Research', in N.K. Denzin and Y.S. Lincoln (eds), *Handbook of Qualitative Research*. Thousand Oaks, CA: Sage.

Athayde, R. and Blackburn, R.A. (1999) 'Learning to Use the Internet: SME and Business Centre Experiences', paper presented to the National Small Firms Policy and Research Conference, Leeds, November.

Atkinson, J. (1984) 'Jobs for the Few', *The Economist*, September 29: 79.

Atkinson, J. and Meager, N. (1994) 'Running to Stand Still: the Small Business in the Labour Market', in J. Atkinson and D.J. Storey (eds), *Employment, the Small Firm and the Labour Market*. London: Routledge.

Bank of England (1999) *Quarterly Report on Small Business Statistics*, July, London.

Bannock, G. and Albach, H. (1991) *Small Business Policy in Europe, Britain, Germany and the European Commission*. London: Anglo-German Foundation.

Barad, M. (1996) 'Total Quality Management', in M. Warner (ed.), *International Encyclopaedia of Business and Management*. London: Routledge and International Thomson Publishing.

Barkham, R., Gudgin, G., Hart, M. and Hanvey, E. (1996) *The Determinants of Small Business Growth, An Inter-Regional Study in the United Kingdom 1986–90*. London: Jessica Kingsley and the Regional Studies Association.

Batstone, E.V. (1969) *Aspects of Stratification in a Community Context: a Study of Class Attitudes and the 'Size Effect'*. PhD thesis, University of Wales.

Bechhofer, F. and Elliott, B. (eds) (1981) *The Petite Bourgeoisie: Comparative Studies in the Uneasy Stratum*. London: The Macmillan Press.

Bechhofer, F., Elliott, B., Rushworth, M. and Bland, R. (1974) 'The Petits Bourgeois in the Class Structure: the Case of the Small Shopkeepers', in F. Parkin (ed.), *Social Analysis of Class Structure*. London: Tavistock.

Beesley, M. and Wilson, P. (1981) 'Government Aid to Small Firms in Britain', in

P. Gorb, P. Dowell and P. Wilson (eds), *Small Business Perspectives*. London: Armstrong Publishing Company and the London Business School.

Bennett, R. and Robson, P. (1999) 'Business Link: Use, Satisfaction and Comparison with Business Shop and Business Connect', *Policy Studies*, 20 (2): 107–31.

Birch, D. (1979) *The Job Generation Process*. Cambridge, MA: MIT Programme on Neighbourhood and Regional Change.

Blackburn, R.A. (1996) *The Future of the Small Firm in the UK Economy*. The Third Midland Bank Small Business Lecture, Kingston Upon Thames, Kingston University, July.

Blackburn, R.A., Berney, R. and Kuusisto, J. (1999) *A Critical Evaluation of Industry SME Support Policies in the United Kingdom and the Republic of Ireland, Stage Two Report an In-Depth Delphi Study of Selected SME Support Policies and their Evaluation*. Helsinki, Ministry of Trade and Industry, Finland, Studies and Reports, 6/1999.

Blackburn, R.A., Curran, J., Woods, A. and Associates (1990) *Exploring Enterprise Cultures: Small Service Sector Enterprise Owners and Their Views*. Kingston upon Thames, Small Business Research Centre, Kingston University.

Blackburn, R. and Stokes, D. (in press) 'Breaking Down the Barriers: Using Focus Groups to Research Small and Medium-Sized Enterprises', *International Small Business Journal*.

Bolton Report, The (1971) *Report of the Committee of Inquiry on Small Firms*, Cmnd, 4811, London: HMSO.

Boswell, J. (1973) *The Rise and Decline of Small Firms*. London: Allen and Unwin.

British Chambers of Commerce (1999) *National Minimum Wage Survey, October 1999*. London: British Chambers of Commerce.

Bryman, A. and Burgess, R.G. (1994) 'Reflections on Qualitative Data Analysis', in A. Bryman and R.G. Burgess (eds), *Analyzing Qualitative Data*. London: Routledge.

Bryman, A. and Cramer, D. (1990) *Quantitative Data Analysis for Social Scientists*. London: Routledge.

Burgess, R.G. (1984) *In the Field: an Introduction to Field Research*. London: Allen and Unwin.

Burrows, R. (ed.) (1991a) *Deciphering the Enterprise Culture, Entrepreneurship, Petty Capitalism and the Restructuring of Britain*. London: Routledge.

Burrows, R. (1991b) 'A Socio-Economic Anatomy of the British Petty Bourgeoisie: a Multivariate Analysis', in R. Burrows (ed.), *Deciphering the Enterprise Culture, Entrepreneurship, Petty Capitalism and the Restructuring of Britain*. London: Routledge.

Burrows, R. and Curran, J. (1989) 'Sociological Research on Service Sector Small Businesses: Some Conceptual Considerations', *Work, Employment and Society*, 3 (4): 527–39.

Burrows, R. and Curran, J. (1991) 'Not Such a Small Business: Reflections on the Rhetoric, the Reality and the Future of the Enterprise Culture', in M. Cross and G. Payne (eds), *Work and the Enterprise Culture*. London: The Falmer Press.

Burrows, R. and Ford, J. (1998) 'Self-Employment and Home Ownership After the Enterprise Culture', *Work, Employment and Society*, 12 (1): 97–119.

Business Link Directorate (1999) *Creating the SBS Gateway and Associated Portfolio of Services*. London: Department of Trade and Industry.

Carter, S. and Cannon, T. (1988) *Female Entrepreneurs: a Study of Female Business*

Owners, Their Motivations, Experiences and Strategies for Success. Research Paper No. 65, London: Department of Employment.

Chell, E., Haworth, J. and Brearley, S. (1991) *The Entrepreneurial Personality: Concepts, Cases and Categories*. London: Routledge.

Chittenden, F., Masooda Mukhtar, S. and Poutziouris, P. (1996) 'BS 5750 and Quality Management in SMEs', in R. Blackburn and P. Jennings (eds), *Small Firms: Contributions to Economic Regeneration*. London: Paul Chapman.

Collins, O.F., Moore, D.G. with Unwalla, D.B. (1964) *The Enterprising Man*. East Lansing: Michigan State University Press.

Cosh, A. and Hughes, A. (1998) *Enterprise Britain: Growth, Innovations and Public Policy in the Small and Medium-Sized Sector 1994–1997*. Cambridge: ESRC Centre for Business Research, Cambridge University.

Cramer, D. (1994) *Introducing Statistics for Social Research*. London: Routledge.

Curran, J. (1990) 'Rethinking Economic Structure: Exploring the Role of the Small Firm and Self-Employment in the British Economy', *Work, Employment and Society*, Special Issue, May: 125–46.

Curran, J. (1991) 'Employment and Employment Relations in the Small Enterprise', in J. Stanworth and C. Gray (eds), *Bolton 20 Years On: The Small Firm in the 1990s*. London: Paul Chapman.

Curran, J. (1993) *TECs and Small Firms: Can TECs Reach the Small Firms Other Strategies Have Failed to Reach?* Paper presented to the All Party Social Science and Policy Group, House of Commons, April. Available from the Small Business Research Centre, Kingston University.

Curran, J. (1997) 'Small Business Strategy', in M. Warner (ed.), *The Concise International Encyclopaedia of Business and Management*. London: International Thomson Business Press.

Curran, J. (1999) *The Role of the Small Firm in the UK Economy: Hot Stereotypes and Cool Assessments*. Milton Keynes, Small Business Research Trust: Open University, May.

Curran, J. (2000) 'What is Small Business Policy in the UK for? Evaluation and Assessing Small Business Policies', *International Small Business Journal*, 18 (3): 36–50.

Curran, J., Berney, R. and Kuusisto, J. (1999) *A Critical Evaluation of Industry SME Support Policies in the United Kingdom and the Republic of Ireland Stage One Report, Introduction to SME Policies and Their Evaluation*. Helsinki, Ministry of Trade and Industry, Finland, Studies and Reports, 5/1999.

Curran, J. and Blackburn R.A. with Associates (1992) 'Exploring Enterprise Cultures; Small Service Sector Enterprise Owners and Their Views', in M. Robertson, E. Chell and C. Mason (eds), *Towards the Twenty First Century, the Challenge for Small Businesses*. Macclesfield and London: Nadamal Books and Paul Chapman.

Curran, J. and Blackburn, R.A. (1993) *Ethnic Enterprise and the High Street Bank: A Survey of Ethnic Businesses in Two Localities*. Kingston upon Thames: Small Business Research Centre, Kingston University.

Curran, J. and Blackburn, R.A. (1994) *Small Firms and Local Economic Networks: The Death of the Local Economy?* London: Paul Chapman.

Curran, J., Blackburn, R.A. and Klett-Davies, M. (1994) *Soft Loan Schemes and the Finance Gap: An Evaluation Study*. Kingston upon Thames, Small Business Research Centre: Kingston University, August.

Curran, J., Blackburn, R.A. and Woods, A. (1991) *Profiles of the Small Enterprise in the Service Sector*. Kingston upon Thames, Small Business Research Centre: Kingston University.

Curran, J. and Burrows, R. (1988) *Enterprise Britain: a National Profile of Small Business Owners and the Self-Employed*. London and Milton Keynes: The Small Business Research Trust and the Open University.

Curran, J. and Burrows, R. (1989) 'National Profiles of the Self-Employed', *Employment Gazette*, 97 (7): 376–85.

Curran, J., Jarvis, R., Blackburn, R.A. and Black, S. (1993a) 'Networks and Small Firms: Constructs, Methodological Strategies and Some Findings', *International Small Business Journal*, 11 (2): 13–25.

Curran, J., Kitching, J., Abbott, B. and Mills, V. (1993b) *Employment and Employment Relations in the Small Service Sector Enterprise – A Report*. Kingston upon Thames, ESRC Centre for Research on the Small Service Sector Enterprises: Kingston University, February.

Curran, J. and Stanworth, J. (1979) 'Self-Selection and the Small Firm Worker – A Critique and an Alternative View', *Sociology*, 13 (3): 427–44.

Curran, J. and Stanworth, J. (1981a) 'A New Look at Job Satisfaction in the Small Firm', *Human Relations*, 34 (5): 343–66.

Curran, J. and Stanworth, J. (1981b) 'Size of Workplace and Attitudes to Industrial Relations in the Printing and Electronics Industries', *British Journal of Industrial Relations*, XIX (1): 14–25.

Curran, J. and Stanworth, J. (1986) 'Small Firms, Large Firms: Theoretical and Research Strategies for the Comparative Analysis of Small and Large Firms', in M. Scott, A. Gibb, J. Lewis and T. Faulkner (eds), *Small Firms: Growth and Development*. Aldershot: Gower.

Curran, J. and Storey, D. (eds) (1994) *Small Firms in Urban and Rural Locations*. London: Routledge.

Curran, J., Woods, A. and Blackburn R.A. (1995) 'A Longitudinal Study of Small Enterprises in the Service Sector', in F. Chittenden, M. Robertson and I. Marshall (eds), *Small Firms, Partnerships for Growth*. London: Paul Chapman.

Curran, J., Blackburn, R.A., Kitching, J. and North, J. (1996) *Establishing Small Firms' Training Practices, Needs, Difficulties and Use of Industry Training Organisations*. London: DfEE Research Studies RS17, HMSO.

Daly, M., Campbell, M., Robson, G. and Gallagher, C. (1991) 'Job Creation 1987–9: The Contribution of Small and Large Firms', *Employment Gazette*, November: 589–96.

Deakins, D. and Hussain G. (1994) *Risk Assessment by Bank Managers*. Birmingham: The Business School, Birmingham Polytechnic/University of Central England.

Denzin, N. (1970) *The Research Act in Sociology, A Theoretical Introduction to Sociological Methods*. London: Butterworths.

Dewhurst, J. and Burns, P. (1993) *Small Business Management*. London: Macmillan, third edition.

Dey, I. (1993) *Qualitative Data Analysis, A User-Friendly Guide for Social Scientists*. London: Routledge.

DfEE (1997) *Labour Market and Skill Trends 1997–1998*. Nottingham: Skills and Enterprise Network, Department for Education and Employment.

DfEE (1998) *Labour Market and Skill Trends 1998/1999*. Sudbury, Suffolk: DfEE Publications.

DfEE (1999) *Evaluation of the Iip Small Firm Development Projects*. Nottingham: DfEE Research Report, RR135.

Department of Employment (1989) *Small Firms in Britain*. London: Department of Employment.

DTI (1996) *Small Firms in Britain Report 1996*. London: Department of Trade and Industry.

DTI (1998) *Our Competitive Future Building the Knowledge Driven Economy*. London: HMSO, Cm 4176.

DTI (1999a) *Small and Medium-Sized Enterprise (SME) Statistics for the United Kingdom, 1998*. Sheffield: Small Firms Statistics Unit, Department of Trade and Industry, August.

DTI (1999b) *The Small Business Service: a Public Consultation*. London: Department of Trade and Industry, June.

Downing, S. (1997) 'A Narrative Analysis of Managerial and Business Performance: New Concepts to Examine Entrepreneurship', paper presented to the 20th National Small Firms Policy and Research Conference, Belfast, November.

Downing, S. (1998) 'Relationship Interaction Skills of Entrepreneurs and Business Advisers', paper presented to the 21st National Small Firms Policy and Research Conference, Durham, November.

Drucker, J. and Macallan, H. (1996) *Work Status and Self-Employment in the British Construction Industry*. Milton Keynes: Small Business Research Trust/the Open University.

Drucker, P.F. (1964) *Managing for Results: Economic Tasks and Risk Taking Decisions*. Oxford: Heinemann.

Drucker, P.F. (1970) 'Entrepreneurship in Business Enterprise', *Journal of Business Enterprise*, 1 (1): 3–13.

Drucker, P.F. (1985) *Innovation and Entrepreneurship: Practices and Principles*. Oxford: Butterworth Heinemann.

During, W. and Oakey, R. (1998) *New Technology Based Firms in the 1990s Vol. IV*. London: Sage.

Fletcher, M. (1996) 'How Bank Managers Make Lending Decisions to Small Firms', in R.A. Blackburn and P. Jennings (eds), *Small Firms' Contributions to Economic Generation*. London: Paul Chapman.

Fontana, A. and Frey, J.H. (1994) 'Interviewing, the Art of Science', in N.K. Denzin and Y.S. Lincoln (eds), *Handbook of Qualitative Research*. Thousand Oaks, CA: Sage.

Ford, J., Kiel, T., Bryman, A. and Beardsworth, A. (1984) 'Internal Labour Market Processes', *Industrial Relations Journal*, 13 (3): 257–77.

Foreman-Peck, J. (1985) 'Seedcorn of Chaff: New Firm Formation and the Performance of the Interwar Economy', *Economic History Review*, XXXVIII, 402–22.

Freedman, J. and Godwin, M. (1994) 'Incorporating the Micro-Business: Perceptions and Misperceptions', in A. Hughes and D. Storey (eds), *Finance and the Small Firm*. London: Routledge.

Freund, J., Williams, F.J. and Perles, B.M. (1993) *Elementary Business Statistics, the Modern Approach*. Englewood Cliffs, NJ: Prentice-Hall, sixth edition.

Gavron, R., Cowling, M., Holtham, G. and Westall, A. (1998) *The Entrepreneurial Society*. London: Institute for Public Policy Research.

Gibb, A. (1998) 'Academic Research and the Growth of Ignorance SME Policy:

Mythical Concepts, Myths, Assumptions, Rituals and Confusions', paper presented to the National Small Firms Policy and Research Conference, Durham, November.

Gill, J. (1985) *Factors Affecting the Survival and Growth of the Smaller Company*. Aldershot: Gower.

Gill, J. and Johnson, P. (1997) *Research Methods for Managers*. London: Paul Chapman, second edition.

Glaser, B.G. (1978) *Theoretical Sensitivity*. San Francisco: The Sociology Press.

Glaser, B.G. and Strauss, A.L. (1965) *Awareness of Dying*. Chicago: Aldine.

Glaser, B.G. and Strauss, A.L. (1967) *The Discovery of Grounded Theory, Strategies for Qualitative Research*. London: Weidenfeld and Nicolson.

Glesne, C. and Pershkin, A. (1992) *Becoming Qualitative Researchers, An Introduction*. White Plains, New York: Longman.

Goffee, R. and Scase, R. (1985) *Women in Charge: the Experiences of Female Entrepreneurs*. London: Allen and Unwin.

Goffee, R. and Scase, R. (1995) *Corporate Realities: the Dynamics of Large and Small Organisations*. London: Routledge.

Goss, D. (1986) *Social Structure of the Small Firm*. PhD thesis, University of Kent.

Goss, D. (1991) *Small Business and Society*. London: Routledge.

Goss, D. (1994) *Principles of Human Resource Management*. London: Routledge.

Graham Bannock & Partners (1994) *The Future of Small Business Banking: a Report*. London: Graham Bannock & Partners and the National Westminster Bank, February.

Gray, C. (1998) *Enterprise and Culture*. London: Routledge.

Gray, C. and Stanworth, J. (1986) *Allowing for Enterprise: A Qualitative Assessment of the Enterprise Allowance Scheme*. London: Small Business Research Trust.

Guedalla, M., Iles, J., Stanworth, J. and Dykes, J. (1997) 'A Longitudinal Saturation Study of Marylebone High Street London: A Preliminary Report', paper presented to the 20th National Small Firms Policy and Research Conference, Belfast, November.

Hakim, C. (1987) *Research Design, Strategies and Choices in the Design of Social Research*. London: Allen and Unwin.

Hammersley, M. (1990) *Reading Ethnographic Research: A Critical Guide*. London: Longman.

Hammersley, M. and Atkinson, P. (1983) *Ethnography, Principles in Practice*. London: Tavistock Publications.

Handy, C. (1992) *Understanding Organizations*. London, Penguin Books.

Handy, C. (1995) *The Empty Raincoat*. London: Arrow.

Harding, P. and Jenkins, R. (1989) *The Myth of the Hidden Economy*. Milton Keynes: The Open University Press.

Harding, T. (1998) *The Normative Value Orientations of Collaborative Entrepreneurs*. Unpublished PhD thesis, University of Cambridge.

Harrison, B. (1994) *Lean and Mean: the Changing Landscape of Corporate Power in the Age of Flexibility*. New York: Basic Books.

Harrison, R. and Mason, C. (1986) 'The Regional Impact of the Small Firms Guarantee Scheme in the United Kingdom', *Regional Studies*, 20: 535–50.

Harrison, R. and Mason, C. (1991) 'Regional Variations in the Take-Up and Impact of Small Firms Policy in the United Kingdom: Analysis and Future Prospects', in R.T. Harrison and M. Hart (eds), *Spatial Policy in a Divided Nation*. London: Jessica Kingsley.

Hart, M. and Gudgin, G. (1999) 'Small Firm Growth and Public Policy in Northern Ireland', *Environment and Planning C: Government and Policy*, 17: 511–25.

Hart, M., Harrison, R.T. and Gallagher, C. (1993) 'Enterprise Creation, Job Generation and Regional Policy in the UK', in R.T. Harrison and M. Hart (eds), *Spatial Policy in a Divided Nation*. London: Jessica Kingsley.

Holliday, R. (1993) *Small Firms and the Organization of Production*. PhD thesis, Staffordshire University.

Holliday, R. (1995) *Investigating Small Firms, Nice Work?* London: Routledge.

Holliday, R. and Letherby, G. (1993) 'Happy Families or Poor Relations? An Exploration of Familial Analogies in the Small Firm', *International Small Business Journal*, 11 (2): 54–63.

Howard, K. and Sharp, J.A. (1983) *The Management of a Student Project*. Aldershot: Gower.

Huberman, A.M. and Miles, M.B. (1994) 'Data Management and Analytic Methods', in N.K. Denzin and Y.S. Lincoln (eds), *Handbook of Qualitative Research*. Thousand Oaks, CA: Sage.

Hughes, J. (1992) *The Philosophy of Social Research*. London: Longman, second edition.

Hussey, J. and Hussey, R. (1997) *Business Research, A Practical Guide for Undergraduate and Postgraduate Students*. Basingstoke: Macmillan Business.

Ingham, G.K. (1968) *Organizational Size, Orientation to Work and Industrial Behaviour*. PhD thesis, University of Cambridge.

Ingham, G.K. (1970) *Size of Industrial Organization and Worker Behaviour*. Cambridge: Cambridge University Press.

Institute of Directors (1996) *Your Business Matters Report of the Regional Conferences*. London: Institute of Directors, March

Jankowicz, A.D. (1995) *Business Research Projects*. London: Chapman and Hall, second edition.

Jarvis, R. (1996) *Users and Uses of Unlisted Companies' Financial Statements: a Literature Review*. London: The Institute of Chartered Accountants in England and Wales.

Jarvis, R., Kitching, J., Curran, J. and Lightfoot, G. (1996) *The Financial Management Practices of Small Firms: an Alternative Perspective*. London: ACCA and the Certified Accountants Educational Trust.

Keasey, K. and Watson, R. (1993) *Small Firm Management, Ownership, Finance and Performance*. Oxford: Blackwell.

Keeble, D., Bryson, J. and Wood, P. (1992) 'Entrepreneurship and Flexibility in Business Services: The Rise of Small Management Consultancy and Market Research Firms in the United Kingdom', in K. Caley, E. Chell, F. Chittenden and C. Mason (eds), *Small Enterprise Development: Policy and Practice in Action*. London: Paul Chapman.

Keeble, D., Tyler, P., Broom, G. and Lewis, J. (1992) *Business Success in the Countryside: the Performance of Rural Enterprise*. London: Department of the Environment/HMSO.

Kidder, L.H. and Judd, C.M. (1986) *Research Methods in Social Relations*. London: Holt, Rinehart and Winston, eighth edition.

Kitching, J. (1997) *Labour Regulation in the Small Service Sector Enterprise*. PhD thesis, Kingston University.

Kitching, J. and Blackburn, R. (1999a) 'Intellectual Property Management in the

Small and Medium Enterprise (SME)', *Journal of Small Business Management and Enterprise Development*, 5 (4): 327–35.

Kitching, J. and Blackburn, R. (1999b) 'Management Training and Networking in Small and Medium-Sized Enterprises in Three European Regions: Implications for Business Support', *Environment and Planning C: Government and Policy*, 17: 621–35.

Kosmin, B. (1981) 'Exclusion and Opportunity: Traditions of Work Amongst British Jews', in P. Braham, E. Rhodes and M. Pearn (eds), *Discrimination and Disadvantage in Employment: the Experience of Black Workers*. London: Harper and Row and the Open University Press.

Leach, P. (1994) *The Stoy Hayward Guide to the Family Business*. London: Kogan Page, second edition.

Leslie Hays Consultants (1990) *Evaluation of Regional Enterprise Grants*. London: HMSO.

Lightfoot, G. (1998) *Financial Management and Small Firm Owner-Managers*. PhD thesis, Kingston upon Thames.

London Business School (1983) *Small Business Bibliography*. London: London Business School, second edition.

London Business School (1983) *The London Business School Small Business Bibliography 1983/84 Update*. London: London Business School Library.

London Business School (1990) *London Business School Small Business Bibliography 1989*. London: London Business School Library.

McClelland, D.C. (1961) *The Achieving Society*. New York: Van Nostrand.

McGregor, A. and Fletcher, R. (1993) 'Generating Enterprise and Employment in Disadvantaged Urban Areas', in J. Atkinson and D.J. Storey (eds), *Employment in the Small Firm and the Labour Market*. London: Routledge.

McLennan, E. (1986) 'Women and Employment Legislation in Small Firms', in T. Faulkner (ed.), *Readings in Small Business*. Aldershot: Gower.

Marcus, G.E. (1994) 'What Comes (Just) After "Post"? The Case of Ethnography', in N. Denzin and Y.S. Lincoln (eds), *Handbook of Qualitative Research*. Thousand Oaks, CA: Sage.

Mars, G. and Nicod, M. (1984) *The World of Waiters*. London: Allen and Unwin.

Mason, D. (1988) 'Gissa a Project', *Times Higher Education Supplement*, 18 March.

Meager, N. (1991) *Self-Employment in the United Kingdom*. Report 205, Sussex, Institute of Manpower Studies, University of Sussex, May.

Meager, N., Kaiser, M. and Dietrich, H. (1992) *Self-Employment in the United Kingdom and Germany*. London: Anglo-German Foundation.

Mueller, D.C. (1972) 'A Life Cycle Theory of the Firm', *Journal of Industrial Economics*, XX (2): 109–219.

Miles, M.B. and Huberman, A.M. (1994) *Qualitative Data Analysis: a New Sourcebook of Methods*. Newbury Park, CA: Sage.

North, J., Curran, J. and Blackburn, R.A. (1995) 'Small Firms and BS 5750: A Preliminary Investigation', in F. Chittenden, M. Robertson and I. Marshall (eds), *Small Firms, Partnerships for Growth*. London: Paul Chapman.

North, J., Curran, J. and Blackburn, R.A. (1998) *The Quality Business*. London: Routledge.

Oakey, R. (1991) 'Government Policy Towards High Technology: Small Firms Beyond Year 2000', in J. Curran and R.A. Blackburn (eds), *Paths of Enterprise, The Future of the Small Business*. London: Routledge.

Oakey, R. (1994) *New Technology Based Firms in the 1990s*. London: Paul Chapman/Sage.

Oakey, R. (1996) *New Technology Based Firms in the 1990s, Vol II*. London: Paul Chapman/Sage.

Oakey, R. and During, W. (1998) *New Technology Based Firms in the 1990s, Vol V*. London: Sage.

Oakey, R., Faulkner, W., Cooper, S. and Walsh, V. (1990) *New Firms in the Biotechnology Industry: their Contribution to Innovation and Growth*. London: Pinter.

Oakey, R. and Mukhtar, S. (1997) *New Technology Based Firms in the 1990s, Vol III*. London: Sage.

O'Farrell, P.N. and Hitchens, D.M.W.N. (1988) 'The Relative Competitiveness and Performance of Small Manufacturing Companies in Scotland and the Mid-West of Ireland', *Regional Studies*, 22 (5): 399–416.

O'Farrell, P.N. and Hitchens, D.M.W.N. (1989) 'The Competitiveness and Performance of Small Manufacturing Firms: An Analysis of Matched Pairs in Scotland and England', *Environment and Planning A*, 21: 1241–63.

Olesen, V. (1994) 'Feminisms and Models of Qualitative Research', in N. Denzin and Y.S. Lincoln (eds), *Handbook of Qualitative Research*. Thousand Oaks, CA: Sage.

Oppenheim, A.N. (1966) *Questionnaire Design and Attitude Measurement*. London: Heinemann.

PA Cambridge Economic Consultants (1995) *Evaluation of DTI-Funded TEC Services in Support of Small and Medium-Sized Businesses*. London: HMSO.

Penrose, E.T. (1959) *The Theory of the Growth of the Firm*. Oxford: Blackwell.

Phillips, E.M. and Pugh, D.S. (1987) *How to Get a PhD*. Milton Keynes: Open University Press.

Popper, K. (1972) *Objective Knowledge*. London: Oxford University Press.

Porter, M. (1985) *Competitive Advantage: Creating and Sustaining Superior Performance*. New York: The Free Press.

Pratt, A. (1990) 'Enterprise Culture: Rhetoric and Reality – The Case of "Small Firms" and "Rural" Localities', in P. Lowe (ed.), *Petit Capitalism in Rural Areas: East-West Perspectives*. London: David Fulton.

QSR NUDIST4 (2000) *QSR NUDIST Software for Qualitative Data Analysis*.

Rainnie, A. (1989) *Industrial Relations in Small Firms: Small Isn't Beautiful*. London: Routledge.

Ram, M. and Holliday, R. (1993) '"Keeping it in the Family": Small Firms and Familial Culture', in F. Chittenden, M. Robertson and I. Marshall (eds), *Small Firms, Recession and Recovery*. London: Paul Chapman.

Rees, H. and Shah, A. (1993) 'The Characteristics of the Self Employed: The Supply of Labour', in A. Atkinson and D.J. Storey (eds), *Employment, the Small Firm and the Labour Market*. London: Routledge.

Reid, G.C., Jacobsen, L.R. and Anderson, M. (1993) *Profiles in Small Business: a Competitive Strategy Approach*. London: Routledge.

Reynolds, P.D. and White, S. (1997) *The Entrepreneurial Process: Economic Growth, Men, Women and Minorities*. Westport, CT: Quorum Books.

Revans, R.W. (1956) 'Industrial Morale and Size of Unit', *Political Quarterly*, 27 (3): 303–10.

Richards, L. and Richards, T. (1994) 'Using Computers in Qualitative Research', in N. Denzin and Y.S. Lincoln (eds), *Handbook of Qualitative Research*. Thousand Oaks, CA: Sage.

Richardson, L. (1994) 'Writing, A Method of Inquiry', in N. Denzin and Y.S. Lincoln (eds), *Handbook of Qualitative Research*. Thousand Oaks, CA: Sage.

Ritchie, J. (1991) 'Enterprise Cultures: A Frame Analysis', in R. Burrows (ed.), *Deciphering the Enterprise Culture, Petty Capitalism and the Restructuring of Britain*. London: Routledge.

Robson, P., Dex, S. and Wilkinson, F. (1997) *The Wage Costs of a National Statutory Minimum Wage in Britain*. Cambridge: ESRC Centre for Business Research, Cambridge University.

Roper, S., Hewitt-Dundas, N. and McFerran, B. (1997) 'Disparities in Quality Perceptions Between Small Firms and Their Customers', *International Small Business Journal*, 15 (4): 64–79.

Rudestam, K.E. and Newton, R.R. (1992) *Surviving Your Dissertation: a Comprehensive Guide to Content and Process*. London: Sage.

SBRT (1998a) *A Register of Small Business Researchers*. Small Business Research Trust, Milton Keynes: Open University Business School.

SBRT (1998b) *The SME Research Database*. Small Business Research Trust, Milton Keynes: Open University Business School.

SBRT (1999) *NatWest SBRT Quarterly Survey of Small Business in Britain*. Small Business Research Trust, Milton Keynes: Open University Business School, 15, 4, December.

Sayer, A. (1992) *Method in Social Science: a Realist Approach*. London: Routledge, second edition.

Scase, R. and Goffee, R. (1980) *The Real World of the Small Business Owner*. London: Croom Helm.

Scase, R. and Goffee, R. (1982) *The Entrepreneurial Middle Class*. London: Croom Helm.

Scott, M., Roberts, I., Holroyd, G. and Sawbridge, G. (1989) *Management and Industrial Relations in Small Firms*. Research Paper No. 70, London: Department of Employment.

Scott, M. and Rosa, P. (1996) 'Has Firm Level Analysis Reached its Limits? Time to Rethink', *International Small Business Journal*, 14 (4): 81–9.

Scott, M. and Rosa, P. (1997) 'New Businesses for Old: The Role of the Portfolio Entrepreneurs in the Start-Up and Growth of Small Businesses', in M. Ram, D. Deakins and D. Smallbone (eds), *Small Firms Enterprising Futures*. London: Paul Chapman/Sage.

Segal Quince Wickstead (1988) *Encouraging Small Business Start-Up and Growth: Creating a Supportive Environment*. London: HMSO.

Small Business Research Centre (1992) *The State of British Enterprise, Growth, Innovation and Competitive Advantage in Small and Medium Sized Firms*. Cambridge: University of Cambridge.

Smallbone, D., North, D. and Leigh, R. (1993) 'The Growth and Survival of Mature Manufacturing SMEs in the 1980s: an Urban-Rural Comparison', in J. Curran and D. Storey (eds), *Small Firms in Urban and Rural Locations*. London: Routledge.

Smith, N.R. (1967) *The Entrepreneur and His Firm: the Relationship Between Type of Man and Type of Company*. East Lansing: Michigan State University.

Spence, L.J. (2000) *Priorities, Practice and Ethics in Small Firms*. London: Institute of Business Ethics.

Stake, R.E. (1995) *The Art of Case Study Research*. Thousand Oaks, CA: Sage.

Stanworth, M.J.K. and Curran, J. (1976) 'Growth and the Small Firm – An Alternative View', *Journal of Management Studies*, 13 (2): 95–110.

Stanworth, M.J.K. and Curran, J. (1973) *Management Motivation and the Smaller Business*. Aldershot: Gower.

Stanworth, J. and Curran, J. (1999) 'Colas, Burger, Shakes, and Shirkers: Towards a Sociological Model of Franchising in the Market Economy', *Journal of Business Venturing*, 14 (4): 323–44.

Stanworth, J. and Gray, C. (eds) (1991) *Bolton 20 Years On: The Small Firm in the 1990s*. London: Paul Chapman.

Storey, D.J. (1981) 'Small Firms and the Regional Problem', in P. Gorb, P. Dowell and P. Wilson (eds), *Small Business Perspectives*. London: Armstrong Publishing Company and the London Business School.

Storey, D.J. (1994) *Understanding the Small Business Sector*. London: Routledge.

Storey, D.J., Keasey, K., Watson, R. and Wynarczyk, P. (1987) *The Performance of Small Firms, Profits, Jobs and Failures*. London: Croom Helm.

Storey, D.J. and Westhead, P. (1994) *Management Training and Small Firm Performance: a Critical Review*. Warwick, Working Paper No. 18: Centre for Small and Medium-Sized Enterprises, Warwick University.

Strauss, A.L. (1987) *Qualitative Analysis for Social Scientists*. Cambridge: Cambridge University Press.

Strauss, A.L. and Corbin, J. (1998) *Basics of Qualitative Research: Techniques and Procedures for Developing Grounded Theory*. Newbury Park, CA: Sage, second edition.

Vogt, P.W. (1999) *A Dictionary of Statistics and Methodology, A Nontechnical Guide for the Social Scientist*. London: Sage, second edition.

Ward, R. and Jenkins, R. (1984) *Ethnic Communities in Business, Strategies for Economic Survival*. Cambridge: Cambridge University Press.

Weber, M. (1952) *The Protestant Ethic and the Spirit of Capitalism*. London: Allen and Unwin.

Werbner, P. (1984) 'Business on Trust: Pakistani Entrepreneurship in the Manchester Garment Trade', in R. Ward and R. Jenkins (eds), *Ethnic Communities in Business: Strategies for Economic Survival*. Cambridge, Cambridge University Press.

Williams, A.J. (1985) 'Stress and the Entrepreneurial Role', *International Small Business Journal*, 3 (4): 11–25.

Wilson Committee (1979) *The Financing of Small Firms: Interim Report of the Committee to Review the Functioning of Financial Institutions*. London: Cmnd. 7503, HMSO.

Wynarczyk, P., Watson, R., Storey, D.J., Short, H. and Keasey, K. (1993) *The Managerial Labour Market in Small and Medium-Sized Enterprises*. London: Routledge.

Yin, R.K. (1994) *Case Study Research, Design and Methods*. London: Sage.

Your Business Matters (1996) Report of the Regional Conferences issued in conjunction with a conference held at the Queen Elizabeth Conference Centre and published by the Institute of Directors, London, March.

Index